ONE WEEK LOAN

Undergraduate Texts in Mathematics

Editors

S. Axler
F.W. Gehring
K.A. Ribet

Springer
New York
Berlin
Heidelberg
Barcelona
Hong Kong
London
Milan
Paris
Singapore
Tokyo

Undergraduate Texts in Mathematics

Anglin: Mathematics: A Concise History and Philosophy.
Readings in Mathematics.

Anglin/Lambek: The Heritage of Thales.
Readings in Mathematics.

Apostol: Introduction to Analytic Number Theory. Second edition.

Armstrong: Basic Topology.

Armstrong: Groups and Symmetry.

Axler: Linear Algebra Done Right. Second edition.

Beardon: Limits: A New Approach to Real Analysis.

Bak/Newman: Complex Analysis. Second edition.

Banchoff/Wermer: Linear Algebra Through Geometry. Second edition.

Berberian: A First Course in Real Analysis.

Bix: Conics and Cubics: A Concrete Introduction to Algebraic Curves.

Brémaud: An Introduction to Probabilistic Modeling.

Bressoud: Factorization and Primality Testing.

Bressoud: Second Year Calculus.
Readings in Mathematics.

Brickman: Mathematical Introduction to Linear Programming and Game Theory.

Browder: Mathematical Analysis: An Introduction.

Buchmann: Introduction to Cryptography.

Buskes/van Rooij: Topological Spaces: From Distance to Neighborhood.

Callahan: The Geometry of Spacetime: An Introduction to Special and General Relativity.

Carter/van Brunt: The Lebesgue–Stieltjes Integral: A Practical Introduction.

Cederberg: A Course in Modern Geometries. Second edition.

Childs: A Concrete Introduction to Higher Algebra. Second edition.

Chung: Elementary Probability Theory with Stochastic Processes. Third edition.

Cox/Little/O'Shea: Ideals, Varieties, and Algorithms. Second edition.

Croom: Basic Concepts of Algebraic Topology.

Curtis: Linear Algebra: An Introductory Approach. Fourth edition.

Devlin: The Joy of Sets: Fundamentals of Contemporary Set Theory. Second edition.

Dixmier: General Topology.

Driver: Why Math?

Ebbinghaus/Flum/Thomas: Mathematical Logic. Second edition.

Edgar: Measure, Topology, and Fractal Geometry.

Elaydi: An Introduction to Difference Equations. Second edition.

Exner: An Accompaniment to Higher Mathematics.

Exner: Inside Calculus.

Fine/Rosenberger: The Fundamental Theory of Algebra.

Fischer: Intermediate Real Analysis.

Flanigan/Kazdan: Calculus Two: Linear and Nonlinear Functions. Second edition.

Fleming: Functions of Several Variables. Second edition.

Foulds: Combinatorial Optimization for Undergraduates.

Foulds: Optimization Techniques: An Introduction.

Franklin: Methods of Mathematical Economics.

Frazier: An Introduction to Wavelets Through Linear Algebra.

Gamelin: Complex Analysis.

Gordon: Discrete Probability.

Hairer/Wanner: Analysis by Its History.
Readings in Mathematics.

Halmos: Finite-Dimensional Vector Spaces. Second edition.

Halmos: Naive Set Theory.

Hämmerlin/Hoffmann: Numerical Mathematics.
Readings in Mathematics.

Harris/Hirst/Mossinghoff: Combinatorics and Graph Theory.

Hartshorne: Geometry: Euclid and Beyond.

(continued after index)

Johannes A. Buchmann

Introduction to Cryptography

Springer

Johannes A. Buchmann
Department of Computer Science
Technical University, Darmstadt
Alexanderstrasse 10
64283 Darmstadt
Germany

Cover: Author photograph by Almut Knaak.
With 7 figures.

Mathematics Subject Classification (2000): 11T71, 14G50, 94A60, 68P25

Library of Congress Cataloging-in-Publication Data
Buchmann, Johannes A.
   Introduction to cryptography / Johannes A. Buchmann.
      p.   cm.—(Undergraduate texts in mathematics)
   Includes bibliographical references and index.
   ISBN 0-387-95034-6 (hc: alk. paper)
      1. Coding theory.   2. Cryptography.   I. Title.   II. Series.
   QA268.B83   2000
   003′–dc21   00-030465

Printed on acid-free paper.

Production managed by Terry Kornak; manufacturing supervised by Joe Quatela.
Typeset by The Bartlett Press, Inc., Marietta, GA.
Printed and bound by Edwards Brothers, Inc., Ann Arbor, MI.
Printed in the United States of America.

9 8 7 6 5 4 3 2 1

ISBN 0-387-95034-6   SPIN 10765385

Springer-Verlag   New York   Berlin   Heidelberg
A member of BertelsmannSpringer Science+Business Media GmbH

Preface

Cryptography is a key technology in electronic security systems. Modern cryptograpic techniques have many uses, such as to digitally sign documents, for access control, to implement electronic money, and for copyright protection. Because of these important uses it is necessary that users be able to estimate the efficiency and security of cryptographic techniques. It is not sufficient for them to know only how the techniques work.

This book is written for readers who want to learn about modern cryptographic algorithms and their mathematical foundation but who do not have the necessary mathematical background. It is my goal to explain the basic techniques of modern cryptography, including the necessary mathematical results from linear algebra, algebra, number theory, and probability theory. I assume only basic mathematical knowledge.

The book is based on courses in cryptography that I have been teaching at the Technical University, Darmstadt, since 1996. I thank all students who attended the courses and who read the manuscript carefully for their interest and support. In particular, I would like to thank Harald Baier, Gabi Barking, Manuel Breuning, Safuat Hamdy, Birgit Henhapl, Michael Jacobson (who also corrected my English), Andreas Kottig, Markus Maurer, Andreas Meyer, Stefan

Neis, Sachar Paulus, Thomas Pfahler, Marita Skrobic, Edlyn Teske, Patrick Theobald, and Ralf-Philipp Weinmann. I also thank the staff at Springer-Verlag, in particular Martin Peters, Agnes Herrmann, Claudia Kehl, Ina Lindemann, and Terry Kornak, for their support in the preparation of this book.

Darmstadt, Germany   Johannes A. Buchmann
September 2000

Contents

Preface   **v**

1 Integers   **1**
   1.1 Basics   1
   1.2 Divisibility   2
   1.3 Representation of Integers   4
   1.4 O- and Ω-Notation   6
   1.5 Cost of Addition, Multiplication, and
         Division with Remainder   7
   1.6 Polynomial Time   9
   1.7 Greatest Common Divisor   9
   1.8 Euclidean Algorithm 12
   1.9 Extended Euclidean Algorithm 16
  1.10 Analysis of the Extended Euclidean Algorithm . . . 18
  1.11 Factoring into Primes 21
  1.12 Exercises 24

2 Congruences and Residue Class Rings   **29**
   2.1 Congruences 29
   2.2 Semigroups 32
   2.3 Groups 34

2.4   Residue Class Rings 35
2.5   Fields 36
2.6   Division in the Residue Class Ring 36
2.7   Analysis of Operations in the Residue Class Ring . . . 38
2.8   Multiplicative Group of Residues 39
2.9   Order of Group Elements 41
2.10 Subgroups 42
2.11 Fermat's Little Theorem 44
2.12 Fast Exponentiation 45
2.13 Fast Evaluation of Power Products 48
2.14 Computation of Element Orders 49
2.15 The Chinese Remainder Theorem 51
2.16 Decomposition of the Residue Class Ring 54
2.17 A Formula for the Euler φ-Function 55
2.18 Polynomials 57
2.19 Polynomials over Fields 59
2.20 Structure of the Unit Group of Finite Fields 62
2.21 Structure of the Multiplicative Group of Residues
      mod a Prime Number 63
2.22 Exercises 64

3 Encryption   69
3.1   Encryption Schemes 69
3.2   Symmetric and Asymmetric Cryptosystems 71
3.3   Cryptanalysis 71
3.4   Alphabets and Words 73
3.5   Permutations 75
3.6   Block Ciphers 77
3.7   Multiple Encryption 78
3.8   Use of Block Ciphers 79
3.9   Stream Ciphers 88
3.10 Affine Cipher 89
3.11 Matrices and Linear Maps 91
3.12 Affine Linear Block Ciphers 96
3.13 Vigenère, Hill, and Permutation Ciphers 97
3.14 Cryptanalysis of Affine Linear Block Ciphers 98
3.15 Exercises 99

4 Probability and Perfect Secrecy 103
4.1 Probability 103
4.2 Conditional Probability 105
4.3 Birthday Paradox 106
4.4 Perfect Secrecy 107
4.5 Vernam One-Time Pad 110
4.6 Random Numbers 111
4.7 Pseudorandom Numbers 112
4.8 Exercises 112

5 DES 115
5.1 Feistel Ciphers 115
5.2 DES Algorithm 116
5.3 An Example 123
5.4 Security of DES 124
5.5 Exercises 125

6 Prime Number Generation 127
6.1 Trial Division 127
6.2 Fermat Test 129
6.3 Carmichael Numbers 130
6.4 Miller-Rabin Test 132
6.5 Random Primes 135
6.6 Exercises 136

7 Public-Key Encryption 139
7.1 Idea 139
7.2 RSA Cryptosystem 141
7.3 Rabin Encryption 153
7.4 Diffie-Hellman Key Exchange 158
7.5 ElGamal Encryption 162
7.6 Exercises 167

8 Factoring 171
8.1 Trial Division 171
8.2 $p-1$ Method 172
8.3 Quadratic Sieve 173
8.4 Analysis of the Quadratic Sieve 178

8.5   Efficiency of Other Factoring Algorithms 181
8.6   Exercises 182

9 Discrete Logarithms   **185**
9.1   DL Problem 185
9.2   Enumeration 186
9.3   Shanks Baby-Step Giant-Step Algorithm 186
9.4   Pollard ρ-Algorithm 189
9.5   Pohlig-Hellman Algorithm 193
9.6   Index Calculus 198
9.7   Other Algorithms 202
9.8   Generalization of the Index Calculus Algorithm . . . 203
9.9   Exercises 203

10 Cryptographic Hash Functions   **205**
10.1 Hash Functions and Compression Functions 205
10.2 Birthday Attack 208
10.3 Compression Functions from Encryption Functions . 209
10.4 Hash Functions from Compression Functions 209
10.5 Efficient Hash Functions 212
10.6 An Arithmetic Compression Function 213
10.7 Message Authentication Codes 214
10.8 Exercises 215

11 Digital Signatures   **217**
11.1 Idea 217
11.2 RSA Signatures 218
11.3 Signatures from Public-Key Systems 222
11.4 ElGamal Signature 223
11.5 Digital Signature Algorithm (DSA) 228
11.6 Exercises 231

12 Other Groups   **233**
12.1 Finite Fields 233
12.2 Elliptic Curves 236
12.3 Quadratic Forms 239
12.4 Exercises 240

13 Identification   241
13.1 Passwords 242
13.2 One-Time Passwords 243
13.3 Challenge-Response Identification 243
13.4 Exercises 247

14 Public-Key Infrastructures   249
14.1 Personal Security Environments 249
14.2 Certification Authorities 251
14.3 Certificate Chains 256

References   257

Solutions to the Exercises   261

Index   277

1

CHAPTER

Integers

Integers play a fundamental role in cryptography. In this chapter we present important properties of integers and describe fundamental algorithms.

1.1 Basics

As usual, $\mathbb{N} = \{1, 2, 3, 4, 5, \ldots\}$ is the set of positive integers and $\mathbb{Z} = \{0, \pm 1, \pm 2, \pm 3, \ldots\}$ is the set of *integers*. The rational numbers are denoted by $\mathbb{Q}$ and the real numbers by $\mathbb{R}$.

Clearly, we have $\mathbb{N} \subset \mathbb{Z} \subset \mathbb{Q} \subset \mathbb{R}$. Real numbers (including integers and rational numbers) can be added and multiplied. We assume that this is known.

We use the following rules.

If the product of two real numbers is zero, then at least one factor is zero so it is impossible that both factors are nonzero but the product is zero.

Real numbers can be compared. For example, $\sqrt{2}$ is less than 2 but greater than 1. If a real number α is less than another real number β, then we write $\alpha < \beta$. If α is less than or equal to β, we write $\alpha \leq \beta$. If α is greater than β, we write $\alpha > \beta$. If α is greater than or equal to β we write $\alpha \geq \beta$. If γ is another real number, then $\alpha < \beta$ implies $\alpha + \gamma < \beta + \gamma$. Analogous statements hold for $\leq, >$, and $\geq$. If $0 < \alpha$ and $0 < \beta$, then $0 < \alpha\beta$.

A set M of real numbers is called *bounded from below* if there is a real number γ such that all elements of M are greater than γ. We also say that M is bounded from below by γ. For example, the set of positive integers is bounded from below by 0, but the set of even integers is not bounded from below. An important property of the integers is the fact that every set of integers that is bounded from below contains a smallest element. For example, the smallest positive integer is 1. In an analogous way one defines sets of real numbers that are bounded from above. Every set of integers that is bounded from above contains a greatest element.

For any real number α, we write

$$\lfloor \alpha \rfloor = \max\{b \in \mathbb{Z} : b \leq \alpha\}.$$

Hence, $\lfloor \alpha \rfloor$ is the greatest integer, which is less than or equal to α. This number exists because the set $\{b \in \mathbb{Z} : b \leq \alpha\}$ is bounded from above.

Example 1.1.1
We have $\lfloor 3.43 \rfloor = 3$ and $\lfloor -3.43 \rfloor = -4$.

Finally, we need *induction*: If a statement, which depends on a positive integer n, is true for $n = 1$ and if the truth for any integer m with $1 \leq m \leq n$ (or just for n) implies the truth for $n+1$, then the statement is true for any positive integer n.

In this chapter, lower case italic letters denote integers.

1.2 Divisibility

Definition 1.2.1
We say that *a divides n* if there is an integer b with $n = ab$.

If a divides n, then a is called a *divisor* of n, n is called a *multiple* of a, and we write $a \mid n$. We also say that n is *divisible* by a. If a is not a divisor of n, then we write $a \nmid n$.

Example 1.2.2
We have $13 \mid 182$ because $182 = 14 * 13$. Likewise, we have $-5 \mid 30$ because $30 = (-6) * (-5)$. The divisors of 30 are ± 1, ± 2, ± 3, ± 5, ± 6, ± 10, ± 15, ± 30.

Any integer a divides 0 because $0 = a * 0$. The only integer that is divisible by 0 is 0 because $a = 0 * b$ implies $a = 0$.
We prove a few simple rules.

Theorem 1.2.3
1. If $a \mid b$ and $b \mid c$, then $a \mid c$.
2. If $a \mid b$, then $ac \mid bc$ for all c.
3. If $c \mid a$ and $c \mid b$, then $c \mid da + eb$ for all d and e.
4. If $a \mid b$ and $b \neq 0$, then $|a| \leq |b|$.
5. If $a \mid b$ and $b \mid a$, then $|a| = |b|$.

Proof. 1. If $a \mid b$ and $b \mid c$, then there are f, g with $b = af$ and $c = bg$. This implies $c = bg = (af)g = a(fg)$. 2. If $a \mid b$, then there is f with $b = af$. Hence, $bc = (af)c = f(ac)$. 3. If $c \mid a$ and $c \mid b$, then there is f, g with $a = fc$ and $b = gc$. This implies $da + eb = dfc + egc = (df + eg)c$. 4. If $a \mid b$ and $b \neq 0$, then there is $f \neq 0$ with $b = af$. This implies $|b| = |af| \geq |a|$. 5. Suppose that $a \mid b$ and $b \mid a$. If $a = 0$, then $b = 0$ and vice versa. If $a \neq 0$ and $b \neq 0$, then 4. implies $|a| \leq |b|$ and $|b| \leq |a|$, and hence $|a| = |b|$. □

The following result is very important. It shows that division with remainder of integers is possible.

Theorem 1.2.4
If a and b are integers, $b > 0$, then there are uniquely determined integers q and r such that $a = qb + r$ and $0 \leq r < b$, namely $q = \lfloor a/b \rfloor$ and $r = a - bq$.

Proof. If $a = qb + r$ and $0 \leq r < b$, then $0 \leq r/b = a/b - q < 1$. This implies $a/b - 1 < q \leq a/b$; hence $q = \lfloor a/b \rfloor$. Conversely, $q = \lfloor a/b \rfloor$ and $r = a - bq$ satisfy the assertion. □

In the situation of Theorem 1.2.4, the integer q is called the (integral) *quotient* and r the *remainder* of the division of a by b. We write $r = a \bmod b$. If a is replaced by $a \bmod b$, then we say that a is *reduced* modulo b.

Example 1.2.5
If $a = 133$ and $b = 21$, then $q = 6$ and $r = 7$, so $133 \bmod 21 = 7$. Likewise, we have $-50 \bmod 8 = 6$.

1.3   Representation of Integers

In books, integers are written in decimal expansion. On computers, the binary expansion is used. More generally, integers can be represented using the so-called g-adic expansion, which is explained in this section. For an integer $g > 1$ and a positive real number α, denote by $\log_g \alpha$ the logarithm for base g of α. For a set M, let M^k be the set of all sequences of length k with entries from M.

Example 1.3.1
We have $\log_2 8 = 3$ because $2^3 = 8$. Also, $\log_8 8 = 1$ because $8^1 = 8$.

Example 1.3.2
The sequence $(0, 1, 1, 1, 0)$ is an element of $\{0, 1\}^5$. Also $\{1, 2\}^2 = \{(1, 1), (1, 2), (2, 1), (2, 2)\}$.

Theorem 1.3.3
Let g be an integer, $g > 1$. For each positive integer a, there is a uniquely determined positive integer k and a uniquely determined sequence

$$(a_1, \ldots, a_k) \in \{0, \ldots, g-1\}^k$$

with $a_1 \neq 0$ and

$$a = \sum_{i=1}^{k} a_i g^{k-i}. \tag{1.1}$$

In addition, $k = \lfloor \log_g a \rfloor + 1$, and $a_i = \lfloor (a - \sum_{j=1}^{i-1} a_j g^{k-j})/g^{k-i} \rfloor$ for $1 \leq i \leq k$.

Proof. Let a be a positive integer. If a_i, $1 \leq i \leq k$, is chosen as in the theorem, then (1.1) is satisfied. We prove the uniqueness. If a can be represented as in (1.1), then $g^{k-1} \leq a = \sum_{i=1}^{k} a_i g^{k-i} \leq (g-1) \sum_{i=1}^{k} g^{k-i} = g^k - 1 < g^k$. Hence, $k = \lfloor \log_g a \rfloor + 1$. This proves the uniqueness of k. We prove the uniqueness of the sequence $(a_1, \ldots, a_k)$ by induction on k.

For $k = 1$, we have $a_1 = a$ and there is no other choice for a_1.

Let $k > 1$. If there is a representation as in (1.1), then $0 \leq a - a_1 g^{k-1} < g^{k-1}$ and therefore $0 \leq a/g^{k-1} - a_1 < 1$. Therefore, a_1 is the integral quotient of a divided by g^{k-1} and is hence uniquely determined. Set $a' = a - a_1 g^{k-1} = \sum_{i=2}^{k} a_i g^{k-i}$. Either we have $a' = 0$, in which case $a_i = 0$, $2 \leq i \leq n$ or $a' = \sum_{i=2}^{k} a_i g^{k-i}$ is the uniquely determined representation of a' by the induction hypothesis. $\square$

Definition 1.3.4

The sequence $(a_1, \ldots, a_k)$ from Theorem 1.3.3 is called the *g-adic expansion* of a. Its elements are called *digits*. Its *length* is $k = \lfloor \log_g a \rfloor + 1$. If $g = 2$, the sequence is called the *binary expansion* of a. If $g = 16$, then the sequence is called the *hexadecimal expansion* of a.

The g-adic expansion of a positive integer is only uniquely determined if its first digit is nonzero. Instead of $(a_1, \ldots, a_k)$, we also write $a_1 a_2 \ldots a_k$.

Example 1.3.5

The sequence 10101 is the binary expansion of $2^4 + 2^2 + 2^0 = 21$. When writing the hexadecimal expansion, we use instead of the digits $10, 11, \ldots, 15$ the letters A, B, C, D, E, F, so A1C is the hexadecimal expansion of $10 * 16^2 + 16 + 12 = 2588$.

Theorem 1.3.3 contains a procedure for computing the g-adic expansion of a positive integer. This is applied in the next example.

Example 1.3.6

We determine the binary expansion of 105. Since $64 = 2^6 < 105 < 128 = 2^7$, it is of length 7. We find the following: $a_1 = \lfloor 105/64 \rfloor = 1$; $105 - 64 = 41$; $a_2 = \lfloor 41/32 \rfloor = 1$; $41 - 32 = 9$; $a_3 = \lfloor 9/16 \rfloor = 0$; $a_4 = \lfloor 9/8 \rfloor = 1$; $9 - 8 = 1$. $a_5 = a_6 = 0$; $a_7 = 1$. Hence, the binary expansion of 105 is the sequence 1101001.

The transformation of hexadecimal expansions to binary expansions is particularly simple. Let $(h_1, h_2, \ldots, h_k)$ be the hexadecimal expansion of a positive integer n. For $1 \le i \le k$, let $(b_{1,i}, b_{2,i}, b_{3,i}, b_{4,i})$ be the bitstring of length 4, which represents h_i (i.e., $h_i = b_{1,i}2^3 + b_{2,i}2^2 + b_{3,i}2 + b_{4,i}$). Then $(b_{1,1}, b_{2,1}, b_{3,1}, b_{4,1}, b_{1,2}, \ldots, b_{4,k})$ is the binary expansion of n.

Example 1.3.7
Consider the hexadecimal number $n = 6EF$. The length 4 normalized binary expansions of the digits are $6 = 0110$, $E = 1110$, $F = 1111$. Therefore, 011011101111 is the binary expansion of n.

The length of the binary expansion of a positive integer is also referred to as its *binary length*. The binary length of 0 is defined to be 1. The binary length of an integer is defined to be the binary length of its absolute value. It is denoted by size (a) or size a.

1.4 O- and Ω-Notation

When designing a cryptographic algorithm, it is necessary to estimate how much computing time and how much storage it requires. To simplify such estimates, we introduce the O- and the Ω-notation.

Let k be a positive integer, $X, Y \subset \mathbb{N}^k$ and $f : X \to \mathbb{R}_{\ge 0}$, $g : Y \to \mathbb{R}_{\ge 0}$ functions. We write $f = O(g)$ if there are positive integers B and C such that for all $(n_1, \ldots, n_k) \in \mathbb{N}^k$ with $n_i > B$, $1 \le i \le k$ the following is true:

1. $(n_1, \ldots, n_k) \in X \cap Y$; that is, $f(n_1, \ldots, n_k)$ and $g(n_1, \ldots, n_k)$ are defined,

2. $f(n_1, \ldots, n_k) \le Cg(n_1, \ldots, n_k)$.

This means that almost always $f(n_1, \ldots, n_k) \le Cg(n_1, \ldots, n_k)$. We also write $g = \Omega(f)$. If g is constant, then we write $f = O(1)$.

Example 1.4.1
We have $2n^2 + n + 1 = O(n^2)$ because $2n^2 + n + 1 \le 4n^2$ for all $n \ge 1$. Also, $2n^2 + n + 1 = \Omega(n^2)$ because $2n^2 + n + 1 \ge 2n^2$ for all $n \ge 1$.

Example 1.4.2

If g is an integer, $g > 2$, and if $f(n)$ denotes the length of the g-adic expansion of a positive integer n, then $f(n) = O(\log n)$, where $\log n$ is the natural logarithm of n. In fact, this length is $\lfloor \log_g n \rfloor + 1 \leq \log_g n + 1 = \log n / \log g + 1$. If $n > 3$, then $\log n > 1$ and therefore $\log n / \log g + 1 < (1/\log g + 1) \log n$.

1.5   Cost of Addition, Multiplication, and Division with Remainder

In many cryptographic applications, multiprecision integers must be added, multiplied, and divided with remainder. To estimate the running time of such applications, we must study how long such operations take. To do so, one has to choose a model of computation that is as similar as possible to real computers. This is described in detail in [3] and [4]. Here, we only use a naive model, which, however, yields reasonable estimates.

Let a and b be positive integers, which are given by their binary representations. Let m be the binary length of a and let n be the binary length of m. To compute $a + b$, we use the school method, which adds bit by bit with carry.

Example 1.5.1

Let $a = 10101$, $b = 111$. We compute $a + b$.

		1	0	1	0	1
+				1	1	1
carry			1	1	1	
	1	1	1	0	0	

We assume that the addition of two bits takes time $O(1)$. Then the whole addition requires time $O(\max\{m, n\})$. Analogously, one can show that the difference $b - a$ can be computed in time $O(\max\{m, n\})$.

We use the school method also for multiplication.

Example 1.5.2

Let $a = 10101$, $b = 101$. We compute $a * b$.

$$
\begin{array}{ccccccccc}
 & & 1 & 0 & 1 & 0 & 1 & * & 1 & 0 & 1 \\
\hline
 & & & & 1 & 0 & 1 & 0 & 1 \\
+ & & & 1 & 0 & 1 & 0 & 1 \\
\text{carry} & & & & 1 & & 1 \\
\hline
 & & & 1 & 1 & 0 & 1 & 0 & 0 & 1
\end{array}
$$

We scan b from right to left. For each 1, we write a such that the rightmost bit of a is below the current 1. Then this a is added to the previous result. Any such addition takes time $O(m)$, and $O(n)$ additions are necessary. The computation takes time $O(mn)$. In [3], the algorithm of Schönhage and Strassen is explained, which can multiply two n-bit numbers in time $O(n \log n \log \log n)$. In practice, this algorithm is less efficient than the school method for operands that have fewer than 10,000 bits.

We also use the school method to divide a by b with remainder.

Example 1.5.3

Let $a = 10101$, $b = 101$. We divide a with remainder by b.

$$
\begin{array}{rcccccccccccccc}
 & 1 & 0 & 1 & 0 & 1 & = & 1 & 0 & 1 & * & 1 & 0 & 0 & + & 1 \\
- & 1 & 0 & 1 \\
\hline
 & & 0 & 0 & 0 \\
- & & 0 & 0 & 0 \\
\hline
 & & & 0 & 0 & 1 \\
- & & & 0 & 0 & 0 \\
\hline
 & & & & & 1
\end{array}
$$

When analyzing the algorithm, we see the following. Let k be the binary length of the quotient. Then one has to subtract at most k times two numbers of binary length $\le n + 1$. This takes time $O(kn)$. We therefore obtain the following bounds, which will be used henceforth:

Let a and b be integers.

1. Adding a and b requires time $O(\max\{\text{size } a, \text{size } b\})$.

2. Multiplying a and b requires time $O((\text{size } a)(\text{size } b))$.

3. Dividing a with remainder by b requires time $O((\text{size } b)(\text{size } q))$, where q is the quotient.

All algorithms require space $O(\text{size } a + \text{size } b)$.

1.6 Polynomial Time

When analyzing a cryptographic algorithm, we must show that it works efficiently but is difficult to break. We make the notion of "efficiency" more precise.

Suppose an algorithm receives as input integers $z_1, \ldots, z_n$. We say that the algorithm has *polynomial running time* if there are nonnegative integers $e_1, \ldots, e_n$ such that the running time of the algorithm is

$$O((\text{size } z_1)^{e_1}(\text{size } z_2)^{e_2} \cdots (\text{size } z_n)^{e_n}).$$

An algorithm is considered to be efficient if it has polynomial running time. Observe, however, that in order for the algorithm to be efficient in practice, the exponents e_i and the O-constant must be small.

1.7 Greatest Common Divisor

We define the greatest common divisor of two integers.

Definition 1.7.1
A *common divisor* of a and b is an integer that divides both a and b.

Theorem 1.7.2
Among all common divisors of two integers a and b, which are not both zero, there is exactly one greatest (with respect to $\leq$). It is called the greatest common divisor (gcd) of a and b.

Proof. Let $a \neq 0$. By Theorem 1.2.3, all divisors of a are bounded by $|a|$. Therefore, among the common divisors of a and b there is a unique greatest. □

For completeness, we set the greatest common divisor of 0 and 0 to 0 (i.e., $\gcd(0, 0) = 0$). Hence, the greatest common divisor of two numbers is never negative.

Example 1.7.3

The greatest common divisor of 18 and 30 is 6. The greatest common divisor of -10 and 20 is 10. The greatest common divisor of -20 and -14 is 2. The greatest common divisor of 12 and 0 is 12.

The greatest common divisor of integers $a_1, \ldots, a_k$, $k \geq 1$ is defined as follows. If at least one of the a_i is nonzero, then $\gcd(a_1, \ldots, a_k)$ is the greatest positive integer that divides all the a_i. If all the a_i are zero, then we set $\gcd(a_1, \ldots, a_k) = 0$.

Next, we present an important way of representing a greatest common divisor. We need the following notation.

If $\alpha_1, \ldots, \alpha_k$ are real numbers, then we write

$$\alpha_1 \mathbb{Z} + \ldots + \alpha_k \mathbb{Z} = \{\alpha_1 z_1 + \ldots + \alpha_k z_k : z_i \in \mathbb{Z}, 1 \leq i \leq k\}.$$

This is the set of all *integer linear combinations* of the a_i.

Example 1.7.4

The set of all integer linear combinations of 3 and 4 is $3\mathbb{Z} + 4\mathbb{Z}$. It contains $1 = 3 * (-1) + 4$. It therefore also contains all integer multiples of 1. Hence, this set is $\mathbb{Z}$.

The next theorem shows that the result in the previous example was not an accident.

Theorem 1.7.5

The set of all integer linear combinations of a and b is the set of all integer multiples of $\gcd(a, b)$; i.e.,

$$a\mathbb{Z} + b\mathbb{Z} = \gcd(a, b)\mathbb{Z}.$$

Proof. For $a = b = 0$, the assertion is obviously correct, so let a or b be nonzero.

Set

$$I = a\mathbb{Z} + b\mathbb{Z}.$$

Let g be the smallest positive integer in I. We claim that $I = g\mathbb{Z}$. To see this, choose a nonzero element c in I. We must show that $c = qg$ for some q. By Theorem 1.2.4, there are q, r with $c = qg + r$ and $0 \leq r < g$. Therefore, $r = c - qg$ belongs to I. But since g is the smallest positive integer in I, we must have $r = 0$ and $c = qg$.

It remains to be shown that $g = \gcd(a, b)$. Since $a, b \in I$, it follows from $I = g\mathbb{Z}$ that g is a common divisor of a and b. Moreover, since $g \in I$ there are x, y with $g = xa + yb$. Therefore, if d is a common divisor of a and b, then d is also a divisor of g. Theorem 1.2.3 implies $|d| \leq g$. This shows that $g = \gcd(a, b)$. □

We could have obtained the result of Example 1.7.4 directly from Theorem 1.7.5. Since $\gcd(3, 4) = 1$, it follows that $3\mathbb{Z} + 4\mathbb{Z} = 1\mathbb{Z} = \mathbb{Z}$.

Theorem 1.7.5 has important implications.

Corollary 1.7.6

For all a, b, n the equation $ax + by = n$ is solvable in integers x and y if and only if $\gcd(a, b)$ divides n.

Proof. If there are x and y with $n = ax + by$, then $n \in a\mathbb{Z} + b\mathbb{Z}$ and by Theorem 1.7.5 $n \in \gcd(a, b)\mathbb{Z}$. Therefore, we can write $n = c\gcd(a, b)$, which implies that n is a multiple of $\gcd(a, b)$.

Conversely, if n is a multiple of $\gcd(a, b)$, then n is an element of $\gcd(a, b)\mathbb{Z}$. By Theorem 1.7.5, we also have $n \in a\mathbb{Z} + b\mathbb{Z}$. Therefore, there are integers x and y with $n = ax + by$. □

Corollary 1.7.6 tells us that the equation

$$3x + 4y = 123$$

has a solution, because $\gcd(3, 4) = 1$. But so far, we have not explained an efficient method for finding a solution x and y. This can be done using the euclidean algorithm, which is explained in the next section.

Corollary 1.7.7

There are integers x and y with $ax + by = \gcd(a, b)$.

Proof. Since $\gcd(a, b)$ divides itself, the assertion follows immediately from Corollary 1.7.6. □

We present another useful characterization of the greatest common divisor. It is frequently used to define the gcd.

Corollary 1.7.8

There is exactly one nonnegative common divisor of a and b, which is divisible by all other common divisors of a and b, namely the greatest common divisor of a and b.

Proof. The greatest common divisor of a and b is a nonnegative common divisor of a and b. Moreover, by Corollary 1.7.7 there are integers x and y with $ax + by = \gcd(a, b)$. Therefore, every common divisor of a and b is a divisor of $\gcd(a, b)$. This shows that there exists a common divisor of a and b that is divisble by any common divisor of a and b.

Conversely, let g be a nonnegative divisor of a and b that is divisible by every common divisor of a and b. If $a = b = 0$, then $g = 0$ since 0 is only divisible by 0. If a or b is nonzero, then by Theorem 1.2.3 every common divisor of a and b is $\leq g$. Therefore, $g = \gcd(a, b)$. □

The question remains how to compute $\gcd(a, b)$ and integers x and y with $ax + by = \gcd(a, b)$. The fact that both problems admit efficient solutions is crucial for many cryptographic systems. In the next sections we present and analyze the euclidean algorithm, which solves both problems.

1.8   Euclidean Algorithm

The euclidean algorithm determines the greatest common divisor of two integers very efficiently. It is based on the following theorem.

Theorem 1.8.1
1. *If $b = 0$, then $\gcd(a, b) = |a|$.*
2. *If $b \neq 0$, then $\gcd(a, b) = \gcd(|b|, a \bmod |b|)$.*

Proof. The first assertion is obviously correct. We prove the second assertion. By Theorem 1.2.4, there is an integer q with $a = q|b| + (a \bmod |b|)$. Therefore, the greatest common divisor of a and b divides the greatest common divisor of $|b|$ and $a \bmod |b|$ and vice versa. Since both greatest common divisors are nonnegative, the assertion follows from Theorem 1.2.3. □

We explain the euclidean algorithm in an example.

Example 1.8.2

We want to compute gcd(100, 35). From Theorem 1.8.1, we obtain gcd(100, 35) = gcd(35, 100 mod 35) = gcd(35, 30) = gcd(30, 5) = gcd(5, 0) = 5.

First, the euclidean algorithm replaces a by $|a|$ and b by $|b|$. This has no effect in our example. As long as b is nonzero, the algorithm replaces a by b and b by a mod b. As soon as $b = 0$, the algorithm returns a. We show what the euclidean algorithm looks like as a C++ program. We use the class `bigint` from the C++ library LiDIA [22], which implements multiprecision integers. Our algorithm uses the method `n.abs()`, which yields the absolute value of n.

```
bigint euclid(bigint a, bigint b) {

   bigint r;
   a.abs();
   b.abs();

   while (b != 0) {
      r = a%b;
      a = b;
      b = r;
   }

   return a;
}
```

We prove the correctness of the euclidean algorithm.

Theorem 1.8.3

The euclidean algorithm computes the greatest common divisor of a and b.

Proof. To prove that the euclidean algorithm terminates and yields gcd(a, b), we introduce some notation that will also be used later. We set

$$r_0 = |a|, r_1 = |b| \tag{1.2}$$

and for $k \geq 1$ and $r_k \neq 0$

$$r_{k+1} = r_{k-1} \bmod r_k. \tag{1.3}$$

Then $r_2, r_3, \ldots$ is the sequence of remainders that are computed in the `while`-loop of the euclidean algorithm. Also, after the kth iteration of the `while`-loop, we have

$$a = r_k, \quad b = r_{k+1}.$$

It follows from Theorem 1.8.1 that the greatest common divisor of a and b is not changed in the algorithm, so we only need to prove that there is k such that $r_k = 0$. But this follows from the fact that by (1.3) the sequence $(r_k)_{k \geq 1}$ is strictly decreasing. This concludes the correctness proof for the euclidean algorithm.   □

The euclidean algorithm computes $\gcd(a, b)$ very efficiently. This is important for cryptographic applications. To prove the efficiency, we estimate the number of iterations required by the euclidean algorithm. For simplicity, we assume

$$a > b > 0.$$

This is no restriction, since the euclidean algorithm requires one step to determine $\gcd(a, b)$ (if $b = 0$) or to produce this situation.

Let r_n be the last nonzero remainder in the sequence (r_k). Then n is the number of iterations, which the euclidean algorithm requires to compute $\gcd(a, b)$. Furthermore, let

$$q_k = \lfloor r_{k-1}/r_k \rfloor, \quad 1 \leq k \leq n. \tag{1.4}$$

Then q_k is the quotient of r_{k-1} divided by r_k, and we have

$$r_{k-1} = q_k r_k + r_{k+1}. \tag{1.5}$$

Example 1.8.4
If $a = 100$ and $b = 35$, then we obtain the remainder sequence

k	0	1	2	3	4
r_k	100	35	30	5	0
q_k			2	1	6

To estimate the number n of iterations, we prove the following auxiliary result. Here we assume $a > b > 0$.

Lemma 1.8.5
We have $q_k \geq 1$ for $1 \leq k \leq n-1$ and $q_n \geq 2$.

Proof. Since $r_{k-1} > r_k > r_{k+1}$, it follows from (1.5) that $q_k \geq 1$ for $1 \leq k \leq n$. Suppose $q_n = 1$. Then $r_{n-1} = r_n$, and this is impossible because the sequence of remainders is strictly decreasing. Therefore, $q_n \geq 2$. □

Theorem 1.8.6
In the euclidean algorithm, let $a > b > 0$. Also, let $\Theta = (1 + \sqrt{5})/2$. Then the number of iterations in the euclidean algorithm is at most $(\log b)/(\log \Theta) + 1$.

Proof. By Exercise 1.12.19, we may assume that $\gcd(a, b) = r_n = 1$. We prove

$$r_k \geq \Theta^{n-k}, \quad 0 \leq k \leq n. \tag{1.6}$$

Then

$$b = r_1 \geq \Theta^{n-1}.$$

Taking logarithms, we obtain

$$n \leq (\log b)/(\log \Theta) + 1,$$

as asserted.

We now prove (1.6) by induction. First, we have

$$r_n = 1 = \Theta^0$$

and by Lemma 1.8.5

$$r_{n-1} = q_n r_n = q_n \geq 2 > \Theta.$$

Let $n - 2 \geq k \geq 0$, and assume that the assertion is true for $k' > k$. Then Lemma 1.8.5 implies

$$r_k = q_{k+1} r_{k+1} + r_{k+2} \geq r_{k+1} + r_{k+2}$$
$$\geq \Theta^{n-k-1} + \Theta^{n-k-2} = \Theta^{n-k-1}\left(1 + \frac{1}{\Theta}\right) = \Theta^{n-k},$$

so (1.6) and the theorem are proved. □

1.9   Extended Euclidean Algorithm

In the previous section, we have seen how the greatest common divisor of two integers can be computed. Corollary 1.7.7 tells us that there are integers x, y with $\gcd(a, b) = ax + by$. In this section, we extend the euclidean algorithm in such a way that it also determines such coefficients x and y. As in Section 1.8, we denote by $r_0, \ldots, r_{n+1}$ the sequence of remainders and by $q_1, \ldots, q_n$ the sequence of quotients that are computed in the course of the euclidean algorithm.

We now explain the construction of two sequences (x_k) and (y_k), such that $x = (-1)^n x_n$ and $y = (-1)^{n+1} y_n$ are the required coefficients.

We set

$$x_0 = 1, \quad x_1 = 0, \quad y_0 = 0, \quad y_1 = 1.$$

Furthermore, we let

$$x_{k+1} = q_k x_k + x_{k-1}, \quad y_{k+1} = q_k y_k + y_{k-1}, \quad 1 \le k \le n. \quad (1.7)$$

We assume that a and b are nonnegative.

Theorem 1.9.1
We have $r_k = (-1)^k x_k a + (-1)^{k+1} y_k b$ for $0 \le k \le n+1$.

Proof.   We note first that

$$r_0 = a = 1 * a - 0 * b = x_0 * a - y_0 * b.$$

Moreover,

$$r_1 = b = -0 * a + 1 * b = -x_1 * a + y_1 * b.$$

Now let $k \ge 2$ and suppose that the assertion is true for $k' < k$. Then

$$
\begin{aligned}
r_k &= r_{k-2} - q_{k-1} r_{k-1} \\
&= (-1)^{k-2} x_{k-2} a + (-1)^{k-1} y_{k-2} b - q_{k-1}((-1)^{k-1} x_{k-1} a + (-1)^k y_{k-1} b) \\
&= (-1)^k a(x_{k-2} + q_{k-1} x_{k-1}) + (-1)^{k+1} b(y_{k-2} + q_{k-1} y_{k-1}) \\
&= (-1)^k x_k a + (-1)^{k+1} y_k b,
\end{aligned}
$$

so our theorem is proved.   □

We see that in particular

$$r_n = (-1)^n x_n a + (-1)^{n+1} y_n b,$$

so we have represented the greatest common divisor of a and b as a linear combination of a and b.

Example 1.9.2
Choose $a = 100$ and $b = 35$. Then the values r_k, q_k, x_k, and y_k are listed in the following table.

k	0	1	2	3	4
r_k	100	35	30	5	0
q_k		2	1	6	
x_k	1	0	1	1	7
y_k	0	1	2	3	20

We find therefore that $n = 3$ and $\gcd(100, 35) = 5 = -1*100 + 3*35$.

The extended euclidean algorithm also computes the coefficients

$$x = (-1)^n x_n, \quad y = (-1)^{n+1} y_n.$$

This is done in the next C++ program. It stores x and y as x[0] and y[0].

```
bigint xeuclid(bigint a, bigint b, bigint x[], bigint y[])
        {
  bigint q, r, xx, yy, sign;

  // Initializes the coefficients

  x[0] = 1; x[1] = 0;
  y[0] = 0; y[1] = 1;
  sign = 1;

  // As long as b != 0 we replace  a by b and b by a%b.
  // We also update the coefficients x and y.

  while (b != 0) {
    r = a%b;
    q = a/b;
```

```
    a = b;
    b = r;
    xx = x[1];
    yy = y[1];
    x[1] = q*x[1] + x[0];
    y[1] = q*y[1] + y[0];
    x[0] = xx;
    y[0] = yy;
    sign = -sign;
  }
  // Final computation of the coefficients.

  x[0] = sign*x[0];
  y[0] = -sign*y[0];

  // Return gcd(a,b)

  return a;
}
```

1.10   Analysis of the Extended Euclidean Algorithm

First, we estimate the size of the coefficients x and y. We use the matrices

$$E_k = \begin{pmatrix} q_k & 1 \\ 1 & 0 \end{pmatrix}, \quad 1 \le k \le n,$$

$$T_k = \begin{pmatrix} y_k & y_{k-1} \\ x_k & x_{k-1} \end{pmatrix}, \quad 1 \le k \le n+1.$$

We have

$$T_{k+1} = T_k E_k, \quad 1 \le k \le n,$$

and since T_1 is the identity matrix, we have

$$T_{n+1} = E_1 E_2 \cdots E_n.$$

If we set

$$S_k = E_{k+1}E_{k+2}\cdots E_n, \quad 0 \le k \le n,$$

where S_n is the identity matrix, then

$$S_0 = T_{n+1}.$$

We use the matrix S_0 to estimate x_n and y_n. If we write

$$S_k = \begin{pmatrix} u_k & v_k \\ u_{k+1} & v_{k+1} \end{pmatrix}, \quad 0 \le k \le n,$$

then because of

$$S_{k-1} = E_k S_k, \quad 1 \le k \le n,$$

we obtain the recursions

$$u_{k-1} = q_k u_k + u_{k+1}, \quad v_{k-1} = q_k v_k + v_{k+1}, \quad 1 \le k \le n. \tag{1.8}$$

The remainders r_k satisfy the same recursion.

Now we estimate the entries v_k of the matrices S_k.

Lemma 1.10.1
We have $0 \le v_k \le r_k/(2\gcd(a,b))$ for $0 \le k \le n$.

Proof. Note that $0 = v_n < r_n/(2\gcd(a,b))$, $q_n \ge 2$ by Lemma 1.8.5, and $v_{n-1} = 1$. Therefore, $r_{n-1} = q_n r_n \ge 2\gcd(a,b) = 2\gcd(a,b)v_{n-1}$. Suppose that the assertion is true for $k' \ge k > 0$. Then $v_{k-1} = q_k v_k + v_{k+1} \le (q_k r_k + r_{k+1})/(2\gcd(a,b)) = r_{k-1}/(2\gcd(a,b))$, so the asserted estimate is proved. □

From Lemma 1.10.1, we can deduce the estimates for the coefficients x_k and y_k.

Corollary 1.10.2
We have $x_k \le b/(2\gcd(a,b))$ and $y_k \le a/(2\gcd(a,b))$ for $1 \le k \le n$.

Proof. It follows from $S_0 = T_{n+1}$ that $x_n = v_1$ and $y_n = v_0$. Therefore, we obtain the asserted estimate for $k = n$ from Lemma, 1.10.1. But since $(x_k)_{k \ge 1}$ and $(y_k)_{k \ge 0}$ are increasing sequences, the assertion is proved for $1 \le k \le n$. □

For the coefficients x and y, which are computed by the extended euclidean algorithm, we obtain the following estimate.

Corollary 1.10.3
We have $|x| \leq b/(2 \gcd(a, b))$ and $|y| \leq a/(2 \gcd(a, b))$.

We are also able to determine the coefficients x_{n+1} and y_{n+1}.

Lemma 1.10.4
We have $x_{n+1} = b/\gcd(a, b)$ and $y_{n+1} = a/\gcd(a, b)$.

We leave the proof to the reader.

We will now estimate the running time of the euclidean algorithm. It turns out that this running time is of the same order of magnitude as the running time for multiplying two integers. This is quite surprising because the euclidean algorithm looks much more difficult than the multiplication algorithm.

Theorem 1.10.5
The extended euclidean algorithm uses time $O((\text{size } a)(\text{size } b))$ to compute $\gcd(a, b)$ including a representation $\gcd(a, b) = xa + yb$.

Proof. We assume that $a > b > 0$. We have already seen that the euclidean algorithm requires one iteration to compute $\gcd(a, b)$ or to generate this situation. The running time for this one iteration is $O(\text{size } (a)\text{size } (b))$.

The euclidean algorithm computes the remainder sequence $(r_k)_{2 \leq k \leq n+1}$ and the quotient sequence $(q_k)_{1 \leq k \leq n}$. The number r_{k+1} is the remainder of the division of r_{k-1} by r_k for $1 \leq k \leq n$. As explained in Section 1.5, the computation of r_{k+1} requires time $O(\text{size } (r_k)\text{size } (q_k))$, where q_k is the quotient of this division.

We know that $r_k \leq b$, hence $\text{size } (r_k) \leq \text{size } (b)$ for $1 \leq k \leq n + 1$. Moreover, we know that $\text{size } (q_k) \leq \log(q_k) + 1$ for $1 \leq k \leq n$. Therefore, the euclidean algorithm takes time

$$T_1(a, b) = O\left(\text{size } (b)\left(n + \sum_{k=1}^{n} \log q_k\right)\right). \tag{1.9}$$

By Theorem 1.8.6, we have

$$n = O(\text{size } b). \tag{1.10}$$

Also,

$$a = r_0 = q_1 r_1 + r_2 \geq q_1 r_1 = q_1(q_2 r_2 + r_3)$$
$$\geq q_1 q_2 r_2 > \dots \geq q_1 q_2 \cdots q_n.$$

This implies

$$\sum_{k=1}^{n} \log q_k = O(\text{size } a). \tag{1.11}$$

If we use (1.10) and (1.11) in (1.9), then the running time of the simple euclidean algorithm is proven.

We also estimate the time that the extended euclidean algorithm needs to compute the coefficients x and y. In the first iteration, we have

$$x_2 = q_1 x_1 + x_0 = 1, \quad y_2 = q_1 y_1 + y_0 = q_1.$$

This takes time $O(\text{size } (q_1)) = O(\text{size } (a))$. Then,

$$x_{k+1} = q_k x_k + x_{k-1}, \quad y_{k+1} = q_k y_k + y_{k-1}$$

is computed for $2 \leq k \leq n$. By Lemma 1.10.2, we have $x_k, y_k = O(a)$ for $0 \leq k \leq n$. The time to compute x and y is therefore

$$T_2(a, b) = O\left(\text{size } (a) \left(1 + \sum_{k=2}^{n} \text{size } (q_k) \right) \right)$$

$$= O\left(\text{size } (a) \left(n + \sum_{k=2}^{n} \log q_k \right) \right). \tag{1.12}$$

As above, it is easy to see that

$$\prod_{k=2}^{n} q_k \leq b. \tag{1.13}$$

If this is used in (1.12), then the assertion is proved. □

1.11   Factoring into Primes

A central notion of elementary number theory is that of a prime number. Prime numbers are used in many cryptographic algorithms. In this section, we introduce prime numbers and prove that every positive integer is a product of primes in which the factors are unique up to permutation.

Definition 1.11.1

An integer $p > 1$ is called a *prime number* if it has exactly two positive divisors, namely 1 and p.

Instead of "prime number" we also simply say "prime". The first nine prime numbers are $2, 3, 5, 7, 11, 13, 17, 19, 23$. We denote the set of all primes by $\mathbb{P}$. An integer $a > 1$ that is not a prime is called *composite* . If the prime p divides the integer a, then p is called *prime divisor* of a.

Theorem 1.11.2

Every integer $a > 1$ has a prime divisor.

Proof.   The integer a has a divisor that is greater than 1, namely a. Among all divisors of a that are greater than 1, let p be the smallest. Then p must be prime. Otherwise, p would have a divisor b with

$$1 < b < p \leq a.$$

This contradicts the assumption that p is the smallest divisor of a that is greater than 1.   □

The following result is crucial for the proof of the decomposition theorem.

Lemma 1.11.3

If a prime number divides the product of two integers, then it divides at least one factor.

Proof.   Suppose the prime number p divides ab but not a. Since p is a prime number, we must have $\gcd(a, p) = 1$. By Corollary 1.7.7, there are x, y with $1 = ax + py$. This implies

$$b = abx + pby.$$

Since p divides abx and pby, Theorem 1.2.3 implies that p is a divisor of b.   □

Corollary 1.11.4

If a prime number p divides a product $\prod_{i=1}^{k} q_i$ of prime numbers, then p is equal to one of the factors $q_1, q_2, \ldots, q_k$.

Proof.   The proof uses induction on k. If $k = 1$, then p is a divisor of q_1 which is greater than 1, hence $p = q_1$. If $k > 1$, then p divides

$q_1 (q_2 \cdots q_k)$. By Lemma 1.11.3, the prime p divides q_1 or $q_2 \cdots q_k$. Because both products have fewer than k factors, the assertion follows from the induction hypothesis. ☐

Now we prove the main theorem of elementary number theory.

Theorem 1.11.5
Every integer $a > 1$ can be written as the product of prime numbers. Up to permutation, the factors in this product are uniquely determined.

Proof.   The theorem is proved by induction on a. For $a = 2$, the theorem is true. Let $a > 2$. By Theorem 1.11.2, there is a prime divisor p of a. If $a/p = 1$, then $a = p$ and the assertion holds. Let $a/p > 1$. By the induction hypothesis, a/p is a product of primes. Therefore, a is also a product of primes. This proves the existence of the prime factor decomposition of a. We must still show the uniqueness, so let $a = p_1 \cdots p_k$ and $a = q_1 \cdots q_l$ be factorizations of a into prime numbers. By Corollary 1.11.4, the prime p_1 is equal to one of the primes $q_1, \ldots, q_k$. By permuting the q_i, we can make sure that $p_1 = q_1$. But by the induction hypothesis, the factorization of $a/p_1 = a/q_1$ into prime numbers is unique. Hence, $k = l$ and $q_i = p_i$ for $1 \leq i \leq k$ after an appropriate permutation of the q_i. ☐

The *prime factorization* of an integer a is the representation of $|a|$ as the product of prime numbers. The problem of finding the prime factorization of an integer a is referred to as the integer factorization problem. Efficient algorithms for solving the integer factorization problem are not known. This fact is the basis of the security of the RSA cryptosystem and other important cryptographic schemes. But we have no proof that the integer factorization problem is difficult. It is therefore quite possible that in the future someone will invent an efficient integer factoring algorithm. The cryptographic schemes based on the difficulty of integer factorization are insecure and must be replaced by others.

Example 1.11.6
The French mathematician Pierre de Fermat (1601 to 1665) thought that all of the so-called *Fermat numbers*

$$F_i = 2^{2^i} + 1$$

are primes. In fact, $F_0 = 3$, $F_1 = 5$, $F_2 = 17$, $F_3 = 257$, and $F_4 = 65537$ are prime numbers. However, in 1732 Euler discovered that $F_5 = 641 * 6700417$ is composite. Both factors in this decomposition are primes. F_6, F_7, F_8, and F_9 are also composite. The factorization of F_6 was found in 1880 by Landry and Le Lasseur. The factorization of F_7 was found in 1970 by Brillhart and Morrison. The factorization of F_8 was computed in 1980 by Brent and Pollard and F_9 was factored in 1990 by Lenstra, Lenstra, Manasse, and Pollard. This shows the the difficulty of the factoring problem. But on the other hand, we also see that there is considerable progress. It took until 1970 to factor the 39-digit number F_7, but only 20 years later the 155-digit number F_9 was factored.

1.12　Exercises

Exercise 1.12.1
Let α be a real number. Show that $\lfloor \alpha \rfloor$ is the uniquely determined integer z with $0 \leq \alpha - z < 1$.

Exercise 1.12.2
Determine the number of divisors of 2^n, $n \in \mathbb{Z}_{\geq 0}$.

Exercise 1.12.3
Determine all divisors of 195.

Exercise 1.12.4
Prove the following modification of division with remainder: If a, b are integers, $b > 0$, then there are uniquely determined integers q and r such that $a = qb + r$ and $-b/2 < r \leq b/2$. Write a program that determines the remainder r.

Exercise 1.12.5
Compute 1243 mod 45 and -1243 mod 45.

Exercise 1.12.6
Find an integer a with a mod $2 = 1$, a mod $3 = 1$, and a mod $5 = 1$.

Exercise 1.12.7
Let m be a positive integer and let a, b be integers. Prove that a mod $m = b$ mod m if and only if m divides the difference $b - a$.

Exercise 1.12.8
Determine the binary length of the nth Fermat number $2^{2^n} + 1$, $n \in \mathbb{Z}_{\geq 0}$.

Exercise 1.12.9
Determine the binary expansion and the hexadecimal expansion of 225.

Exercise 1.12.10
Write a program that computes the g-adic expansion of a positive integer n for any integer $g > 1$.

Exercise 1.12.11
Let $f(n) = a_d X^d + a_{d-1} X^{d-1} + \ldots + a_0$ be a polynomial with real coefficients and let $a_d > 0$. Prove that $f(n) = O(n^d)$.

Exercise 1.12.12
Let $k \in \mathbb{N}$ and $X \subset \mathbb{N}^k$. Assume that $f, g, F, G : X \to \mathbb{R}_{\geq 0}$ with $f = O(F)$ and $g = O(G)$. Prove that $f \pm g = O(F + G)$ and $fg = O(FG)$.

Exercise 1.12.13
Let $a_1, \ldots, a_k$ be integers. Prove the following assertions:

1. $\gcd(a_1, \ldots, a_k) = \gcd(a_1, \gcd(a_2, \ldots, a_k))$.

2. $a_1 \mathbb{Z} + \ldots + a_k \mathbb{Z} = \gcd(a_1, \ldots, a_k) \mathbb{Z}$.

3. The equation $x_1 a_1 + \ldots + x_k a_k = n$ has integer solutions $x_1, \ldots, x_k$ if and only if $\gcd(a_1, \ldots, a_k)$ divides n.

4. There are integers $x_1, \ldots, x_k$ with $a_1 x_1 + \ldots + a_k x_k = \gcd(a_1, \ldots, a_k)$.

5. The greatest common divisor of $a_1, \ldots, a_k$ is the uniquely determined nonnegative common divisor of $a_1, \ldots, a_k$ which is divisible by all common divisors of $a_1, \ldots, a_k$.

Exercise 1.12.14
Show that the euclidean algorithm also works if the division with remainder is modified as in Exercise 1.12.4.

Exercise 1.12.15
Use the euclidean algorithm to compute gcd(235, 124) including its representation.

Exercise 1.12.16
Use the modified euclidean algorithm from Exercise 1.12.14 to compute gcd(235, 124) including its representation. Compare this computation with the computation in Exercise 1.12.15.

Exercise 1.12.17
Prove Lemma 1.10.4.

Exercise 1.12.18
Let $a > b > 0$. Prove that the modified euclidean algorithm from Exercise 1.12.14 requires $O(\log b)$ iterations to compute gcd(a, b).

Exercise 1.12.19
Let $a > b > 0$. Prove that the number of iterations that the euclidean algorithm needs to compute gcd(a, b) depends only on the ratio a/b.

Exercise 1.12.20
Find a sequence $(a_i)_{i \geq 1}$ of positive integers such that the euclidean algorithm needs exactly i iterations to compute gcd(a_{i+1}, a_i).

Exercise 1.12.21
Prove that gcd$(a, m) = 1$ and gcd$(b, m) = 1$ implies gcd$(ab, m) = 1$.

Exercise 1.12.22
Compute the prime factorization of 37800.

Exercise 1.12.23
Prove that a composite integer n, $n > 1$ has a prime divisor p with $p \leq \sqrt{n}$.

Exercise 1.12.24
The *sieve of Eratosthenes* determines all prime numbers p below a given bound C. It works as follows. Write the list of integers

$2, 3, 4, 5, \ldots, \lfloor C \rfloor$. Then iterate the following procedure for $i = 2, 3, \ldots, \lfloor \sqrt{C} \rfloor$. If i is still in the list, delete all proper multiples $2i, 3i, 4i, \ldots$ in the list. The numbers remaining in the list are the prime numbers $\leq C$. Prove the correctness of this algorithm. Write a program that implements it.

2

CHAPTER

Congruences and Residue Class Rings

In this chapter, we show how to compute in residue class rings and prime residue class groups. We also discuss algorithms for finite abelian groups. These techniques are of great importance in cryptographic algorithms.

In this chapter, m is a positive integer and lowercase italic letters denote integers.

2.1 Congruences

Definition 2.1.1
We say that a is *congruent* to b modulo m, and we write $a \equiv b \bmod m$, if m divides the $b - a$.

Example 2.1.2
We have $-2 \equiv 19 \bmod 21$, $10 \equiv 0 \bmod 2$.

It can be easily verified that congruence modulo m is an equivalence relation on the integers. This means that

1. any integer is congruent to itself modulo m (reflexivity),

2. $a \equiv b \bmod m$ implies $b \equiv a \bmod m$ (symmetry),

3. $a \equiv b \bmod m$ and $b \equiv c \bmod m$ implies $a \equiv c \bmod m$ (transitivity).

Moreover, we have the following characterizations.

Lemma 2.1.3
The following statements are equivalent:
1. *$a \equiv b \bmod m$.*
2. *There is $k \in \mathbb{Z}$ with $a = b + km$.*
3. *When divided by m, both a and b leave the same remainder.*

The *equivalence class* of a consists of all integers that are obtained from a by adding integer multiples of m; i.e.,

$$\{b : b \equiv a \bmod m\} = a + m\mathbb{Z}.$$

This equivalence class is called the *residue class* of a mod m.

Example 2.1.4
The residue class of 1 mod 4 is the set $\{1, 1 \pm 4, 1 \pm 2*4, 1 \pm 3*4, \ldots\} = \{1, -3, 5, -7, 9, -11, 13, \ldots\}$. The residue class of 0 mod 2 is the set of all even integers. The residue class of 1 mod 2 is the set of all odd integers. The residue classes mod 4 are $0 + 4\mathbb{Z}, 1 + 4\mathbb{Z}, 2 + 4\mathbb{Z}, 3 + 4\mathbb{Z}$.

The set of residue classes mod m is denoted by $\mathbb{Z}/m\mathbb{Z}$. It has m elements, since $0, 1, 2, \ldots, m - 1$ are the possible remainders of the division by m. A *set of representatives* for those residue classes is a set of integers that contains exactly one element of each residue class mod m.

Example 2.1.5
A set of representatives mod 3 contains an element of each of the residue classes $3\mathbb{Z}, 1 + 3\mathbb{Z}, 2 + 3\mathbb{Z}$. Hence, $\{0, 1, 2\}, \{3, -2, 5\}, \{9, 16, 14\}$ are such sets.

One set of representatives mod m is the set $\{0, 1, \ldots, m - 1\}$. Its elements are called the *least nonnegative residues* mod m. This set is denoted by $\mathbb{Z}_m$. Likewise, $\{1, 2, \ldots, m\}$ is a set of representatives mod m. Its elements are called the *least positive residues* mod m. Finally, $\{n + 1, n + 2, \ldots, n + m\}$ with $n = -\lceil m/2 \rceil$ is a set of representatives mod m.

Example 2.1.6

$$\{0, 1, 2, 3, 4, 5, 6, 7, 8, 9, 10, 11, 12\}$$

is the set of least nonnegative residues mod 13.

We need a few rules for computing with congruences. They will later allow us to define a ring structure on the residue classes mod m.

Theorem 2.1.7
$a \equiv b \bmod m$ and $c \equiv d \bmod m$ implies $-a \equiv -b \bmod m$, $a + c \equiv b + d \bmod m$, and $ac \equiv bd \bmod m$.

Proof. Since m divides $a - b$, m also divides $-a + b$. Therefore, $-a \equiv -b \bmod m$. Since m divides $a - b$ and $c - d$, m also divides $a - b + c - d = (a + c) - (b + d)$. Therefore, $a + c \equiv b + d \bmod m$. To show that $ac \equiv bd \bmod m$, we write $a = b + lm$ and $c = d + km$. Then we obtain $ac = bd + m(ld + kb + lkm)$, as asserted. $\square$

Example 2.1.8
We apply Theorem 2.1.7 to prove that the fifth Fermat number $2^{2^5} + 1$ is divisible by 641. First,

$$641 = 640 + 1 = 5 * 2^7 + 1.$$

This implies

$$5 * 2^7 \equiv -1 \bmod 641.$$

From Theorem 2.1.7, we deduce that this congruence remains valid if both sides are raised to the fourth power; i.e.,

$$5^4 * 2^{28} \equiv 1 \bmod 641. \tag{2.1}$$

On the other hand,

$$641 = 625 + 16 = 5^4 + 2^4.$$

This implies

$$5^4 \equiv -2^4 \bmod 641.$$

If we use this congruence in (2.1), we obtain

$$-2^{32} \equiv 1 \bmod 641;$$

hence,

$$2^{32} + 1 \equiv 0 \bmod 641.$$

This proves that 641 is a divisor of the fifth Fermat number.

We want to prove that the residue classes modulo m form a ring. In the following sections, we review a few basic notions of algebra.

2.2   Semigroups

Definition 2.2.1
If X is a set, a map $\circ : X \times X \to X$ which sends a pair (x_1, x_2) of elements from X to the element $x_1 \circ x_2$ is called an *operation* on X.

Example 2.2.2
On the set of real numbers, we already know the operations addition and multiplication.

On the set $\mathbb{Z}/m\mathbb{Z}$ of residue classes mod m, we introduce two operations, addition and multiplication.

Definition 2.2.3
The sum of the residue classes $a + m\mathbb{Z}$ and $b + m\mathbb{Z}$ is $(a + m\mathbb{Z}) + (b + m\mathbb{Z}) = (a + b) + m\mathbb{Z}$. The product of the residue classes $a + m\mathbb{Z}$ and $b + m\mathbb{Z}$ is $(a + m\mathbb{Z}) \cdot (b + m\mathbb{Z}) = (a \cdot b) + m\mathbb{Z}$.

Observe that the sum and product of residue classes modulo m are defined using representatives. From Theorem 2.1.7, it follows, however, that these definitions are independent of the representatives. In practice, the residue classes are represented using fixed representatives. The computations are done with those representatives.

Example 2.2.4
We use the least nonnegative representatives mod $m = 5$. We obtain $(3 + 5\mathbb{Z}) + (2 + 5\mathbb{Z}) = (5 + 5\mathbb{Z}) = 5\mathbb{Z}$ and $(3 + 5\mathbb{Z})(2 + 5\mathbb{Z}) = 6 + 5\mathbb{Z} = 1 + 5\mathbb{Z}$. We can also write this computation in the form $3 + 2 \equiv 0 \bmod 5$ and $3 * 2 \equiv 1 \bmod 5$.

Definition 2.2.5
Let $\circ$ be an operation on the set X. It is called *associative* if $(a \circ b) \circ c = a \circ (b \circ c)$ holds for all $a, b, c \in X$. It is called *commutative* if $a \circ b = b \circ a$ for all $a, b \in X$.

Example 2.2.6
Addition and multiplication on the set of real numbers are associative and commutative. The same is true for addition and multiplication in $\mathbb{Z}/m\mathbb{Z}$.

Definition 2.2.7
A pair $(H, \circ)$ consisting of a set H and an associative operation $\circ$ on H is called a *semigroup*. The semigroup is called *commutative* or *abelian* if the operation $\circ$ is commutative.

Example 2.2.8
Commutative semigroups are $(\mathbb{Z}, +)$, $(\mathbb{Z}, \cdot)$, $(\mathbb{Z}/m\mathbb{Z}, +)$, $(\mathbb{Z}/m\mathbb{Z}, \cdot)$.

Let $(H, \circ)$ be a semigroup, and set $a^1 = a$ and $a^{n+1} = a \circ a^n$ for $a \in H$ and $n \in \mathbb{N}$. Then the following are true:

$$a^n \circ a^m = a^{n+m}, \quad (a^n)^m = a^{nm}, \quad a \in H, n, m \in \mathbb{N}. \tag{2.2}$$

If $a, b \in H$ and $a \circ b = b \circ a$, then

$$(a \circ b)^n = a^n \circ b^n. \tag{2.3}$$

If the semigroup is commutative, then (2.3) is true in general.

Definition 2.2.9
A *neutral element* of the semigroup $(H, \circ)$ is an element $e \in H$ which satisfies $e \circ a = a \circ e = a$ for all $a \in H$. If the semigroup contains a neutral element, then it is called *monoid*.

A semigroup has at most one neutral element (see Exercise 2.22.3).

Definition 2.2.10
If e is the neutral element of the semigroup $(H, \circ)$ and if $a \in H$, then $b \in H$ is called an *inverse* of a if $a \circ b = b \circ a = e$. If a has an inverse, then a is called *invertible* in the semigroup H.

In a monoid, each element has at most one inverse (see Exercise 2.22.5).

Example 2.2.11
1. The neutral element of the semigroup $(\mathbb{Z}, +)$ is 0. The inverse of a is $-a$.
2. The neutral element of the semigroup $(\mathbb{Z}, \cdot)$ is 1. The only invertible elements are 1 and -1.
3. The neutral element of the semigroup $(\mathbb{Z}/m\mathbb{Z}, +)$ is the residue class $m\mathbb{Z}$. The inverse of $a + m\mathbb{Z}$ is $-a + m\mathbb{Z}$.
4. The neutral element of the semigroup $(\mathbb{Z}/m\mathbb{Z}, \cdot)$ is $1 + m\mathbb{Z}$. The invertible elements will be determined later.

2.3   Groups

Definition 2.3.1
A *group* is a monoid in which any element is invertible. The group is called *commutative* or *abelian* if the monoid is commutative.

Example 2.3.2
1. The monoid $(\mathbb{Z}, +)$ is an abelian group.
2. The monoid $(\mathbb{Z}, \cdot)$ is not a group because not every element is invertible.
3. The monoid $(\mathbb{Z}/m\mathbb{Z}, +)$ is an abelian group.

Let $(G, \cdot)$ be a group. Denote by a^{-1} the inverse of $a \in G$, and set $a^{-n} = (a^{-1})^n$ for each positive integer n. Then (2.2) holds for all integral exponents. If the group is abelian, then (2.3) is true for all integers n.

In a group, the following *cancellation rules* can be easily verified.

Theorem 2.3.3
Let $(G, \cdot)$ be a group and $a, b, c \in G$. Then $ca = cb$ implies $a = b$ and $ac = bc$ implies $a = b$.

Definition 2.3.4
The *order* of a group or a semigroup is the number of its elements.

Example 2.3.5
The additive group $\mathbb{Z}$ has infinite order. The additive group $\mathbb{Z}/m\mathbb{Z}$ has order m.

2.4   Residue Class Rings

Definition 2.4.1
A *ring* is a triplet $(R, +, \cdot)$ such that $(R, +)$ is an abelian group and $(R, \cdot)$ is a semigroup. In addition, $x \cdot (y + z) = (x \cdot y) + (x \cdot z)$ and $(x + y) \cdot z = (x \cdot z) + (y \cdot z)$ for all $x, y, z \in R$. The ring is called *commutative* if the semigroup $(R, \cdot)$ is commutative. A *unit element* of the ring is a neutral element of the semigroup $(R, \cdot)$.

Example 2.4.2
The triplet $(\mathbb{Z}, +, \cdot)$ is a commutative ring with unit element 1. This implies that $(\mathbb{Z}/m\mathbb{Z}, +, \cdot)$ is a commutative ring with unit element $1 + m\mathbb{Z}$. The latter ring is called the *residue class ring* modulo m.

Instead of writing $(R, +, \cdot)$ for a ring, we also write R if it is clear which operations are meant. For example, we write $\mathbb{Z}/m\mathbb{Z}$ for the residue class ring modulo m.

Definition 2.4.3
Let R be a ring with unit element. An element a of R is called *invertible* or a *unit* if it is invertible in the multiplicative semigroup of R. The element a is called a *zero divisor* if it is nonzero and there is a nonzero $b \in R$ with $ab = 0$ or $ba = 0$.

In Exercise 2.22.9, it is shown that the units of a commutative ring R form a group. It is called the *unit group* of R and is denoted by R^*.

Example 2.4.4
The ring of integers contains no zero divisors.

The zero divisors of the residue class ring $\mathbb{Z}/m\mathbb{Z}$ are the residue classes $a + m\mathbb{Z}$ with $1 < \gcd(a, m) < m$. In fact, if $a + m\mathbb{Z}$ is a zero divisor of $\mathbb{Z}/m\mathbb{Z}$, then there is an integer b with $ab \equiv 0 \bmod m$ but neither $a \equiv 0 \bmod m$ nor $b \equiv 0 \bmod m$. Hence, m is a divisor of ab but neither of a nor of b. This means that $1 < \gcd(a, m) < m$. If, conversely, $1 < \gcd(a, m) < m$ and $b = m/\gcd(a, m)$, then $a \not\equiv 0 \bmod m$, $ab \equiv 0 \bmod m$, and $b \not\equiv 0 \bmod m$. Therefore, $a + m\mathbb{Z}$ is a zero divisor of $\mathbb{Z}/m\mathbb{Z}$.

If m is a prime, then $\mathbb{Z}/m\mathbb{Z}$ contains no zero divisors.

2.5   Fields

Definition 2.5.1

A *field* is a commutative ring in which every nonzero element is invertible.

Example 2.5.2

The set of integers is not a field because most integers are not invertible, but it is contained in the field of rational numbers. Also, the real and complex numbers form a field. As we will see later, the residue class ring modulo a prime number is a field.

2.6   Division in the Residue Class Ring

Divisibility in rings is defined as divisibility in $\mathbb{Z}$. To explain this in more detail, we let R be a ring and let $a, n \in R$.

Definition 2.6.1

We say that *a divides n* if there is a, $b \in R$ such that $n = ab$.

If the ring element a divides n, then a is called a *divisor* of n and n is called a *multiple* of a, and we write $a|n$. We also say that n is *divisible* by a. If a is not a divisor of n, then we write $a \nmid n$.

We study which elements of the residue class ring mod m are invertible.

First, we note that the residue class $a + m\mathbb{Z}$ is invertible in $\mathbb{Z}/m\mathbb{Z}$ if and only if the congruence

$$ax \equiv 1 \bmod m \tag{2.4}$$

is solvable. The next theorem answers the question when this is the case.

Theorem 2.6.2

The residue class $a + m\mathbb{Z}$ is invertible in $\mathbb{Z}/m\mathbb{Z}$ (i.e., the congruence (2.4) is solvable) if and only if $\gcd(a, m) = 1$. If $\gcd(a, m) = 1$, then the inverse of $a + m\mathbb{Z}$ is uniquely determined (i.e., the solution x of (2.4) is uniquely determined mod m).

Proof. Let $g = \gcd(a, m)$ and let x be a solution of (2.4). Then g is a divisor of m and therefore it is a divisor of $ax - 1$. But g is also a divisor of a. Hence, g is a divisor of 1 (i.e., $g = 1$ because g, being a gcd, is positive). Conversely, let $g = 1$. Then by Corollary 1.7.7 there are numbers x, y with $ax + my = 1$ (i.e., $ax - 1 = -my$). This shows that x is a solution of the congruence (2.4) and that $x + m\mathbb{Z}$ is an inverse of $a + m\mathbb{Z}$ in $\mathbb{Z}/m\mathbb{Z}$.

To prove the uniqueness, let $v + m\mathbb{Z}$ be another inverse of $a + m\mathbb{Z}$. Then $ax \equiv av \bmod m$. Therefore, m divides $a(x - v)$. Because $\gcd(a, m) = 1$, this implies that m is a divisor of $x - v$. This proves $x \equiv v \bmod m$. □

A residue class $a + m\mathbb{Z}$ with $\gcd(a, m) = 1$ is called *an invertible residue class* modulo m. Theorem 2.6.2 implies that a residue class $a + m\mathbb{Z}$ with $1 \le a < m$ is either a zero divisor or an invertible residue class (i.e., a unit in the residue class ring mod m).

In the proof of Theorem 2.6.2, we have shown that we can solve the congruence $ax \equiv 1 \bmod m$ with the extended euclidean algorithm (see Section 1.9) since it computes the representation $1 = ax + my$. In fact, we only need the coefficient x. By Theorem 1.10.5, the solution of the congruence can be computed efficiently.

Example 2.6.3
Let $m = 12$. The residue class $a + 12\mathbb{Z}$ is invertible in $\mathbb{Z}/12\mathbb{Z}$ if $\gcd(a, 12) = 1$. The invertible residue classes mod 12 are therefore $1 + 12\mathbb{Z}, 5 + 12\mathbb{Z}, 7 + 12\mathbb{Z}, 11 + 12\mathbb{Z}$. To find the inverse of $5 + 12\mathbb{Z}$, we use the extended euclidean algorithm. We obtain $5 * 5 \equiv 1 \bmod 12$. Analogously, we have $7 * 7 \equiv 1 \bmod 12$ and $11 * 11 \equiv 1 \bmod 12$.

We also introduce the residue class field modulo a prime number, which is frequently used in cryptography.

Theorem 2.6.4
The residue class ring $\mathbb{Z}/m\mathbb{Z}$ is a field if and only if m is a prime number.

Proof. By Theorem 2.6.2, the ring $\mathbb{Z}/m\mathbb{Z}$ is a field if and only if $\gcd(k, m) = 1$ for all k with $1 \le k < m$. This is true if and only if m is a prime number. □

2.7 Analysis of Operations in the Residue Class Ring

In all algorithms of public-key cryptography, computing in residue class rings is very time-consuming. Frequently, those computations must be carried out on smart cards. It is therefore important to know how efficiently those computations can be carried out. This is described in this section.

We assume that the elements of the residue class ring $\mathbb{Z}/m\mathbb{Z}$ are represented by their smallest nonnegative representatives. Under this assumption, we estimate the running time of the operations in the residue class ring.

Let $a, b \in \{0, 1, \ldots, m-1\}$.

To compute $(a + m\mathbb{Z}) + (b + m\mathbb{Z})$, we must determine $(a + b) \bmod m$. First, we compute $c = a + b$. The required sum is $c + m\mathbb{Z}$, but c may be the wrong representative since we only know that $0 \leq c < 2m$. If $0 \leq c < m$, then c is the correct representative. If $m \leq c < 2m$, then the correct representative is $c - m$ because $0 \leq c - m < m$. In this case, we replace c by $c - m$. Likewise, $(a + m\mathbb{Z}) - (b + m\mathbb{Z})$ is computed. We determine $c = a - b$. Then $-m < c < m$. If $0 \leq c < m$, then c is the correct representative of the difference. If $-m < c < 0$, then the correct representative is $c + m$. Hence, c must be replaced by $c + m$. The results in Section 1.5 imply that the sum and difference of two residue classes modulo m can be computed in time $O(\text{size } m)$.

Now we wish to compute $(a + m\mathbb{Z})(b + m\mathbb{Z})$. We determine $c = ab$. Then $0 \leq c < m^2$. We divide c with remainder by m and replace c by the remainder of this division. For the quotient q of this division, we have $0 \leq q < m$. By the results of Section 1.5, we can perform the multiplication and the division in time $O((\text{size } m)^2)$. Hence, two residue classes mod m can be multiplied in time $O((\text{size } m)^2)$.

Finally, we discuss how to invert $a + m\mathbb{Z}$. Using the extended euclidean algorithm, we compute $g = \gcd(a, m)$ and x with $ax \equiv g \bmod m$ and $0 \leq x < m$. By Corollary 1.10.3, we have $|x| \leq m/(2g)$. Possibly, the algorithm yields a negative x. Then x is replaced by $x + m$. By Theorem 1.10.5, this computation requires time $O((\text{size } m)^2)$. The residue class $a + m\mathbb{Z}$ is invertible if and only if $g = 1$.

In this case, x is the least nonnegative representative of the inverse class. The total computing time is $O((\text{size } m)^2)$. This implies that the division by an invertible residue class mod m takes time $O((\text{size } m)^2)$.

In all algorithms, only constantly many numbers of size $O(\text{size } m)$ must be stored. Therefore, the algorithms require space $O(\text{size } m)$. We remark that there are algorithms for multiplying and dividing residue classes that are asymptotically more efficient. They require time $O(\log m (\log \log m)^2)$ (see [3]). For numbers of the sizes relevant in cryptography, these algorithms are, however, slower than the ones that we have analyzed here. In many situations, the $O((\text{size } m)^2)$ algorithms admit optimizations. An overview can be found in [24].

We have proved the following theorem.

Theorem 2.7.1
Suppose the residue classes modulo m are represented by their least non-negative representatives. Then two residue classes mod m can be added and subtracted using time and space $O(\text{size } m)$. They can be multiplied and divided using time $O((\text{size } m)^2)$ and space $O(\text{size } m)$.

2.8 Multiplicative Group of Residues

The following result is of crucial importance in cryptography.

Theorem 2.8.1
The set of all invertible residue classes modulo m is a finite abelian group with respect to multiplication.

Proof. By Theorem 2.6.2, this set is the unit group of the residue class rings mod m. □

The group of invertible residue classes modulo m is called the *multiplicative group of residues* modulo m and is written $(\mathbb{Z}/m\mathbb{Z})^*$. Its order is denoted by $\varphi(m)$. The function

$$\mathbb{N} \to \mathbb{N}, \quad m \mapsto \varphi(m)$$

is called the *Euler φ-function*. Observe that $\varphi(m)$ is the number of integers a in $\{1, 2, \ldots, m\}$ with $\gcd(a, m) = 1$. In particular, $\varphi(1) = 1$.

TABLE 2.1   Values of the Euler φ-function.

m	1	2	3	4	5	6	7	8	9	10	11	12	13	14	15
$\varphi(m)$	1	1	2	2	4	2	6	4	6	4	10	4	12	6	8

Example 2.8.2
The multiplicative group of residues mod 12 is $(\mathbb{Z}/12\mathbb{Z})^* = \{1 + 12\mathbb{Z}, 5 + 12\mathbb{Z}, 7 + 12\mathbb{Z}, 11 + 12\mathbb{Z}\}$. Hence, $\varphi(12) = 4$.

A few values of the Euler φ-function can be found in Table 2.1.

In this table, we see that $\varphi(p) = p - 1$ for the prime numbers p. This is in general true for any prime numbers p because all numbers a between 1 and $p - 1$ are prime to p. This proves the following theorem.

Theorem 2.8.3
If p is a prime number, then $\varphi(p) = p - 1$.

The Euler φ-function has the following useful property.

Theorem 2.8.4

$$\sum_{d|m, d>0} \varphi(d) = m.$$

Proof. We have

$$\sum_{d|m, d>0} \varphi(d) = \sum_{d|m, d>0} \varphi(m/d)$$

because the set of positive divisors of m is $\{m/d : d|m, d > 0\}$. Now $\varphi(m/d)$ is the number of integers a in the set $\{1, \ldots, m/d\}$ with $\gcd(a, m/d) = 1$. Hence, $\varphi(m/d)$ is the number of integers b in $\{1, 2, \ldots, m\}$ with $\gcd(b, m) = d$. Therefore,

$$\sum_{d|m, d>0} \varphi(d) = \sum_{d|m, d>0} |\{b : 1 \le b \le m \text{ with } \gcd(b, m) = d\}|.$$

But

$$\{1, 2, \ldots, m\} = \cup_{d|m, d>0}\{b : 1 \le b \le m \text{ with } \gcd(b, m) = d\}.$$

This implies the assertion. $\square$

2.9 Order of Group Elements

Next, we introduce element orders and their properties. Let G be a group that is multiplicatively written with neutral element 1.

Definition 2.9.1
Let $g \in G$. If there is a positive integer e with $g^e = 1$, then the smallest such integer is called the *order* of g in G. Otherwise, we say that the order of g in G is infinite. The order of g in G is denoted by order$_G g$. If it is clear which group we mean, we also write order g.

Theorem 2.9.2
Let $g \in G$ and $e \in \mathbb{Z}$. Then $g^e = 1$ if and only if e is divisible by the order of g in G.

Proof. Let $n = $ order g. If $e = kn$, then

$$g^e = g^{kn} = (g^n)^k = 1^k = 1.$$

Conversely, let $g^e = 1$ and $e = qn + r$ with $0 \leq r < n$. Then

$$g^r = g^{e-qn} = g^e (g^n)^{-q} = 1.$$

Because n is the least positive integer with $g^n = 1$, and since $0 \leq r < n$, we have $r = 0$ and therefore $e = qn$. Hence, n is a divisor of e, as asserted. $\qquad\square$

Corollary 2.9.3
Let $g \in G$ and let k, l be integers. Then $g^l = g^k$ if and only if $l \equiv k \bmod$ order g.

Proof. Set $e = l - k$ and apply Theorem 2.9.2. $\qquad\square$

Example 2.9.4
We determine the order of $2 + 13\mathbb{Z}$ in $(\mathbb{Z}/13\mathbb{Z})^*$. For this purpose, we use the following table:

k	0	1	2	3	4	5	6	7	8	9	10	11	12
$2^k \bmod 13$	1	2	4	8	3	6	12	11	9	5	10	7	1

We see that the order of $2 + 13\mathbb{Z}$ is 12. This order is equal to the group order of $(\mathbb{Z}/13\mathbb{Z})^*$, but this is not true for any group element. For example, the order of $4 + 13\mathbb{Z}$ is 6.

We determine the order of powers.

Theorem 2.9.5

If $g \in G$ is of finite order e and if n is an integer, then order $g^n = e/\gcd(e, n)$.

Proof. We have

$$(g^n)^{e/\gcd(e,n)} = (g^e)^{n/\gcd(e,n)} = 1,$$

so Theorem 2.9.3 implies that $e/\gcd(e, n)$ is a multiple of the order of g^n. Suppose

$$1 = (g^n)^k = g^{nk}.$$

Then Theorem 2.9.3 implies that e is a divisor of nk. Therefore, $e/\gcd(e, n)$ is a divisor of k, which implies the assertion. $\square$

2.10 Subgroups

We introduce subgroups. By G we denote a group.

Definition 2.10.1

A subset U of G is called a *subgroup* of G if U together with the group operation of G is a group.

Example 2.10.2

For all $g \in G$, the set $\{g^k : k \in \mathbb{Z}\}$ is a subgroup of G. It is called the *subgroup generated* by g and is denoted by $\langle g \rangle$.

If g has finite order e, then $\langle g \rangle = \{g^k : 0 \leq k < e\}$. In fact, for any integer x we have $g^x = g^{x \bmod e}$ by Corollary 2.9.3. Corollary 2.9.3 also implies that e is the order of $\langle g \rangle$.

Example 2.10.3

By Example 2.9.4, the subgroup generated by $2 + 13\mathbb{Z}$ in $(\mathbb{Z}/13\mathbb{Z})^*$ is the full group $(\mathbb{Z}/13\mathbb{Z})^*$. The subgroup generated by $4 + 13\mathbb{Z}$ has order 6. It is $\{k + 13\mathbb{Z} : k = 1, 4, 3, 12, 9, 10\}$.

Definition 2.10.4

If $G = \langle g \rangle$ for some $g \in G$, then G is called *cyclic* and g is called a *generator* of G.

Example 2.10.5

The additive group $\mathbb{Z}$ is cyclic. It has two generators, namely 1 and -1.

Theorem 2.10.6

If G is finite and cyclic, then G has exactly $\varphi(|G|)$ generators and they are all of order $|G|$.

Proof. Let $g \in G$ be an element of order e. Then the subgroup generated by g has order e. Hence, an element of G is a generator of G if and only if it is of order $|G|$. We determine the number of elements of order $|G|$ in G. Let g be a generator of G. Then $G = \{g^k : 0 \le k < |G|\}$. By Theorem 2.9.5 an element of this set is of order $|G|$ if and only if $\gcd(k, |G|) = 1$. This means that the number of generators of G is exactly $\varphi(|G|)$. $\qquad\qquad\square$

Example 2.10.7

Since the order of $2 + 13\mathbb{Z}$ in $(\mathbb{Z}/13\mathbb{Z})^*$ is 12, the group $(\mathbb{Z}/13\mathbb{Z})^*$ is cyclic. We will prove later that $(\mathbb{Z}/p\mathbb{Z})^*$ is always cyclic if p is a prime number. By Example 2.9.4, the generators of this group are the residue classes $a + 13\mathbb{Z}$ with $a \in \{2, 6, 7, 11\}$.

To prove the next result, we need a few notions. A map $f : X \to Y$ is called *injective* if $f(x) = f(y)$ implies $x = y$ for all $x, y \in X$. This means that two different elements of X can never have the same image under f. The map is called *surjective* if for any $y \in Y$ there is $x \in X$ with $f(x) = y$. The map is called *bijective* if it is injective and surjective. A bijective map is also called a *bijection*. If there is a bijection between two finite sets, then the sets have the same number of elements.

Example 2.10.8

Consider the map $f : \mathbb{N} \to \mathbb{N}$, $n \mapsto f(n) = n$. This map is obviously bijective.

Consider the map $f : \mathbb{N} \to \mathbb{N}$, $n \mapsto f(n) = n^2$. Since positive integers have pairwise distinct squares, the map is injective. But since 3 is not the square of a positive integer, the map is not surjective.

Consider the map $f : \{1, 2, 3, 4, 5, 6\} \to \{0, 1, 2, 3, 4, 5\}$, $n \mapsto f(n) = n \bmod 6$. Since both sets are sets of representatives modulo 6, the map is bijective.

We prove a theorem of Lagrange.

Theorem 2.10.9
If G is a finite group, then the order of each subgroup of G divides the order of G.

Proof. Let H be a subgroup of G. We say that two elements a and b of G are equivalent if $a/b = ab^{-1}$ belongs to H. This is an equivalence relation. In fact, $a/a = 1 \in H$; hence the relation is reflexive. Since $a/b \in H$, the inverse b/a also belongs to H, so the relation is symmetric. Finally, since $a/b \in H$ and $b/c \in H$, it follows that $a/c = (a/b)(b/c) \in H$. This proves the transitivity of the relation.

We show that all the equivalence classes have the same cardinality. The equivalence class of $a \in G$ is $\{ha : h \in H\}$. Let a, b be two elements of G. Consider the map

$$\{ha : h \in H\} \to \{hb : h \in H\}, ha \mapsto hb.$$

The map is injective because in the group G cancellation is possible. Moreover, the map is surjective since an inverse image of $g \in G$ is ga/b. Therefore, all equivalence classes have the same number of elements. Since G is the disjoint union of all the equivalence classes, the number of elements in one equivalence class must divide $|G|$. But the equivalence class of 1 is H; hence $|H|$ divides $|G|$.   □

Definition 2.10.10
If H is a subgroup of G, then the positive integer $|G|/|H|$ is called the *index* of H in G.

2.11   Fermat's Little Theorem

We formulate the famous theorem of Fermat.

Theorem 2.11.1
If $gcd(a, m) = 1$, then $a^{\varphi(m)} \equiv 1 \bmod m$.

If $gcd(a, m) = 1$, then by Theorem 2.11.1 we have

$$a^{\varphi(m)-1} \cdot a \equiv 1 \bmod m.$$

This implies that $a^{\varphi(m)-1} + m\mathbb{Z}$ is the inverse residue class of $a + m\mathbb{Z}$. Hence, we have a new method for computing inverses mod m. If we apply fast exponentiation as explained in Section 2.12, this method can compete with the algorithm that is based on the extended euclidean algorithm.

We prove Fermat's little theorem in a more general context. Let G be a finite group of order $|G|$, multiplicatively written, with neutral element 1.

Theorem 2.11.2
The order of every group element divides the group order.

Proof. The order of a group element g is the order of the subgroup generated by g. Therefore, the assertion follows from Theorem 2.10.9. □

From this result, we deduce the following general version of Fermat's little theorem.

Corollary 2.11.3
We have $g^{|G|} = 1$ for all $g \in G$.

Proof. The assertion follows from Theorem 2.11.2 and Theorem 2.9.3. □

Since $(\mathbb{Z}/m\mathbb{Z})^*$ is a finite abelian group of order $\varphi(m)$, Theorem 2.11.1 follows from Corollary 2.11.3.

2.12 Fast Exponentiation

Theorem 2.11.1 shows that an integer x with $x \equiv a^{\varphi(m)-1} \bmod m$ solves the congruence (2.4). In order for this new method of solving (2.4) to be efficient, we must be able to compute quickly powers mod m.

We now describe an efficient algorithm for computing powers in a monoid G. This algorithm and its variants are central ingredients of many cryptographic protocols. Let $g \in G$ and e be a positive integer.

Let

$$e = \sum_{i=0}^{k} e_i 2^i$$

be the binary expansion of e. Observe that the coefficients e_i are either 0 or 1. Therefore,

$$g^e = g^{\sum_{i=0}^{k} e_i 2^i} = \prod_{i=0}^{k} (g^{2^i})^{e_i} = \prod_{0 \le i \le k, e_i = 1} g^{2^i}.$$

From this formula, we obtain the following idea:

1. Compute the successive squares g^{2^i}, $0 \le i \le k$.

2. Determine g^e as the product of those g^{2^i} for which $e_i = 1$.

Observe that

$$g^{2^{i+1}} = (g^{2^i})^2.$$

Therefore, $g^{2^{i+1}}$ can be computed from g^{2^i} by one squaring. Before we explain the algorithm in more detail, we give an example to show that this method is much faster than the naive one.

Example 2.12.1
We determine 6^{73} mod 100. We write the binary expansion of the exponent:

$$73 = 1 + 2^3 + 2^6.$$

Then we determine the successive squares of 6, $6^2 = 36$, $6^{2^2} = 36^2 \equiv -4 \bmod 100$, $6^{2^3} \equiv 16 \bmod 100$, $6^{2^4} \equiv 16^2 \equiv 56 \bmod 100$, $6^{2^5} \equiv 56^2 \equiv 36 \bmod 100$, $6^{2^6} \equiv -4 \bmod 100$. Hence, $6^{73} \equiv 6 * 6^{2^3} * 6^{2^6} \equiv 6 * 16 * (-4) \equiv 16 \bmod 100$. We have only computed 6 squares and two products $(\mathbb{Z}/m\mathbb{Z})^*$ to obtain the result. If we would have computed 6^{73} mod 100 as $6 * 6 * \cdots * 6$ mod 100, 72 multiplications modulo 100 would have been necessary.

Here is a C++ implementation of the algorithm. It uses the LiDIA types `bigmod` and `bigint`. The class `bigmod` implements the residue class ring $\mathbb{Z}/m\mathbb{Z}$. The class `bigint` implements multiprecision integers.

```
bigmod pow(bigmod base, bigint exponent) {

  bigmod result = 1;

  while (exponent > 0) {
    if (!exponent.is_even())
      result = result * base;
    square(base, base);
    exponent = exponent/2;
  }
  return result;
}
```

This program works as follows. The variable `result` contains the current value of the result. The variable `base` contains the successive squares. The new square is obtained by squaring the old one. The result is multiplied by that square if the corresponding bit in the exponent is 1. The following theorem states the complexity of the fast exponentiation algorithm.

Theorem 2.12.2
pow *computes* base^{exponent} *using at most* size exponent-1 *squarings and multiplications.* pow *only stores a constant number of group elements.*

From Theorem 2.12.2 and Theorem 2.7.1, we obtain an estimate for the time necessary to compute powers in the multiplicative group of residues mod m.

Corollary 2.12.3
If e is an integer and $a \in \{0, \ldots, m-1\}$, then the computation of a^e mod m requires time $O((\text{size } e)(\text{size } m)^2)$ and space $O(\text{size } e + \text{size } m)$.

We see that exponentiation in the multiplicative group of residues is possible in polynomial time. Variants of the fast exponentiation algorithm are described in [24]. Under certain circumstances, they may be more efficient than the basic variant.

2.13   Fast Evaluation of Power Products

Let G be a finite abelian group, $g_1, \ldots, g_k$ be elements of G, and $e_1, \ldots, e_k$ be nonnegative integers. We want to evaluate the power product

$$A = \prod_{i=1}^{k} g_i^{e_i}.$$

We need the binary expansion of the exponents e_i. They are normalized to equal length. Let

$$b_{i,n-1} b_{i,n-2} \ldots b_{i,0}, \quad 1 \le i \le k$$

be the binary expansion of e_i. For at least one i, let $b_{i,n-1}$ be nonzero. For $1 \le i \le k$ and $0 \le j < n$, let $e_{i,j}$ be the integer with binary expansion $b_{i,n-1} b_{i,n-2} \ldots b_{i,j}$. Moreover, let $e_{i,n} = 0$ for $1 \le i \le k$. Then $e_i = e_{i,0}$ for $1 \le i \le k$. Finally, set

$$A_j = \prod_{i=1}^{k} g_i^{e_{i,j}}, \quad 0 \le j \le n.$$

Then $A_0 = A$ is the required power product. We compute $A_n, A_{n-1}, \ldots, A_0 = A$ iteratively. Observe that

$$e_{i,j} = 2 * e_{i,j+1} + b_{i,j}, \quad 1 \le i \le k, 0 \le j < n.$$

Therefore,

$$A_j = A_{j+1}^2 \prod_{i=1}^{k} g_i^{b_{i,j}}, \quad 0 \le j < n.$$

For all $\vec{b} = (b_1, \ldots, b_k) \in \{0, 1\}^k$, we determine

$$G_{\vec{b}} = \prod_{i=1}^{k} g_i^{b_i}.$$

Then

$$A_j = A_{j+1}^2 G_{(b_{1,j}, \ldots, b_{k,j})}, \quad 0 \le j < n.$$

We analyze this algorithm. The computation of the $G_{\vec{b}}$, $\vec{b} \in \{0, 1\}^k$ requires $2^k - 2$ multiplications in G. Then the computation of A

requires $n - 1$ squarings and multiplications in G. Therefore, the following result is proved.

Theorem 2.13.1

Let $k \in \mathbb{N}$, $g_i \in G$, $e_i \in \mathbb{Z}_{\geq 0}$, $1 \leq i \leq k$, and let n be the maximal binary length of the e_i. Then the power product $\prod_{i=1}^{k} g_i^{e_i}$ can be computed using $2^k + n - 3$ multiplications and $n - 1$ squarings in G.

For the case $k = 1$, the algorithm just described is an alternative method for fast exponentiation. Wheras in the method from Section 2.12 the binary expansion of the exponents is scanned from right to left, here we work from left to right.

2.14 Computation of Element Orders

In cryptographic protocols, group elements of large order are frequently used. In this section, we discuss the problem of finding the order of an element g of a finite group G or to check whether a given positive integer is the order of g.

The following theorem shows how to compute the order of g if the prime factorization

$$|G| = \prod_{p||G|} p^{e(p)}$$

of the order of G is known. If this prime factorization is unknown, then it is not easy to find the order of g. However, in public-key cryptography, the group order and its factorization typically are known.

Theorem 2.14.1

For a prime divisor p of $|G|$, let $f(p)$ be the greatest integer such that $g^{|G|/p^{f(p)}} = 1$. Then

$$\text{order } g = \prod_{p||G|} p^{e(p)-f(p)}. \tag{2.5}$$

Proof. Exercise 2.22.22. $\qquad\qquad\qquad\qquad\qquad\qquad\qquad\qquad$ □

Theorem 2.14.1 yields an algorithm that computes the order of an element $g \in G$.

Example 2.14.2

Let G be the multiplicative group of residues modulo 101. Its order is $100 = 2^2 * 5^2$. Hence,

$$e(2) = e(5) = 2.$$

We compute the order of $2 + 101\mathbb{Z}$. First, we compute the numbers $f(p)$ from Theorem 2.14.1. We obtain

$$2^{2*5^2} \equiv 2^{50} \equiv -1 \bmod 101.$$

Hence, $f(2) = 0$. Moreover,

$$2^{2^2*5} \equiv 2^{20} \equiv -6 \bmod 101.$$

Hence, $f(5) = 0$, so the order of $2 + 101\mathbb{Z}$ is 100. This means that $\mathbb{Z}/101\mathbb{Z}$ is cyclic and $2 + 101\mathbb{Z}$ is a generator of this group.

The algorithm for computing the order of g determines the numbers $f(p)$ for all prime divisors p of $|G|$. Then it determines the element order. The implementation details are left to the reader.

Next, we discuss the problem of testing whether a given number is the order of $g \in G$. This is necessary if we want to find a generator of a cyclic group. We need the following result, which is an immediate consequence of Theorem 2.14.1.

Corollary 2.14.3

Let $n \in \mathbb{N}$. If $g^n = 1$ and $g^{n/p} \neq 1$ for each prime divisor p of n, then n is the order of g.

We illustrate the verification algorithm in an example.

Example 2.14.4

We claim that 25 is the order of the residue class $5 + 101\mathbb{Z}$ in the multiplicative group of residues modulo 101. In fact, $5^{25} \equiv 1 \bmod 101$ and $5^5 \equiv -6 \bmod 101$. Hence, the assertion follows from Corollary 2.14.3.

2.15   The Chinese Remainder Theorem

Let $m_1, \ldots, m_n$ be positive integers that are pairwise coprime. Let $a_1, \ldots, a_n$ be integers. We explain how to solve the following *simultaneous congruence*:

$$x \equiv a_1 \bmod m_1, \quad x \equiv a_2 \bmod m_2, \quad \ldots, \quad x \equiv a_n \bmod m_n. \quad (2.6)$$

Set

$$m = \prod_{i=1}^{n} m_i, \quad M_i = m/m_i, \quad 1 \leq i \leq n.$$

We will see that the solution of the congruence (2.6) is unique modulo m. Since the m_i are pairwise coprime, we have

$$\gcd(m_i, M_i) = 1, \quad 1 \leq i \leq n.$$

We use the extended euclidean algorithm to compute numbers $y_i \in \mathbb{Z}$, $1 \leq i \leq n$ with

$$y_i M_i \equiv 1 \bmod m_i, \quad 1 \leq i \leq n. \quad (2.7)$$

Then we set

$$x = \left(\sum_{i=1}^{n} a_i y_i M_i \right) \bmod m. \quad (2.8)$$

We show that x is a solution of the simultaneous congruence (2.6). From (2.7), we obtain

$$a_i y_i M_i \equiv a_i \bmod m_i, \quad 1 \leq i \leq n, \quad (2.9)$$

and because for $j \neq i$ the integer m_i is a divisor of M_j, we have

$$a_j y_j M_j \equiv 0 \bmod m_i, \quad 1 \leq i, j \leq n, i \neq j. \quad (2.10)$$

From (2.8), (2.9), and (2.10), we deduce

$$x \equiv a_i y_i M_i + \sum_{j=1, j \neq i}^{n} a_j y_j M_j \equiv a_i \bmod m_i, \quad 1 \leq i \leq n. \quad (2.11)$$

Hence, x solves the congruence (2.6).

Example 2.15.1

We solve the simultaneous congruence

$$x \equiv 2 \bmod 4, \quad x \equiv 1 \bmod 3, \quad x \equiv 0 \bmod 5.$$

We have $m_1 = 4$, $m_2 = 3$, $m_3 = 5$, $a_1 = 2$, $a_2 = 1$, $a_3 = 0$. Therefore, $m = 60$, $M_1 = 60/4 = 15$, $M_2 = 60/3 = 20$, $M_3 = 60/5 = 12$. We solve $y_1 M_1 \equiv 1 \bmod m_1$ (i.e., $-y_1 \equiv 1 \bmod 4$). A solution is $y_1 = -1$. We solve $y_2 M_2 \equiv 1 \bmod m_2$ (i.e., $-y_2 \equiv 1 \bmod 3$). A solution is $y_2 = -1$. Finally, we solve $y_3 M_3 \equiv 1 \bmod m_3$ (i.e., $2y_3 \equiv 1 \bmod 5$). A solution is $y_3 = 3$. Therefore, $x \equiv -2 * 1520 \equiv 10 \bmod 60$ (i.e., $x = 10$ is a solution of the simultaneous congruence).

Observe that in the algorithm just described, the numbers y_i and M_i do not depend on the a_i. Therefore, if the integers y_i and M_i are precomputed, then (2.8) can be used to solve (2.6) for any selection of the a_i.

Here is a C++ program for solving simultaneous congruences that uses the preceding ideas. The function xgcd_left(inverse,M,m) computes the inverse of M mod m.

```
bigint crtPrecomputation(bigint moduli[],
                         bigint multiplier[], int number)
                {
    int i;
    bigint modulus = 1;
    bigint m;
    bigint M;
    bigint inverse;

    for(i = 0; i < number; i++) modulus=modulus*moduli[i];

    for(i = 0; i < number; i++) {
      m = moduli[i];
      M = modulus/m;
      xgcd_left(inverse,M,m);
      multiplier[i] = inverse*M%modulus;
    }
    return modulus;
}
```

```
bigint crt(bigint moduli[], bigint x[], int number) {

    bigint multiplier[number];
    bigint result = 0;
    bigint modulus = crtPrecomputation(moduli, multiplier,
                                        number);
    int i;

    for(i = 0; i < number; i++)
        result = (result + multiplier[i]*x[i])%modulus;

    return result;
}
```

Now we formulate the *Chinese remainder theorem*.

Theorem 2.15.2

Let $m_1, \ldots, m_n$ be pairwise coprime positive integers and let $a_1, \ldots, a_n$ be integers. Then the simultaneous congruence (2.6) has a solution x which is unique mod $m = \prod_{i=1}^{n} m_i$.

Proof. The existence has been proved in (2.11). Hence, we must prove the uniqueness. Let x and x' be two such solutions. Then $x \equiv x' \bmod m_i$, $1 \leq i \leq n$. Because the numbers m_i are pairwise coprime, it follows that $x \equiv x' \bmod m$.   □

The following theorem estimates the effort that is necessary to construct a solution of a simultaneous congruence.

Theorem 2.15.3

The algorithm for solving the simultaneous congruence (2.6) requires time $O((\text{size } m)^2)$ and space $O(\text{size } m)$.

Proof. By the results of Section 1.5, the computation of m requires time $O(\text{size } m \sum_{i=1}^{n} \text{size } m_i) = O((\text{size } m)^2)$. The computation of all M_i and y_i and of x takes the same time. This follows from the results of Section 1.5 and from Theorem 1.10.5. The upper bound for the space is easy to verify.   □

2.16 Decomposition of the Residue Class Ring

We use the Chinese remainder theorem to decompose the residue class ring $\mathbb{Z}/m\mathbb{Z}$. Using this decomposition, we can reduce computations in a large residue class ring $\mathbb{Z}/m\mathbb{Z}$ to computations in many small residue class rings $\mathbb{Z}/m_i\mathbb{Z}$. Frequently, this is more efficient. This method can, for example, be used to speed up decryption in the RSA cryptosystem.

We define the *product of rings*.

Definition 2.16.1
Let $R_1, R_2, \ldots, R_n$ be rings. Their *direct product* $\prod_{i=1}^{n} R_i$ is the set of all tuples $(r_1, r_2, \ldots, r_n) \in R_1 \times \cdots \times R_n$ together with component-wise addition and multiplication.

It is easy to verify that $R = \prod_{i=1}^{n} R_i$ is a ring. If the R_i are commutative rings with unit elements e_i, $1 \leq i \leq n$, then R is a commutative ring with unit element $(e_1, \ldots, e_n)$.

The direct product of groups is defined analogously.

Example 2.16.2
Let $R_1 = \mathbb{Z}/2\mathbb{Z}$ and $R_2 = \mathbb{Z}/9\mathbb{Z}$. Then $R = R_1 \times R_2$ consists of all pairs $(a + 2\mathbb{Z}, b + 9\mathbb{Z})$, $0 \leq a < 2, 0 \leq b < 9$. Hence, $R = R_1 \times R_2$ has exactly 18 elements. The unit element in R is $(1 + 2\mathbb{Z}, 1 + 9\mathbb{Z})$.

We also need the notion of a homomorphism and an isomorphism.

Definition 2.16.3
Let $(X, \perp_1, \ldots, \perp_n)$ and $(Y, \top_1, \ldots, \top_n)$ be sets with n operations. A map $f : X \to Y$ is called a *homomorphism* if $f(a \perp_i b) = f(a) \top_i f(b)$ for all $a, b \in X$ and $1 \leq i \leq n$. If the map is bijective, it is called an *isomorphism*.

If we know an isomorphism between two rings which can be efficiently computed in both directions, then computational tasks in the one ring can be solved in the other ring. This may result in a more efficient algorithm.

Example 2.16.4

If m is a positive integer, then the map $\mathbb{Z} \to \mathbb{Z}/m\mathbb{Z}$, $a \mapsto a + m\mathbb{Z}$ is a ring homomorphism.

If G is a cyclic group of order n with generator g, then $\mathbb{Z}/n\mathbb{Z} \to G$, $e + n\mathbb{Z} \mapsto g^e$ is an isomorphism of groups (see Exercise 2.22.24).

Theorem 2.16.5

Let $m_1, \ldots, m_n$ be pairwise coprime integers and let $m = m_1 m_2 \cdots m_n$. Then the map

$$\mathbb{Z}/m\mathbb{Z} \to \prod_{i=1}^{n} \mathbb{Z}/m_i\mathbb{Z}, \quad a + m\mathbb{Z} \mapsto (a + m_1\mathbb{Z}, \ldots, a + m_n\mathbb{Z}) \quad (2.12)$$

is an isomorphism of rings.

Proof. First, we note that (2.12) is well defined. In fact, if $a \equiv b \bmod m$, then $a \equiv b \bmod m_i$ for $1 \leq i \leq n$. It is easy to verify that (2.12) is a homomorphism of rings. To prove surjectivity, let $(a_1 + m_1\mathbb{Z}, \ldots, a_n + m_n\mathbb{Z}) \in \prod_{i=1}^{n} \mathbb{Z}/m_i\mathbb{Z}$. Then Theorem 2.15.2 implies that this tuple has an inverse image under (2.12). The injectivity follows from the uniqueness in Theorem 2.15.2. $\square$

Theorem 2.16.5 shows that computations in $\mathbb{Z}/m\mathbb{Z}$ can be reduced to computations in $\prod_{i=1}^{n} \mathbb{Z}/m_i\mathbb{Z}$. For a residue class mod m, the corresponding tuple of residue classes mod m_i is determined. The computation is carried out using those tuples, and the Chinese remainder theorem is used to compute the residue class mod m that corresponds to the result of the computation.

2.17 A Formula for the Euler φ-Function

We prove a formula for the Euler φ-function.

Theorem 2.17.1

Let $m_1, \ldots, m_n$ be pairwise coprime positive integers and $m = \prod_{i=1}^{n} m_i$. Then $\varphi(m) = \varphi(m_1)\varphi(m_2) \cdots \varphi(m_n)$.

Proof. Theorem 2.16.5 implies that the map

$$(\mathbb{Z}/m\mathbb{Z})^* \rightarrow \prod_{i=1}^{n}(\mathbb{Z}/m_i\mathbb{Z})^*, a+m\mathbb{Z} \mapsto (a+m_1\mathbb{Z}, \ldots, a+m_n\mathbb{Z}) \quad (2.13)$$

is an isomorphism of groups. In particular, this map is bijective. Therefore, the number $\varphi(m)$ of the elements of $(\mathbb{Z}/m\mathbb{Z})^*$ is equal to the number $\prod_{i=1}^{n}\varphi(m_i)$ of elements of $\prod_{i=1}^{n}(\mathbb{Z}/m_i\mathbb{Z})^*$.   □

Theorem 2.17.2
Let m be a positive integer and $m = \prod_{p|m}p^{e(p)}$ its prime factorization. Then

$$\varphi(m) = \prod_{p|m}(p-1)p^{e(p)-1} = m\prod_{p|m}\frac{p-1}{p}.$$

Proof. By Theorem 2.17.1,

$$\varphi(m) = \prod_{p|m}\varphi(p^{e(p)}).$$

Hence, we only need to compute $\varphi(p^e)$ for a prime number p and a positive integer e. By Theorem 1.3.3, any $a \in \{0, 1, 2, \ldots, p^e - 1\}$ can be uniquely written as

$$a = a_e + a_{e-1}p + a_{e-2}p^2 + \ldots + a_1 p^{e-1}$$

with $a_i \in \{0, 1, \ldots, p-1\}$, $1 \le i \le e$. Moreover, $\gcd(a, p^e) = 1$ if and only if $a_e \ne 0$. This implies

$$\varphi(p^e) = (p-1)p^{e-1} = p^e\left(1 - \frac{1}{p}\right),$$

so the assertion is proved.   □

Example 2.17.3
We have $\varphi(2^m) = 2^{m-1}$, $\varphi(100) = \varphi(2^2 * 5^2) = 2 * 4 * 5 = 40$.

If the factorization of m is known, then $\varphi(m)$ can be computed using Theorem 2.17.2 in time $O((\text{size } m)^2)$.

2.18 Polynomials

In Section 2.21, we want to prove that for any prime number p the multiplicative group of residues $(\mathbb{Z}/p\mathbb{Z})^*$ is cyclic of order $p - 1$. For this purpose, we need polynomials, which we introduce in this section. We also need polynomials to introduce finite fields.

Let R be a commutative ring with unit element $1 \neq 0$. A *polynomial* in one variable over R is an expression

$$f(x) = a_n x^n + a_{n-1} x^{n-1} + \cdots + a_1 x + a_0,$$

where x is the variable and the *coefficients* $a_0, \ldots, a_n$ of the polynomial are elements of R. The set of all polynomials over R in the variable x is denoted by $R[x]$.

Let $a_n \neq 0$. Then n is called the *degree* of the polynomial. We write $n = \deg f$. Moreover, a_n is called the *leading coefficient* of f. If all coefficients except for the leading one are zero, then f is called a *monomial*.

Example 2.18.1
The polynomials $2x^3 + x + 1$, x, 1 are elements of $\mathbb{Z}[x]$. The first polynomial has degree 3, the second has degree 1, and the third has degree 0.

If $r \in R$, then

$$f(r) = a_n r^n + \cdots + a_0$$

is the *value* of f at r. If $f(r) = 0$, then r is called *zero* of f.

Example 2.18.2
The value of the polynomial $2x^3 + x + 1 \in \mathbb{Z}[x]$ at -1 is -2.

Example 2.18.3
Denote the elements of $\mathbb{Z}/2\mathbb{Z}$ by 0 and 1. Then $x^2 + 1 \in (\mathbb{Z}/2\mathbb{Z})[x]$. This polynomial has the zero 1.

Let

$$g(x) = b_m x^m + \cdots + b_0$$

be another polynomial over R and let $n \geq m$. If we set the missing coefficients to zero, we can write

$$g(x) = b_n x^n + \cdots + b_0.$$

The *sum* of the polynomials f and g is

$$(f + g)(x) = (a_n + b_n)x^n + \cdots + (a_0 + b_0)$$

and is a polynomial.

Example 2.18.4
If $g(x) = x^2 + x + 1 \in \mathbb{Z}[x]$ and $f(x) = x^3 + 2x^2 + x + 2 \in \mathbb{Z}[x]$, then $(f + g)(x) = x^3 + 3x^2 + 2x + 3$.

The addition of f and g requires $O(\max\{\deg f, \deg g\} + 1)$ additions in R.

The *product* of the polynomials f and g is

$$(fg)(x) = c_{n+m}x^{n+m} + \cdots + c_0,$$

where

$$c_k = \sum_{i=0}^{k} a_i b_{k-i}, \quad 0 \leq k \leq n + m.$$

In this formula, the undefined coefficients a_i and b_i are set to 0.

Example 2.18.5
Let $f(x) = x^2 + x + 1 \in \mathbb{Z}[x]$ and $g(x) = x^3 + 2x^2 + x + 2 \in \mathbb{Z}[x]$. Then $(fg)(x) = (x^2 + x + 1)(x^3 + 2x^2 + x + 2) = x^5 + (2 + 1)x^4 + (1 + 2 + 1)x^3 + (2 + 1 + 2)x^2 + (2 + 1)x + 2 = x^5 + 3x^4 + 4x^3 + 5x^2 + 3x + 2$.

We estimate the number of operations necessary for the multiplication of f and g. We compute the products $a_i b_j$, $0 \leq i \leq \deg f$, $0 \leq j \leq \deg g$. There are $(\deg f + 1)(\deg g + 1)$ many of those products. The sum of all products $a_i b_j$ for which $i + j$ has the same value is the coefficient of x^{i+j}. Since every product appears in exactly one sum, those coefficients can be computed using at most $(\deg f + 1)(\deg g + 1)$ additions. In total, the multiplication of f and g requires $O((\deg f + 1)(\deg g + 1))$ additions and multiplications in R. Faster polynomial operations based on fast Fourier transformations are described in [3]. See also [15].

It is easy to see that $(R[x], +, \cdot)$ is a commutative ring with unit element 1.

2.19 Polynomials over Fields

Let K be a field. Then the ring $K[x]$ of polynomials over K contains no zero divisors. The following lemma is easy to prove.

Lemma 2.19.1
If $f, g \in \mathbb{K}[x]$, $f, g \neq 0$, then $\deg (fg) = \deg f + \deg g$.

As in the ring of integers, also in the polynomial ring $K[x]$ division with remainder is possible.

Theorem 2.19.2
Let $f, g \in K[x]$, $g \neq 0$. Then there are uniquely determined polynomials $q, r \in K[x]$ with $f = qg + r$ and $r = 0$ or $\deg r < \deg g$.

Proof.   If $f = 0$, then set $q = r = 0$. Assume that $f \neq 0$. If $\deg g > \deg f$, then set $q = 0$ and $r = f$. We now also assume that $\deg g \leq \deg f$.

We prove the existence of q and r by induction on the degree of f.

If $\deg f = 0$, then $\deg g = 0$. Hence, $f, g \in K$ and we can set $q = f/g$ and $r = 0$.

Assume that $\deg f = n > 0$, $\deg g = m$, $n \geq m$, and

$$f(x) = a_n x^n + \cdots + a_0, \quad g(x) = b_m x^m + \cdots + b_0.$$

Set

$$f_1 = f - a_n/b_m x^{n-m} g.$$

Then either $f_1 = 0$ or $\deg f_1 < \deg f$. By the induction hypothesis, there are polynomials q_1 and r with $f_1 = q_1 g + r$ and $r = 0$ or $\deg r < \deg g$. This implies

$$f = (a_n/b_m x^{n-m} + q_1)g + r.$$

The polynomials $q = a_n/b_m x^{n-m} + q_1$ and r from earlier satisfy the assertion.

We prove uniqueness. Let $f = qg + r = q'g + r'$ be two representations as described in the theorem. Then $(qq')g = r' - r$. If $r = r'$, then $q = q'$ because $g \neq 0$ and $K[x]$ contains no zero divisors. If $r \neq r'$, then $qq' \neq 0$ and since deg g > deg r and deg g > deg r', Lemma 2.19.1 implies deg $(q - q')g$ > deg$(r'r)$. This is impossible because $(q - q')g = r' - r$.   □

In the situation of Theorem 2.19.2, we call q the *quotient* and r the *remainder* of the division of f by g, and we write $r = f$ mod g.

From the proof of Theorem 2.19.2, we obtain an algorithm for dividing a polynomial f by another polynomial g with remainder. First, we set $r = f$ and $q = 0$. While $r \neq 0$ and deg $r \geq \deg g$, we set $h(x) = (a/b)x^{\deg - r\deg g}$, where a is the leading coefficient of r, and b is the leading coefficient of g. Then r is replaced by $r - hg$ and q by $q + h$. As soon as $r = 0$ or deg r < deg g, the algorithm returns the quotient q and the remainder r. This is illustrated in the following example.

Example 2.19.3
Let $K = \mathbb{Z}/2\mathbb{Z}$ be the residue class ring mod 2. This ring is a field. The elements are represented by their least nonnegative representatives, so we write $\mathbb{Z}/2\mathbb{Z} = \{0, 1\}$.
Let

$$f(x) = x^3 + x + 1, \quad g(x) = x^2 + x.$$

We divide f with remainder by g. We first set $r = f$ and $q = 0$. Then we eliminate x^3 in r. We set $h(x) = x$ and replace r by $r - hg = x^3 + x + 1x(x^2 + x) = x^2 + x + 1$ and q by $q + h = x$. Then deg $r =$ deg g. Hence, the algorithm requires another iteration. Again, we eliminate the leading coefficient in r. We set $h(x) = 1$, and we replace r by $r - hg = 1$ and q by $q + h = x + 1$. Now $0 =$ deg r < deg $g = 2$, so we are finished and have found the quotient $q = x + 1$ and the remainder $r = 1$.

We estimate how many operations in K are necessary to divide f by g with remainder. The computation of the monomials h requires one operation in K. The number of monomials h is at most deg $q + 1$ because their degree is strictly decreasing. Every time h is computed, $r - hg$ is also determined. The computation of hg requires deg $g+1$ multiplications in K. The degree of the polynomials r and hg is the same, and the number of nonzero coefficients in hg is at most deg $g+1$. Therefore, the computation of $r-hg$ requires at most deg $g+1$ additions in K. In total, the division with remainder requires $O((\deg\ g+1)(\deg\ q+1))$ operations in K.

Theorem 2.19.4
If $f, g \in K[x]$ with $g \neq 0$, then the division with remainder of f by g requires $O((\deg\ g+1)(\deg\ q+1))$ operations in K, where q is the quotient of the division.

Theorem 2.19.2 implies the following.

Corollary 2.19.5
If f is a nonzero polynomial in $K[x]$ and if a is a zero of f, then $f = (x-a)q$ with $q \in K[x]$ (i.e., f is divisible by the polynomial $x-a$).

Proof. By Theorem 2.19.2, there are polynomials $q, r \in K[x]$ with $f = (x-a)q + r$ and $r = 0$ or deg $r < 1$. This implies $0 = f(a) = r$; hence $f = (x-a)q$. $\qquad\square$

Example 2.19.6
The polynomial $x^2 + 1 \in (\mathbb{Z}/2\mathbb{Z})[x]$ has the zero 1 and therefore $x^2 + 1 = (x-1)^2$.

Corollary 2.19.7
A polynomial $f \in K[x]$, $f \neq 0$, has at most deg f zeros.

Proof. We prove the assertion by induction on $n = \deg f$. For $n = 0$, the assertion holds because $f \in K$ and $f \neq 0$. Let $n > 0$. If f has no zeros, then the assertion is true. If f has a zero a, Corollary 2.19.5 implies $f = (x-a)q$ and deg $q = n-1$. By the induction hypothesis, q has at most $n-1$ zeros. Therefore, f has at most n zeros. $\qquad\square$

In the following example, we show that the upper bound in Corollary 2.19.7 is not always sharp.

Example 2.19.8
The polynomial $x^2 + x \in (\mathbb{Z}/2\mathbb{Z})[x]$ has the zeros 0 and 1 in $\mathbb{Z}/2\mathbb{Z}$. By Corollary 2.19.7, it cannot have more zeros.

The polynomial $x^2 + 1 \in (\mathbb{Z}/2\mathbb{Z})[x]$ has the only zero 1 in $\mathbb{Z}/2\mathbb{Z}$. By Corollary 2.19.7, it could have at most two zeros.

The polynomial $x^2 + x + 1 \in (\mathbb{Z}/2\mathbb{Z})[x]$ has no zeros in $\mathbb{Z}/2\mathbb{Z}$. By Corollary 2.19.7, it could also have at most two zeros.

2.20   Structure of the Unit Group of Finite Fields

We now study the structure of the unit group of a finite field (i.e., of the multiplicative group of nonzero elements in a field with finitely many elements). We prove that this group is always cyclic. This is particularly interesting for cryptography because in cryptography groups with elements of high order are used. We already know the finite field $\mathbb{Z}/p\mathbb{Z}$ for a prime number p. Its unit group is of order $p - 1$. Later, we will also construct other finite fields.

In general, the unit group K^* of a field K with q elements has order $q - 1$ because all nonzero elements in K are units in K. We prove a more general result.

Theorem 2.20.1
Let K be a finite field with q elements. Then for any divisor d of $q - 1$ there are exactly $\varphi(d)$ elements of order d in the unit group K^*.

Proof.   Let d be a divisor of $q - 1$. Denote by $\psi(d)$ the number of elements of order d in F.

Assuming that $\psi(d) > 0$, we prove that $\psi(d) = \varphi(d)$. Later, we will show that in fact $\psi(d) > 0$. Let a be an element of order d in K^*. The powers a^e, $0 \leq e < d$, are pairwise distinct and are all zeros of the polynomial $x^d - 1$. By Corollary 2.19.7, there are at most d zeros of this polynomial in F. Hence, that polynomial has exactly d zeros and they are all powers of a. Now each element of F of order d is a zero of $x^d - 1$ and is therefore a power of a. By Theorem 2.9.5, a power a^e is of order d if and only if $\gcd(d, e) = 1$. Hence, we have shown that $\psi(d) > 0$ implies $\psi(d) = \varphi(d)$.

We will now show that $\psi(d) > 0$. Suppose $\psi(d) = 0$ for a divisor d of $q - 1$. Then

$$q - 1 = \sum_{d \mid q-1} \psi(d) < \sum_{d \mid q-1} \varphi(d).$$

This contradicts Theorem 2.8.4.   □

Example 2.20.2
Consider the field $\mathbb{Z}/13\mathbb{Z}$. Its unit group is of order 12. In this group, there is one element of order 1, one element of order 2, two elements of order 3, two elements of order 4, two elements of order 6, and four elements of order 12. In particular, this group is cyclic and has four generators.

If K is a finite field with q elements, then by Theorem 2.20.1 it contains exactly $\varphi(q-1)$ elements of order $q-1$. This implies the following.

Corollary 2.20.3
If K is a finite field with q elements, then its unit group K^* is cyclic of order $q-1$. It has exactly $\varphi(q-1)$ generators.

2.21 Structure of the Multiplicative Group of Residues mod a Prime Number

Let p be a prime number. Corollary 2.20.3 implies the following result.

Corollary 2.21.1
The multiplicative group of residues mod p is cyclic of order $p-1$.

An integer a for which the residue class $a + p\mathbb{Z}$ generates the multiplicative group of residues $(\mathbb{Z}/p\mathbb{Z})^*$ is called a *primitive root* mod p.

Example 2.21.2
For $p = 13$, we have $p-1 = 12$. Theorem 2.17.2 implies that $\varphi(12) = 4$. Therefore, there are four primitive roots mod 13, namely 2, 6, 7, and 11.

We describe how primitive roots modulo a prime number p can be computed. We have seen in Theorem 2.20.3 that there are $\varphi(p-1)$

primitive roots mod p. Now

$$\varphi(n) \geq n/(6 \log \log n)$$

for any positive integer $n \geq 5$ (see [29]). The proof of this inequality is beyond the scope of this book. Hence, the number of generators of a cyclic group of order n is at least $\lceil n/(6 \log \log n) \rceil$. If $n = 2 * q$ with a prime number q, then the number of generators is $q - 1$. Hence, almost half of all group elements generate the group. If we randomly choose an integer g with $1 \leq g \leq p - 1$, then we have a good chance that g is a primitive root mod p. We only need to check whether g is in fact a primitive root mod p. If we know the factorization of $p - 1$, then Corollary 2.14.3 can be used efficiently to carry out this test. If $p - 1 = 2q$ with a prime number q, then we only need to check whether $g^2 \equiv 1 \bmod p$ or $g^q \equiv 1 \bmod p$. If neither of these congruences is satisfied, then g is a primitive root mod p.

Example 2.21.3
Let $p = 23$. Then $p - 1 = 22 = 11 * 2$. To check whether an integer g is a primitive root modulo 23, we must verify that $g^2 \bmod 23 \neq 1$ and that $g^{11} \bmod 23 \neq 1$. Here is a table with the corresponding remainders for the prime numbers between 2 and 17.

g	2	3	5	7	11	13	17
$g^2 \bmod 23$	4	9	2	3	6	8	13
$g^{11} \bmod 23$	1	1	-1	-1	-1	1	-1

It follows that 5, 7, 11, and 17 are primitive roots mod 23 and that 2, 3, and 13 are not primitive roots mod 23.

2.22   Exercises

Exercise 2.22.1
Prove (2.2) and (2.3).

Exercise 2.22.2
Determine all semigroups that are obtained by defining an operation on $\{0, 1\}$.

Exercise 2.22.3
Prove that in a semigroup there is at most one neutral element.

Exercise 2.22.4
Which of the semigroups of Exercise 2.22.2 are monoids? Which are groups?

Exercise 2.22.5
Prove that in a monoid each element can have at most one inverse.

Exercise 2.22.6
Let n be a positive divisor of the positive integer m. Prove that the map $\mathbb{Z}/m\mathbb{Z} \to \mathbb{Z}/n\mathbb{Z}$, $a + m\mathbb{Z} \mapsto a + n\mathbb{Z}$ is a surjective homomorphism of rings.

Exercise 2.22.7
Construct an example which shows that in the semigroup $(\mathbb{Z}/m\mathbb{Z}, \cdot)$ cancellation is in general not possible.

Exercise 2.22.8
Determine the unit group and the zero divisors of $\mathbb{Z}/16\mathbb{Z}$.

Exercise 2.22.9
Prove that the invertible elements of a commutative ring with unit element form a group.

Exercise 2.22.10
Solve $122x \equiv 1 \bmod 343$.

Exercise 2.22.11
Prove that the congruence $ax \equiv b \bmod m$ is solvable if and only if $\gcd(a, m)$ is a divisor of b. When solvable, determine all solutions.

Exercise 2.22.12
Let $d_1 d_2 \ldots d_k$ be the decimal expansion of a positive integer d. Prove that d is divisible by 11 if and only if $\sum_{i=1}^{k}(-1)^{k-i}$ is divisible by 11.

Exercise 2.22.13
Determine all invertible residue classes modulo 25, and compute their inverses.

Exercise 2.22.14
The least common multiple of two nonzero integers a, b is the least positive integer k that is a multiple of a and a multiple of b. It is denoted by lcm (a, b).
1. Prove the existence and uniqueness of lcm (a, b).
2. How can lcm (a, b) be computed using the euclidean algorithm?

Exercise 2.22.15
Let X and Y be finite sets and $f : X \to Y$ a bijection. Prove that the number of elements in X and Y is equal.

Exercise 2.22.16
Compute the subgroup generated by $2 + 17\mathbb{Z}$ in $(\mathbb{Z}/17\mathbb{Z})^*$.

Exercise 2.22.17
Compute the order of 2 mod 1237.

Exercise 2.22.18
Determine the order of all elements in $(\mathbb{Z}/15\mathbb{Z})^*$.

Exercise 2.22.19
Compute 2^{20} mod 7.

Exercise 2.22.20
Let G be a finite cyclic group. Prove that for every divisor d of $|G|$ there is exactly one subgroup of G of order d.

Exercise 2.22.21
Let p be a prime number, $p \equiv 3$ mod 4. Let a be an integer which is a square mod p (i.e., the congruence $a \equiv b^2$ mod p has a solution). Show that $a^{(p+1)/4}$ is a square root of a mod p.

Exercise 2.22.22
Prove Theorem 2.14.1.

Exercise 2.22.23
Construct an element of order 103 in the multiplicative group of residues mod 1237.

Exercise 2.22.24
Let G be a cyclic group of order n with generator g. Prove that $\mathbb{Z}/n\mathbb{Z} \to G, e + n\mathbb{Z} \mapsto g^e$ is an isomorphism of groups.

Exercise 2.22.25

Solve the simultaneous congruence $x \equiv 1 \bmod p$ for all $p \in \{2, 3, 5, 7\}$.

Exercise 2.22.26

For $g = 2, 3, 5, 7, 11$ determine a prime number $p > g$ such that g is a primitive root mod p.

Exercise 2.22.27

Find all multiplicative groups of residues that have four elements.

3

CHAPTER

Encryption

The traditional topic of cryptography is encryption. Encryption schemes are used to keep messages or stored data secret. In this chapter, we introduce fundamental notions that we need to describe encryption schemes. As a first example, we present affine linear ciphers and their cryptanalysis.

3.1 Encryption Schemes

We define encryption schemes.

Definition 3.1.1
An *encryption scheme* or *cryptosystem* is a tuple
$(\mathcal{P}, \mathcal{C}, \mathcal{K}, \mathcal{E}, \mathcal{D})$ with the following properties:
1. $\mathcal{P}$ is a set. It is called the *plaintext space*. Its elements are called *plaintexts*.
2. $\mathcal{C}$ is a set. It is called the *ciphertext space*. Its elements are called *ciphertexts*.
3. $\mathcal{K}$ is a set. Is is called the *key space*. Its elements are called *keys*.

TABLE 3.1   Correspondence between letters and numbers.

A	B	C	D	E	F	G	H	I	J	K	L	M
0	1	2	3	4	5	6	7	8	9	10	11	12
N	O	P	Q	R	S	T	U	V	W	X	Y	Z
13	14	15	16	17	18	19	20	21	22	23	24	25

4. $\mathcal{E} = \{E_k : k \in K\}$ is a family of functions $E_k : \mathcal{P} \to \mathcal{C}$. Its elements are called *encryption functions*.
5. $\mathcal{D} = \{D_k : k \in K\}$ is a family of functions $D_k : \mathcal{C} \to \mathcal{P}$. Its elements are called *decryption functions*.
6. For each $e \in K$, there is $d \in K$ such that $D_d(E_e(p)) = p$ for all $p \in \mathcal{P}$.

As a first example of an encryption scheme, we describe the *Caesar cipher*.

The plaintext space, ciphertext space, and key space are $\Sigma = \{A, B, \ldots, Z\}$. We identify the letters $A, B, \ldots, Z$ according to Table 3.1 with the numbers $0, 1, \ldots, 25$. This enables us to compute with letters. For $e \in \mathbb{Z}_{26}$, the encryption function E_e is

$$E_e : \Sigma \to \Sigma, \quad x \mapsto (x + e) \bmod 26.$$

Analogously, for $d \in \mathbb{Z}_{26}$ decryption function D_d is

$$D_d : \Sigma \to \Sigma, \quad x \mapsto (x - d) \bmod 26.$$

The decryption key for the encryption key e is $d = e$. This is, however, not true for every cryptosystem.

The Caesar cipher can easily be modified such that the plaintext space and the ciphertext space are the set of all sequences $\vec{w} = (w_1, w_2, \ldots, w_n)$ with $w_i \in \Sigma$, $1 \leq i \leq n$. Again, the key space is $\mathbb{Z}_{26}$. The encryption function E_e replaces each letter w_i by $w_i + e \bmod 26$, $1 \leq i \leq n$. This also is called the Caesar cipher.

Example 3.1.2
If we apply the Caesar cipher with key 5 to the word CRYPTOGRA-PHY, then we obtain HWDUYTLWFUMD.

The Caesar cipher uses only 26 keys. It is therefore very easy to determine the plaintext from the ciphertext by trying all possible keys and checking which plaintext makes sense. In this way, we also obtain the key that was used.

3.2 Symmetric and Asymmetric Cryptosystems

We briefly explain the difference between symmetric and asymmetric cryptosystems.

If Alice wants to send an encrypted message to Bob, then she uses an encryption key e and Bob uses the corresponding decryption key to recover the plaintext.

If in a cryptosystem the encryption key e is always equal to the decryption key d, or if d can be easily computed from e, then the cryptosystem is called *symmetric*. If Alice and Bob use a symmetric cryptosystem, they must exchange the secret key e before they start their communication. Secure key exchange is a major problem. The key e must be kept secret since anybody who knows e can determine the corresponding decryption key d. The Caesar cipher is an example of a symmetric cryptosystem. The keys for encryption and decryption are equal in this system.

In *asymmetric cryptosystems*, the keys d and e are distinct, and the computation of d from e is infeasible. In such systems, the encryption key can be made public. If Bob wants to receive encrypted messages, he publishes an encryption key e and keeps the corresponding decryption key d secret. Anybody can use e to encrypt messages for Bob. Therefore, e is called the *public key*. But only Bob can decrypt the messages, so d is called the *private key*. Asymmetric cryptosystems are also called *public-key cryptosystems*.

In public-key cryptosystems, it is frequently useful to introduce two different key spaces since the public and the private keys have different shapes. This changes the definition of cryptosystems only slightly.

In this chapter, we only describe symmetric encryption schemes. Public-key cryptosystems will be described in Chapter 7.

3.3 Cryptanalysis

Cryptanalysis deals with the attacks on cryptosystems. In this section, we classify those attacks.

To make attacks on cryptosystems more difficult, one can keep the cryptosystem secret. However, it is not clear how much security is really gained in this way because an attacker has many ways of finding out which cryptosystem is used. He can try to tell from intercepted ciphertexts which system is used. He can also try to get information from people who have information about the encryption scheme in use.

Modern cryptanalysis therefore assumes that an attacker knows which cryptosystem is used. Only the (private) keys and the plaintexts are assumed to be secret. The attacker tries to recover plaintexts from ciphertexts or even tries to find out which keys are used.

There are the following types of attacks:

- *Ciphertext-only attack*. The attacker knows ciphertexts and tries to recover the corresponding plaintexts or the key.

- *Known-plaintext attack*. The attacker knows a plaintext and the corresponding ciphertext or several such pairs. He tries to find the key used or to decrypt other ciphertexts.

- *Chosen-plaintext attack*. The attacker is able to encrypt plaintexts but does not know the key. He tries to find the key used or to decrypt other ciphertexts.

- *Adaptive chosen-plaintext attack*. The attacker is able to encrypt plaintexts. He is able to choose new plaintexts as a function of the ciphertexts obtained but does not know the key. He tries to find the key used or to decrypt other ciphertexts.

- *Chosen-ciphertext attack*. The attacker can decrypt but does not know the key. He tries to find the key.

There are many ways to mount these attacks. A simple ciphertext-only attack consists of decrypting the ciphertext with all possible keys. This attack is called *exhaustive search*. The correct plaintext is among the few sensible texts that the attacker obtains. Given the speed of modern computers, this attack is successful for many cryptosystems. It works, for example, for the DES system, which until recently was the U.S. encryption standard. The DES is described in Chapter 5.

A known-plaintext attack may use the statistical properties of the plaintext language. For example, if we apply the Caesar cipher, then for a fixed key any plaintext symbol is replaced by the same ciphertext symbol. The most frequent plaintext symbol is encrypted to the most frequent ciphertext symbol. Since we know the most frequent symbol of the plaintext language, we have a good guess how to decrypt the most frequent ciphertext symbol. Analogously, the frequency of other individual symbols, of pairs, triplets, etc., in the plaintext may be reflected in the ciphertext and can be used to decrypt the ciphertext or to recover the key. A number of examples can be found in [32], and [5]. We will see later how affine linear ciphers can be broken by a known-plaintext attack.

3.4 Alphabets and Words

To write texts, we need symbols from an alphabet. By an *alphabet* we mean a finite nonempty set Σ. The *length* of Σ is the number of elements in Σ. The elements of Σ are called *symbols* or *letters*.

Example 3.4.1
A common alphabet is

$$\Sigma = \{A, B, C, D, E, F, G, H, I, J, K, L, M, N, O, P, Q, R, S, T, U, V, W, X, Y, Z\}.$$

It has length 26.

Example 3.4.2
In computing, we use the alphabet $\{0, 1\}$. It has length 2.

Example 3.4.3
A frequently used alphabet is the set of ASCII symbols. This set, including its encoding by the numbers between 0 and 127, can be found in Table 3.2.

Because alphabets are finite sets, their symbols can be identified with nonnegative integers. If an alphabet has length m, then its symbols are identified with the numbers in $\mathbb{Z}_m = \{0, 1, \ldots, m-1\}$. For the alphabet $\{A, B, \ldots, Z\}$ and the ASCII symbols, we have shown this in Tables 3.1 and 3.2. We will mostly use the alphabet $\mathbb{Z}_m$, where m is a positive integer.

TABLE 3.2   The ASCII symbols.

0	NUL	1	SOH	2	STX	3	ETX
4	EOT	5	ENQ	6	ACK	7	BEL
8	BS	9	HT	10	NL	11	VT
12	NP	13	CR	14	SO	15	SI
16	DLE	17	DC1	18	DC2	19	DC3
20	DC4	21	NAK	22	SYN	23	ETB
24	CAN	25	EM	26	SUB	27	ESC
28	FS	29	GS	30	RS	31	US
32	SP	33	!	34	"	35	#
36	$	37	%	38	&	39	'
40	(	41	)	42	*	43	+
44	,	45	-	46	.	47	/
48	0	49	1	50	2	51	3
52	4	53	5	54	6	55	7
56	8	57	9	58	:	59	;
60	¡	61	=	62	¿	63	?
64	@	65	A	66	B	67	C
68	D	69	E	70	F	71	G
72	H	73	I	74	J	75	K
76	L	77	M	78	N	79	O
80	P	81	Q	82	R	83	S
84	T	85	U	86	V	87	W
88	X	89	Y	90	Z	91	[
92		93	]	94	^	95	_
96	`	97	a	98	b	99	c
100	d	101	e	102	f	103	g
104	h	105	i	106	j	107	k
108	l	109	m	110	n	111	o
112	p	113	q	114	r	115	s
116	t	117	u	118	v	119	w
120	x	121	y	122	z	123	{
124	—	125	}	126	~	127	DEL

In the following definition, we need finite sequences, which we briefly recall. An example of a finite sequence is

$$(2, 3, 1, 2, 3).$$

It has five components. The first component is 2, the second is 3, etc. We also write this sequence as

$$23123.$$

For formal reasons, we also need (). It has zero components.

Definition 3.4.4
Let Σ be an alphabet.
1. A *word* or *string* over Σ is a finite sequence of symbols from Σ including the empty sequence, which is denoted by ε and is called the *empty string*.
2. The *length* of a word $\vec{w}$ over Σ is the number of its components. It is denoted by $|\vec{w}|$. The empty word has length 0.
3. The set of all words over Σ including the empty string is denoted by Σ^*.
4. If $\vec{v}, \vec{w} \in \Sigma^*$, then $\vec{v}\vec{w} = \vec{v} \circ \vec{w}$ is the string that is obtained by concatenating $\vec{v}$ and $\vec{w}$. It is called the *concatenation* of $\vec{v}$ and $\vec{w}$. In particular, we have $\vec{v} \circ \varepsilon = \varepsilon \circ \vec{v} = \vec{v}$.
5. If n is a nonnegative integer, then Σ^n is the set of all words of length n over Σ.

In Exercise 3.15.5, it is shown that $(\Sigma^*, \circ)$ is a monoid whose neutral element is the empty word.

Example 3.4.5
A word over the alphabet from Example 3.4.1 is COLA. It has length four. Another word over Σ is COCA. The concatenation of COCA and COLA is COCACOLA.

3.5 Permutations

To characterize a very general class of encryption schemes, called the block ciphers (see the following), we need the notion of a permutation.

Definition 3.5.1
Let X be a set. A *permutation* of X is a bijective map $f : X \to X$. The set of all permutations of X is denoted by $S(X)$.

Example 3.5.2
Let $X = \{0, 1, \ldots, 5\}$. We obtain a permutation of X if we map an element of X in the first row of the following matrix to the number below that element in the second row:

$$\begin{pmatrix} 0 & 1 & 2 & 3 & 4 & 5 \\ 1 & 2 & 4 & 3 & 5 & 0 \end{pmatrix}.$$

Using this method, permutations can always be represented.

The set $S(X)$ of all permutations of X together with composition is a group that, in general, is not commutative.

If n is a positive integer, then S_n denotes the group of permutations of the set $\{1, 2, \ldots, n\}$.

Example 3.5.3
The group S_2 has the elements

$$\begin{pmatrix} 1 & 2 \\ 1 & 2 \end{pmatrix}, \begin{pmatrix} 1 & 2 \\ 2 & 1 \end{pmatrix}.$$

Theorem 3.5.4
The group S_n has order $n! = 1 * 2 * 3 * \cdots * n$.

Proof. We prove the assertion by induction on n. Clearly, S_1 has order 1. Suppose S_{n-1} has order $(n-1)!$. Consider the permutations of the set $\{1, \ldots, n\}$. We count the number of permutations that send 1 to a fixed number x. In such permutations, the numbers $2, \ldots, n$ are bijectively mapped to the numbers $1, 2, \ldots, x-1, x+1, \ldots, n$. By the induction hypothesis, there are $(n-1)!$ such bijections. But since there are n possibilities to map 1 to a number, the order of S_n is $n(n-1)! = n!$. □

Let $X = \{0, 1\}^n$ be the set of all bitstrings of length n. A permutation of X in which just the positions of the bits are permuted is called a *bit permutation*. To formally describe such a bit permutation, we choose $\pi \in S_n$. Then we set

$$f : \{0, 1\}^n \to \{0, 1\}^n, \quad b_1 \ldots b_n \mapsto b_{\pi(1)} \ldots b_{\pi(n)}.$$

This is in fact a bit permutation, and every bit permutation can be uniquely written in this way. Therefore, there are $n!$ bit permutations of bitstrings of length n.

Special bit permutations are *circular left- or rightshifts*. A circular leftshift of i positions maps the bitstring $(b_0, b_1, \ldots, b_{n-1})$ to $(b_{i \bmod n}, b_{(i+1) \bmod n}, \ldots, b_{(i+n-1) \bmod n})$. Circular rightshifts are defined analogously.

3.6 Block Ciphers

We now introduce block ciphers. They encrypt blocks of fixed length as blocks of the same length. Later, we show how to encrypt messages of arbitrary length using block ciphers.

Definition 3.6.1
A cryptosystem is called a *block cipher* if its plaintext space and its ciphertext space are the set Σ^n of words of a fixed length n over an alphabet Σ. The *block length* n is a positive integer.

A simple example of a block cipher is the Caesar cipher. It has block length 1. In general, block ciphers with block length 1 are called *substitution ciphers*.

Theorem 3.6.2
The encryption functions of a block cipher are permutations.

Proof. Since for each encryption function there is a corresponding decryption function, the encryption functions are injective. An injective map $\Sigma^n \rightarrow \Sigma^n$ is bijective.   □

Theorem 3.6.2 implies that the most general block cipher can be described as follows. Fix the block length n and an alphabet Σ. As plaintext space and ciphertext space use $\mathcal{P} = \mathcal{C} = \Sigma^n$. The key space is the set $S(\Sigma^n)$ of all permutations of Σ^n. The encryption function for a key $\pi \in S(\Sigma^n)$ is

$$E_\pi : \Sigma^n \rightarrow \Sigma^n, \quad \vec{v} \mapsto \pi(\vec{v}).$$

The corresponding decryption function is

$$D_\pi : \Sigma^n \rightarrow \Sigma^n, \quad \vec{v} \mapsto \pi^{-1}(\vec{v}).$$

The key space of this scheme is very large. It contains $(|\Sigma|^n)!$ elements. Therefore, the scheme seems quite secure. It is, however, rather inefficient since it is not clear how to represent and evaluate an arbitrary $\pi \in (|\Sigma|^n)!$ efficiently. Therefore, it makes sense to use as the key space only a subset of all possible permutations of Σ^n. Those permutations should be easy to represent and evaluate.

It is, for example, possible to use the *permutation cipher*. It uses only permutations that permute the positions of the symbols. If $\Sigma = \{0, 1\}$, then those are the bit permutations. The key space is the permutations group S_n. For $\pi \in S_n$, set

$$E_\pi : \Sigma^n \rightarrow \Sigma^n, \quad (v_1, \ldots, v_n) \mapsto (v_{\pi(1)}, \ldots v_{\pi(n)}).$$

The corresponding decryption function is

$$D_\pi : \Sigma^n \rightarrow \Sigma^n, \quad (x_1, \ldots, x_n) \mapsto (x_{\pi^{-1}(1)}, \ldots x_{\pi^{-1}(n)}).$$

The key space has $n!$ elements. Each key can be encoded as a sequence of n integers in $\{0, 1, \ldots, n-1\}$.

A method to study the security of block ciphers consists in studying their algebraic properties. Each encryption function is an element of a permutation group. If its order is small, the decryption can be effected by iterating the encryption function a few times.

3.7 Multiple Encryption

To increase the security of a block cipher, it is possible to apply it a few times. Frequently, the E-D-E triple encryption is used. A plaintext p is encrypted as

$$c = E_{k_1}(D_{k_2}(E_{k_3}(p))).$$

Here, $k_i, 1 \leq i \leq 3$ are three keys, E_{k_i} is the encryption function, and D_{k_i} is the decryption function for key $k_i, 1 \leq i \leq 3$. This results in a considerably larger key space. If we only want to double the key length, we use $k_1 = k_3$.

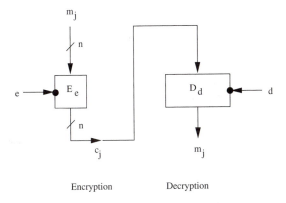

Encryption   Decryption

FIGURE 3.1   ECB mode.

3.8   Use of Block Ciphers

Before explaining classical examples for block ciphers, we discuss the use of block ciphers for encrypting arbitrarily long documents.

3.8.1   ECB mode

In this section, we use a block cipher with alphabet Σ and block length n. Let $\mathcal{K}$ be the key space. Let E_k be the encryption function and let D_k be the decryption function for key $k \in \mathcal{K}$.

First, we explain the *electronic codebook mode* (ECB mode; see Fig. 3.1). An arbitrarily long plaintext is decomposed into blocks of length n. If necessary, the plaintext is supplemented such that its length is divisible by n. This supplement can consist of randomly chosen symbols. If the encryption key e is used, then each block of length n is encrypted using the encryption function E_e. The ciphertext is the sequence of the cipher texts. The ciphertext is decrypted by applying the decryption function D_d with decryption key d, which corresponds to the encryption key e.

Example 3.8.1

We consider the block cipher that applies bit permutations to bit vectors of length 4 (i.e, the permutation cipher with alphabet $\Sigma = \{0, 1\}$ and block length 4). Then $\mathcal{K} = S_4$, and the encryption function for key $\pi \in S_4$ is

$$E_\pi : \{0,1\}^4 \to \{0,1\}^4, \quad b_1 b_2 b_3 b_4 \mapsto b_{\pi(1)} b_{\pi(2)} b_{\pi(3)} b_{\pi(4)}.$$

We encrypt the plaintext

$$m = 101100010100101.$$

It is decomposed into blocks of length four. The last block has length three. It is supplemented to length four by adding one zero. We obtain

$$m = 1011\ 0001\ 0100\ 1010;$$

hence the blocks

$$m_1 = 1011, \quad m_2 = 0001, \quad m_3 = 0100, \quad m_4 = 1010.$$

We use the key

$$\pi = \begin{pmatrix} 1 & 2 & 3 & 4 \\ 2 & 3 & 4 & 1 \end{pmatrix}.$$

The blocks are encrypted separately. We obtain $c_1 = E_\pi(m_1) = 0111, c_2 = E_\pi(m_2) = 0010, c_3 = E_\pi(m_3) = 1000, c_4 = E_\pi(m_4) = 0101$. The ciphertext is

$$c = 0111001010000101.$$

ECB mode can also be used with an encryption algorithm that maps blocks of length n to blocks of greater length. This is, for example, true for the RSA system (see Section 7.2.2).

When using ECB mode, equal plaintext blocks are encrypted into equal ciphertext blocks. It is therefore possible to recognize patterns of the plaintext in the ciphertext. This makes statistical attacks easier. Also, if ECB mode is used, then an attacker can substitute ciphertext blocks with other ciphertext blocks that have been encrypted under the same key. This manipulation of the ciphertext is hard to detect by the receiver. For those reasons, ECB mode should not be used for the encryption of large plaintexts.

The security of ECB mode can be increased if a certain part of each block is random and the remaining part comes from the plaintext. But then many random bits must be generated, and more blocks must be encrypted. This reduces the efficiency of the ECB mode.

3.8.2   CBC mode

The *cipherblock chaining mode* (CBC mode; see Fig. 3.2) avoids the problems of ECB mode. In this mode, the encryption of a block not only depends on the key but also on the previous blocks. Encryption is context-dependent. Equal blocks in different contexts are encrypted differently. The receiver can tell that the ciphertext has been changed because decryption of a manipulated ciphertext does not work.

We now explain CBC mode in detail. We use a block cipher with alphabet $\Sigma = \{0, 1\}$, block length n, key space $\mathcal{K}$, encryption functions E_k, and decryption functions D_k, $k \in \mathcal{K}$.

We need the following definition.

Definition 3.8.2
The map

$$\oplus : \{0, 1\}^2 \to \{0, 1\}, (b, c) \mapsto b \oplus c$$

is defined by the following table:

b	c	$b \oplus c$
0	0	0
1	0	1
0	1	1
1	1	0

It is called the *exclusive or* of two bits or, in shortened form, *XOR*.

For $k \in \mathbb{N}$, $b = (b_1, b_2, \ldots, b_k)$, and $c = (c_1, c_2, \ldots, c_k) \in \{0, 1\}^k$, we set $b \oplus c = (b_1 \oplus c_1, b_2 \oplus c_2, \ldots, b_k \oplus c_k)$.

If the elements of $\mathbb{Z}/2\mathbb{Z}$ are represented by their least nonnegative representatives 0 and 1, then exclusive or is addition in $\mathbb{Z}/2\mathbb{Z}$.

Example 3.8.3
If $b = 0100$ and $c = 1101$, then $b \oplus c = 1001$.

CBC mode uses a fixed *initialization vector*

$$IV \in \Sigma^n,$$

which can be made public. As in ECB mode, the plaintext is decomposed into blocks of length n. If Alice encrypts the sequence

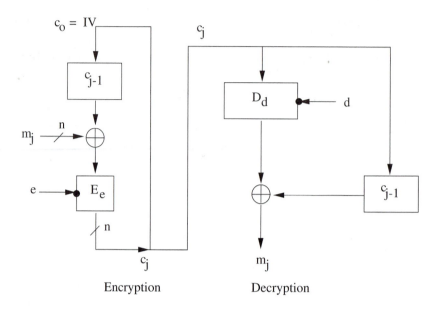

FIGURE 3.2   CBC mode.

$m_1, \ldots, m_t$ of plaintext blocks of length n using the key e, then she sets

$$c_0 = IV, \quad c_j = E_e(c_{j-1} \oplus m_j), \quad 1 \le j \le t.$$

She obtains the ciphertext

$$c = c_1 \ldots c_t.$$

To decrypt this ciphertext, Bob uses the decryption key d, which satisfies $D_d(E_e(w)) = w$ for all plaintext blocks w. Then he computes

$$c_0 = IV, \quad m_j = c_{j-1} \oplus D_d(c_j), \quad 1 \le j \le t. \qquad (3.1)$$

In fact, he obtains $c_0 \oplus D_d(c_1) = c_0 \oplus c_0 \oplus m_1 = m_1$. Analogously, it can be shown that all other plaintexts are correct.

Example 3.8.4

We use the same block cipher, the same plaintext, and the same key as in Example 3.8.1. The plaintext blocks are

$$m_1 = 1011, \quad m_2 = 0001, \quad m_3 = 0100, \quad m_4 = 1010.$$

The key is

$$\pi = \begin{pmatrix} 1 & 2 & 3 & 4 \\ 2 & 3 & 4 & 1 \end{pmatrix}.$$

As initialization vector, we use

$$IV = 1010.$$

Then $c_0 = 1010$, $c_1 = E_\pi(c_0 \oplus m_1) = E_\pi(0001) = 0010$, $c_2 = E_\pi(c_1 \oplus m_2) = E_\pi(0011) = 0110$, $c_3 = E_\pi(c_2 \oplus m_3) = E_\pi(0010) = 0100$, $c_4 = E_\pi(c_3 \oplus m_4) = E_\pi(1110) = 1101$. Also, the ciphertext is

$$c = 0010011001001101.$$

We decrypt this ciphertext and obtain $m_1 = c_0 \oplus E_\pi^{-1}(c_1) = 1010 \oplus 0001 = 1011$, $m_2 = c_1 \oplus E_\pi^{-1}(c_2) = 0010 \oplus 0011 = 0001$, $m_3 = c_2 \oplus E_\pi^{-1}(c_3) = 0110 \oplus 0010 = 0100$, $m_4 = c_3 \oplus E_\pi^{-1}(c_4) = 0100 \oplus 1110 = 1010$.

In general, CBC mode encrypts the same plaintext differently with different initialization vectors. Moreover, the encryption of a plaintext block depends on the preceding plaintext blocks. Therefore, if the order of the ciphertext blocks is changed or if ciphertext blocks are replaced, then decryption becomes impossible. This is an advantage over the ECB mode.

We study the effect of transmission errors. In (3.1), the plaintext block m_j is computed from the ciphertext blocks c_j and c_{j-1}. Therefore, if ciphertext block c_j is transmitted incorrectly, then the plaintext blocks m_j and m_{j+1} may be incorrect. But the following plaintext blocks $m_{j+2}, m_{j+3}, \ldots$ are not influenced. They can be determined correctly.

3.8.3 CFB mode

CBC mode is well suited for the encryption of large messages. In real-time applications (i.e., if Bob wants to decrypt the ciphertext while receiving it), however he may have efficiency problems. Real-time encryption and decryption are, for example, necessary for secure telephone communication. To generate a ciphertext, Alice applies the encryption function. After the encryption is finished, Alice sends the block to Bob, who applies the decryption function. This means that the encryption function and the decryption function must be used sequentially. Those functions may be expensive to compute. Therefore, there may be a considerable time difference between encryption and decryption.

In *cipher feedback mode* (CFB mode; see Fig. 3.3), this is different. To explain this mode, we use the same block cipher as in the CBC mode.

In CFB mode, the encryption function is not used directly for encrypting plaintext blocks but for generating a sequence of key blocks. The plaintext is encrypted by adding those key blocks mod 2. The ciphertext is decrypted by adding the same key blocks mod 2. The key blocks can be simultaneously generated by the sender, Alice, and the receiver, Bob. Only the addition mod 2 must be done sequentially, as follows.

Again, we need an initialization vector $IV \in \{0, 1\}^n$. We also need a positive integer r, $1 \le r \le n$. The plaintext is decomposed into blocks of length r. To encrypt the sequence $m_1, \ldots, m_u$ of plaintexts, Alice sets

$$I_1 = IV,$$

and for $1 \le j \le u$:

1. $O_j = E_k(I_j)$,
2. t_j to the string, which consists of the first r bits of O_j,
3. $c_j = m_j \oplus t_j$,
4. $I_{j+1} = 2^r I_j + c_j \bmod 2^n$, so I_{j+1} is generated by deleting the first r bits in I_j and appending c_j.

   The ciphertext is the sequence $c_1, c_2, \ldots, c_n$.
   Decryption works similarly. Bob sets

$$I_1 = IV,$$

and then for $1 \le j \le u$:

1. $O_j = E_k(I_j)$,
2. t_j to the string, which consists of the first r bits of O_j,
3. $m_j = c_j \oplus t_j$,
4. $I_{j+1} = 2^r I_j + c_j \bmod 2^n$.

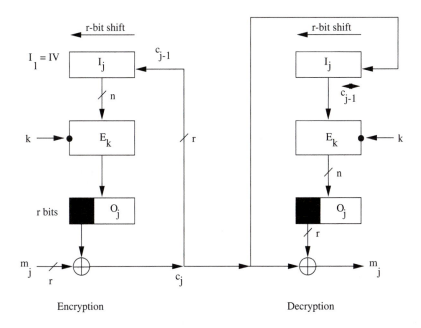

FIGURE 3.3 CFB mode.

Both Alice and Bob can compute the string t_{j+1} as soon as they know the ciphertext block c_j. Therefore, the key block t_1 can be computed by Alice and Bob simultaneously. Then Alice generates the ciphertext block $c_1 = m_1 \oplus t_1$ and sends it to Bob. The computation of c_1 is fast since it only requires an XOR. Then Alice and Bob can simultaneously compute the key block c_2, etc.

Example 3.8.5
We use the block cipher, plaintext, and key from Example 3.8.1 as well as the block length $r = 3$. The plaintext blocks are

$$m_1 = 101, \quad m_2 = 100, \quad m_3 = 010, \quad m_4 = 100, \quad m_5 = 101.$$

The key is

$$\pi = \begin{pmatrix} 1 & 2 & 3 & 4 \\ 2 & 3 & 4 & 1 \end{pmatrix}.$$

As initialization vector, we use

$$IV = 1010.$$

CFB encryption is shown in the following table.

j	I_j	O_j	t_j	m_j	c_j
1	1010	0101	010	101	111
2	0111	1110	111	100	011
3	1011	0111	011	010	001
4	1001	0011	001	100	101
5	1101	1011	101	101	000

In CFB mode, transmission errors spoil decryption as long as parts of the wrong ciphertext block are in the vector I_j. Note that CFB mode cannot be used with public-key cryptosystems because both sender and receiver use the same key e.

3.8.4   OFB mode

Output feedback mode (OFB mode; see Fig. 3.4) is very similar to CFB mode. As in CFB mode, the OFB mode uses a block cipher with block length n, another block length r with $1 \leq r \leq n$, and an initialization vector I_1. If Alice encrypts a plaintext using key e, then she decomposes it into blocks of length r as in CFB mode. Then she sets for $1 \leq j \leq u$:

1. $O_j = E_k(I_j)$,

2. t_j to the string, which consists of the first r bits of O_j,

3. $c_j = m_j \oplus t_j$,

4. $I_{j+1} = O_j$.

Again, decryption works analogously. Step 3 is replaced by $m_j = c_j \oplus t_j$.

If a bit of the ciphertext is transmitted incorrectly, then the plaintext will be wrong in exactly the same position. The wrong bit has no other influence.

The key block t_j only depends on the initialization vector I_1 and on the key k. They can be computed by the sender and the receiver simultaneously. This is even better than in CFB mode. However, the encryption of a plaintext block in OFB mode does not depend on the previous plaintext blocks but only on its position. Therefore,

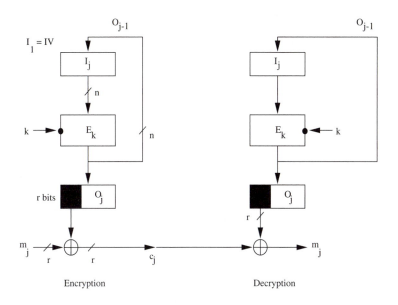

FIGURE 3.4 OFB mode.

manipulation of the ciphertext is easier in OFB mode than in CFB mode.

Example 3.8.6
We use the block cipher, plaintext, and key from Example 3.8.1. Moreover, we use $r = 3$. The plaintext blocks are

$$m_1 = 101, \quad m_2 = 100, \quad m_3 = 010, \quad m_4 = 100, \quad m_5 = 101.$$

The key is

$$\pi = \begin{pmatrix} 1 & 2 & 3 & 4 \\ 2 & 3 & 4 & 1 \end{pmatrix}.$$

As initialization vector, we use

$$IV = 1010.$$

Encryption is shown in the following table.

j	I_j	O_j	t_j	m_j	c_j
1	1010	0101	010	101	111
2	0101	1010	101	100	001
3	1010	0101	010	010	000
4	0101	1010	101	100	001
5	1010	0101	010	101	111

If the same key k is used for encrypting two plaintexts, then the initialization vector must be changed. Otherwise, the same sequence of key blocks t_j is generated, and from two ciphertext blocks $c_j = m_j \oplus t_j$ and $c_j' = m_j' \oplus t_j$ the attacker, Oscar, obtains $c_j \oplus c_j' = m_j \oplus m_j'$. Hence, he can determine m_j' if he knows m_j.

3.9   Stream Ciphers

We have explained how block ciphers can be used to encrypt arbitrarily long plaintexts such that the encryption of the individual plaintext blocks depends on their context. This principle is generalized in stream ciphers.

We only give an example for a stream cipher. A well-known stream cipher works as follows. The alphabet is $\Sigma = \{0, 1\}$. The plaintext- and ciphertext space is Σ^*. The key space is Σ^n for a positive integer n. Words in Σ^* are encrypted bit by bit. This works as follows. Let $k = (k_1, \ldots, k_n)$ be a key and $w = \sigma_1 \ldots \sigma_m$ a word of length m in Σ^*. Alice generates a key stream $z_1, z_2, \ldots, z_m$. She sets

$$z_i = k_i, \quad 1 \leq i \leq n \qquad (3.2)$$

and for $m > n$

$$z_i = \sum_{j=1}^{n} c_j z_{i-j} \bmod 2, \quad n < i \leq m, \qquad (3.3)$$

where $c_1, \ldots, c_n$ are fixed coefficients. Such an equation is called *linear recursion* of degree n. The encryption function E_k and the decryption function D_k are defined by

$$E_k(w) = \sigma_1 \oplus z_1, \ldots, \sigma_m \oplus z_m, D_k(w) = \sigma_1 \oplus z_1, \ldots, \sigma_m \oplus z_m.$$

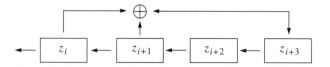

FIGURE 3.5 Linear shift register.

Example 3.9.1

Let $n = 4$. The key stream is generated by the recursion

$$z_{i+4} = z_i + z_{i+1},$$

so we have chosen $c_1 = c_2 = 0$, $c_3 = c_4 = 1$. Let $k = (1, 0, 0, 0)$ be the key. Then we obtain the key stream

$$1, 0, 0, 0, 1, 0, 0, 1, 1, 0, 1, 0, 1, 1, 1, 1, 0, 0, 0, \cdots .$$

This key stream is periodic with period length 15.

The stream cipher that was just described can be implemented in hardware using *linear shift registers*. Figure 3.5 shows such a shift register. The registers contain the last four values of the key stream. In each step, the key from the first register is used for encryption, the contents of the second, third, and fourth registers are shifted by one to the left, and the fourth key is computed by adding those bits for which the coefficient c_i is 1.

We do not discuss stream ciphers in more detail but refer to [30].

3.10 Affine Cipher

Let m be a positive integer. The *affine cipher* with plaintext alphabet $\mathbb{Z}_m$ is a block cipher with block length $n = 1$. The key space consists of all pairs $(a, b) \in \mathbb{Z}_m^2$ for which m is prime to a. The encryption function E_k for key $k = (a, b)$ is

$$E_k : \Sigma \rightarrow \Sigma, \quad x \mapsto ax + b \bmod m.$$

The decryption function for key $k = (a', b)$ is

$$D_k : \Sigma \rightarrow \Sigma, \quad x \mapsto a'(x - b) \bmod m.$$

To compute the decryption key that corresponds to the encryption key (a, b) we solve the congruence $aa' \equiv 1 \bmod m$ with the extended euclidian algorithm. Then this key is (a', b).

Example 3.10.1
If Alice chooses $m = 26$, $(a, b) = (7, 3)$, and encrypts the German word BALD with the affine cipher in ECB mode, then she obtains

B	A	L	D
1	0	11	3
10	3	2	24
K	D	C	Y

Bob computes the corresponding decryption function. He determines an integer a' with $7a' \equiv 1 \bmod 26$. Using the extended euclidean algorithm, he obtains $a' = 15$. Hence, the decryption function maps a symbol σ to $15(\sigma - 3) \bmod 26$. In fact, Bob computes

K	D	C	Y
10	3	2	24
1	0	11	3
B	A	L	D

The key space of the affine cipher with $m = 26$ contains $\varphi(26) * 26 = 312$ elements. Hence, if this block cipher is used in ECB mode, it can be broken with a ciphertext-only attack by an exhaustive key search. If a known plaintext attack is used and two symbols, together with their encryption, are known, then the affine cipher can be broken using an easy linear algebra computation, as the next example shows.

Example 3.10.2
The alphabet $\{A, B, \ldots, Z\}$ is identified with $\mathbb{Z}_{26}$ in the usual way. If the attacker, Oscar, knows that an application of the affine cipher with a fixed key (a, b) maps the letter E to R and S to H, then he obtains the following congruences:

$$4a + b \equiv 17 \bmod 26, \quad 18a + b \equiv 7 \bmod 26.$$

From the first congruence, he obtains $b \equiv 17 - 4a \bmod 26$. If he uses this in the second congruence, then he obtains $18a + 17 - 4a \equiv 7 \bmod 26$ and therefore $14a \equiv 16 \bmod 26$. This implies $7a \equiv$

8 mod 13. He multiplies this congruence by the inverse 2 of 7 mod 13 and obtains $a \equiv 3 \bmod 13$, so he can compute $a = 3$ and $b = 5$.

3.11   Matrices and Linear Maps

In order to generalize affine ciphers, we review a few basic results of linear algebra over rings without proving them. For details, we refer the reader to [26].

Let R be a commutative ring with unit element 1. For example, $R = \mathbb{Z}/m\mathbb{Z}$ for some positive integer m.

3.11.1   Matrices over rings

A $k \times n$ *matrix* over R is a rectangular scheme

$$A = \begin{pmatrix} a_{1,1} & a_{1,2} & \cdots & a_{1,n} \\ a_{2,1} & a_{2,2} & \cdots & a_{2,n} \\ \vdots & \vdots & \cdots & \vdots \\ a_{k,1} & a_{k,2} & \cdots & a_{k,n} \end{pmatrix}.$$

We also write

$$A = (a_{i,j}).$$

If $n = k$, then the matrix is called a *square matrix*. The *i*th *row* of A is the vector $(a_{i,1}, \ldots, a_{i,n})$, $1 \leq i \leq k$. The *j*th *column* of A is the vector $(a_{1,j}, \ldots, a_{k,j})$, $1 \leq j \leq n$. The *entry* in row i and column j is $a_{i,j}$. The set of all $k \times n$ matrices over R is denoted by $R^{(k,n)}$.

Example 3.11.1
Let $R = \mathbb{Z}$. For example,

$$\begin{pmatrix} 1 & 2 & 3 \\ 4 & 5 & 6 \end{pmatrix}$$

is a matrix over $\mathbb{Z}$. It has two rows, namely $(1, 2, 3)$ and $(4, 5, 6)$, and three columns, namely $(1, 4)$, $(2, 5)$, and $(3, 6)$.

3.11.2   Product of matrices and vectors

If $A = (a_{i,j}) \in R^{(k,n)}$ and $\vec{v} = (v_1, \ldots, v_n) \in R^n$, then the product $A\vec{v}$ is defined as the vector $\vec{w} = (w_1, w_2, \ldots, w_k)$ with

$$w_i = \sum_{j=1}^{n} a_{i,j} v_j, \quad 1 \le i \le k.$$

Example 3.11.2

Let $A = \begin{pmatrix} 1 & 2 \\ 2 & 3 \end{pmatrix}$, $\vec{v} = (1, 2)$. Then $A\vec{v} = (5, 8)$.

3.11.3   Sum and product of matrices

Let $n \in \mathbb{N}$ and $A, B \in R^{(n,n)}$, $A = (a_{i,j})$, $B = (b_{i,j})$. The *sum* of A and B is

$$A + B = (a_{i,j} + b_{i,j}).$$

The *product* of A and B is $A \cdot B = AB = (c_{i,j})$ with

$$c_{i,j} = \sum_{k=1}^{n} a_{i,k} b_{k,j}.$$

Example 3.11.3

Let $A = \begin{pmatrix} 1 & 2 \\ 2 & 3 \end{pmatrix}$, $B = \begin{pmatrix} 4 & 5 \\ 6 & 7 \end{pmatrix}$. Then $A + B = \begin{pmatrix} 5 & 7 \\ 8 & 10 \end{pmatrix}$,

$AB = \begin{pmatrix} 16 & 19 \\ 26 & 31 \end{pmatrix}$, $BA = \begin{pmatrix} 14 & 23 \\ 20 & 33 \end{pmatrix}$. Multiplication of matrices is, in general, not commutative.

3.11.4   The ring of matrices

The $n \times n$ *identity matrix* over R is $E_n = (e_{i,j})$ with

$$e_{i,j} = \begin{cases} 1 & \text{for } i = j, \\ 0 & \text{for } i \neq j. \end{cases}$$

The $n \times n$ *zero matrix* over R is the $n \times n$ matrix all of whose entries are zero.

Example 3.11.4

The 2×2 identity matrix over $\mathbb{Z}$ is $\begin{pmatrix} 1 & 0 \\ 0 & 1 \end{pmatrix}$. The 2×2 zero matrix over $\mathbb{Z}$ is $\begin{pmatrix} 0 & 0 \\ 0 & 0 \end{pmatrix}$.

Together with addition and multiplication, the set $R^{(n,n)}$ is a ring with unit element E_n. In general, this ring is not commutative. The neutral element with respect to addition is the zero matrix.

3.11.5 Determinants

The *determinant* $\det A$ of a matrix $A \in R^{(n,n)}$ can be defined recursively. For $n = 1$, $A = (a)$, we have $\det A = a$. Let $n > 1$. For $i, j \in \{1, 2, \ldots n\}$, denote by $A_{i,j}$ the matrix that is obtained from A by deleting the ith row and jth column. Fix $i \in \{1, 2, \ldots, n\}$. Then the determinant of A is

$$\det A = \sum_{j=1}^{n}(-1)^{i+j}a_{i,j}\det A_{i,j}.$$

This value is independent of the choice of i. Also, for all $j \in \{1, 2, \ldots, n\}$, we have

$$\det A = \sum_{i=1}^{n}(-1)^{i+j}a_{i,j}\det A_{i,j}.$$

Example 3.11.5

Let $A = \begin{pmatrix} a_{1,1} & a_{1,2} \\ a_{2,1} & a_{2,2} \end{pmatrix}$. Then $A_{1,1} = (a_{2,2}), A_{1,2} = (a_{2,1}), A_{2,1} = (a_{1,2}), A_{2,2} = (a_{1,1})$. Therefore, $\det A = a_{1,1}a_{2,2} - a_{1,2}a_{2,1}$.

3.11.6 Inverse of matrices

A matrix $A \in R^{(n,n)}$ has a multiplicative inverse if and only if $\det A$ is a unit in R. Here is a formula for this inverse. If $n = 1$, then $(a_{1,1}^{-1})$ is the inverse of A. Let $n > 1$ and $A_{i,j}$ as defined earlier. The *adjoint* of A is an $n \times n$ matrix defined by

$$\operatorname{adj} A = ((-1)^{i+j} \det A_{j,i}).$$

The inverse of A is

$$A^{-1} = (\det A)^{-1} \operatorname{adj} A.$$

Example 3.11.6

Let $A = \begin{pmatrix} a_{1,1} & a_{1,2} \\ a_{2,1} & a_{2,2} \end{pmatrix}$. Then $\operatorname{adj} A = \begin{pmatrix} a_{2,2} & -a_{1,2} \\ -a_{2,1} & a_{1,1} \end{pmatrix}$.

Let $A = (a_{i,j})$, $B = (b_{i,j}) \in \mathbb{Z}^{(n,n)}$ and $m \in \mathbb{N}$. We write

$$A \equiv B \bmod m$$

if $a_{i,j} \equiv b_{i,j} \bmod m$ for $1 \le i, j \le n$.

As an application of the results described in this section, we explain how to solve the congruence

$$AA' \equiv E_n \bmod m. \tag{3.4}$$

First, we give an example.

Example 3.11.7

Let $A = \begin{pmatrix} 1 & 2 \\ 3 & 4 \end{pmatrix}$. We want to solve the congruence

$$AA' \equiv E_2 \bmod 11 \tag{3.5}$$

for $A' \in \mathbb{Z}^{(2,2)}$. Denote by $\overline{A}$ the matrix that is obtained from A by replacing its entries with their residue classes mod m. Solving the congruence (3.5) means finding the inverse $\overline{A'}$ of $\overline{A}$. It exists if the determinant of $\overline{A}$ is a unit in $\mathbb{Z}/11\mathbb{Z}$. This is true if and only if $\det A$ is prime to 11. Now $\det A = -2$, and hence prime to 11. Moreover, $(-2)(-6) \equiv 1 \bmod 11$. If we set

$$A' = (-6) * \operatorname{adj} A \bmod 11 = 5 * \begin{pmatrix} 4 & -2 \\ -3 & 1 \end{pmatrix} \bmod 11 = \begin{pmatrix} 9 & 1 \\ 7 & 5 \end{pmatrix},$$

then a solution of (3.5) is found.

We generalize the result of the preceding example. Let $A \in \mathbb{Z}^{n,n}$ and $m > 1$. The congruence (3.4) is solvable if and only if $\det A$ and

m are coprime. If this is true and if a is an inverse of $\det A$ mod m (i.e., $a \det A \equiv 1 \bmod m$), then

$$A' = a \operatorname{adj} A \bmod m$$

is a solution of the congruence (3.4). This solution is unique mod m. The matrix A' can be computed in polynomial time.

3.11.7 Affine linear functions

We define affine linear functions. They can be used to construct simple block ciphers.

Definition 3.11.8
A function $f : R^n \to R^l$ is called *affine linear* if there is a matrix $A \in R^{(l,n)}$ and a vector $\vec{b} \in R^l$ such that

$$f(\vec{v}) = A\vec{v} + \vec{b}$$

for all $\vec{v} \in R^n$. If $\vec{b} = 0$, then this function is called *linear*.

Affine linear functions $\mathbb{Z}_m^n \to \mathbb{Z}_m^n$ are defined analogously.

Definition 3.11.9
A function $f : \mathbb{Z}_m^n \to \mathbb{Z}_m^l$ is called *affine linear* if there is a matrix $A \in \mathbb{Z}^{(l,n)}$ and a vector $\vec{b} \in \mathbb{Z}^l$ such that

$$f(\vec{v}) = (A\vec{v} + \vec{b}) \bmod m$$

for all $\vec{v} \in \mathbb{Z}_m^n$. If $\vec{b} \equiv 0 \bmod m$, then this function is called *linear*.

Theorem 3.11.10
The affine linear map from Definition 3.11.8 is bijective if and only if $l = n$ and $\det A$ is a unit in R.

Analogously, the map from Definition 3.12 is bijective if and only if $l = n$ and $\det A$ is prime to m.

Example 3.11.11
Consider the map $f : \{0, 1\}^2 \to \{0, 1\}^2$, which is defined by

$$f(0, 0) = (0, 0), f(1, 0) = (1, 1), f(0, 1) = (1, 0), f(1, 1) = (0, 1).$$

This map is linear because $f(\vec{v}) = \begin{pmatrix} 1 & 1 \\ 1 & 0 \end{pmatrix} \vec{v}$ for all $\vec{v} \in \{0, 1\}^2$.

We characterize linear and affine linear functions.

Theorem 3.11.12
A function $f : R^n \to R''''$ is linear if and only if

$$f(a\vec{v} + b\vec{w}) = af(\vec{v}) + bf(w)$$

for all $\vec{v}, \vec{w} \in R^n$ and all $a, b \in R$. It is affine linear if and only if the function $R^n \to R^n, \vec{v} \mapsto f(\vec{v}) - f(\vec{0})$ is linear.

3.12   Affine Linear Block Ciphers

We introduce *affine linear block ciphers*. They are generalizations of the affine cipher. We discuss those ciphers on the one hand for historical reasons. On the other hand, we want to show that affine linear ciphers can be quite easily attacked. This leads to an important design principle for block ciphers: Secure block ciphers must not be linear or easy to approximate by linear functions.

To define linear block ciphers, we need a positive integer n, the block length, and a positive integer m, $m > 2$.

Definition 3.12.1
A block cipher with block length n and plaintext- and ciphertext space $\mathbb{Z}_m$ is called *affine linear* if all of its encryption functions are affine linear. It is called linear if all of its encryption functions are linear.

We describe affine linear block ciphers explicitly. The encryption functions are affine linear, and hence of the form

$$E : \mathbb{Z}_m^n \to \mathbb{Z}_m^n, \quad \vec{v} \mapsto A\vec{v} + \vec{b} \bmod m$$

with $A \in \mathbb{Z}^{(n,n)}$ and $b \in \mathbb{Z}^n$. Moreover, by Theorem 3.6.2, the function E is bijective. Therefore, $\det A$ is prime to m by Theorem 3.11.10. The encryption function is uniquely determined by the pair $(A, \vec{b})$. We can use this pair as the key. By the results of Section 3.11.6, the corresponding decryption function is

$$D : \mathbb{Z}_m^n \to \mathbb{Z}_m^n, \quad \vec{v} \mapsto A'(\vec{v} - \vec{b}) \bmod m,$$

where $A' = (a' \mathrm{adj}\, A) \bmod m$ and a' is an inverse of $\det A \bmod m$.

3.13 Vigenère, Hill, and Permutation Ciphers

We give two examples of affine linear ciphers.

The Vigenère cipher is named after Blaise Vigenère, who lived in the 16th century. The key space is $\mathcal{K} = \mathbb{Z}_m^n$. If $\vec{k} \in \mathbb{Z}_m^n$, then

$$E_{\vec{k}} : \mathbb{Z}_m^n \to \mathbb{Z}_m^n, \quad \vec{v} \mapsto \vec{v} + \vec{k} \bmod m$$

and

$$D_{\vec{k}} : \mathbb{Z}_m^n \to \mathbb{Z}_m^n, \quad \vec{v} \mapsto \vec{v} - \vec{k} \bmod m.$$

The encryption and decryption functions are obviously affine linear. The number of elements in the key space is m^n.

The *Hill cipher* is another classical cryptosystem. It was invented in 1929 by Lester S. Hill. The key space $\mathcal{K}$ is the set of all matrices $A \in \mathbb{Z}_m^{(n,n)}$ with $\gcd(\det A, m) = 1$. The encryption function for key $A \in \mathcal{K}$ is

$$E_A : \mathbb{Z}_m^n \to \mathbb{Z}_m^n, \quad \vec{v} \mapsto A\vec{v} \bmod m. \tag{3.6}$$

Hence, the Hill cipher is the most general linear block cipher.

Finally, we show that the permutation cipher is linear. Let $\pi \in S_n$ and denote by $\vec{e}_i$, $1 \le i \le n$, the row vectors of the identity matrix. They are called *unit vectors*. Moreover, let E_π be the $n \times n$ matrix whose ith row vector is $\vec{e}_{\pi(i)}$, $1 \le i \le n$. This matrix is obtained from the $n \times n$ identity matrix by permuting its rows according to the permutation π. The jth column of E_π is the unit vector $\vec{e}_{\pi(j)}$. For any vector $\vec{v} = (v_1, \ldots, v_n) \in \Sigma^n$, we have

$$(v_{\pi(1)}, \ldots, v_{\pi(n)}) = E_\pi \vec{v}.$$

Therefore, the permutation cipher is a linear cipher (i.e., a special case of the Hill cipher).

3.14 Cryptanalysis of Affine Linear Block Ciphers

We explain how an affine linear cipher with alphabet $\mathbb{Z}_m$ and block length n can be broken by means of a known plaintext attack.

Suppose that Alice and Bob use an affine linear cipher and have agreed on a key. The encryption function is

$$E : \mathbb{Z}_m^n \to \mathbb{Z}_m^n, \quad \vec{v} \mapsto A\vec{v} + \vec{b} \bmod m$$

with $A \in \mathbb{Z}^{(n,n)}$ and $\vec{b} \in \mathbb{Z}^n$. The attacker, Oscar, wants to determine the key $(A, \vec{b})$. Oscar uses $n + 1$ plaintexts $\vec{w}_i$, $0 \le i \le n$ and the corresponding cipher texts $\vec{c}_i = A\vec{w}_i + \vec{b}$, $0 \le i \le n$. Then

$$\vec{c}_i - \vec{c}_0 \equiv A(\vec{w}_i - \vec{w}_0) \bmod m.$$

If W is the matrix

$$W = (\vec{w}_1 - \vec{w}_0, \dots, \vec{w}_n - \vec{w}_0) \bmod m,$$

whose columns are the differences $(\vec{w}_i - \vec{w}_0) \bmod m$, $1 \le i \le n$ and if C is the matrix

$$C = (\vec{c}_1 - \vec{c}_0, \dots, \vec{c}_n - \vec{c}_0) \bmod m$$

whose columns are the differences $(\vec{c}_i - \vec{c}_0) \bmod m$, $1 \le i \le n$, then we have

$$AW \equiv C \bmod m.$$

If $\det W$ is coprime to m, then

$$A \equiv C(w' \mathrm{adj}\, W) \bmod m,$$

where w' is the inverse of $\det W \bmod m$. Moreover, we have

$$\vec{b} = \vec{c}_0 - A\vec{w}_0.$$

Thus, the key has been determined from $n + 1$ plaintext-ciphertext pairs. If the cipher is linear, then Oscar can set $\vec{w}_0 = \vec{c}_0 = \vec{b} = \vec{0}$.

Example 3.14.1

We show how to break a Hill cipher with block length 2. Suppose that we know that the encryption of HAND is FUSS. Then the encryption of $\vec{w}_1 = (7, 0)$ is $\vec{c}_1 = (5, 20)$ and that of $\vec{w}_2 = (13, 3)$ is $\vec{c}_2 = (18, 18)$.

We obtain $W = \begin{pmatrix} 7 & 13 \\ 0 & 3 \end{pmatrix}$ and $C = \begin{pmatrix} 5 & 18 \\ 20 & 18 \end{pmatrix}$. Now $\det W = 21$ is coprime to 26. The inverse of 21 mod 26 is 5. This implies

$$A = 5C(\text{adj } W) \bmod 26 = 5 * \begin{pmatrix} 5 & 18 \\ 20 & 18 \end{pmatrix} \begin{pmatrix} 3 & 13 \\ 0 & 7 \end{pmatrix} \bmod 26 = \begin{pmatrix} 23 & 19 \\ 14 & 6 \end{pmatrix}.$$

In fact, we have $AW = C$.

3.15 Exercises

Exercise 3.15.1
The ciphertext VHFUHW has been generated with the Caesar cipher. Determine the key and the plaintext.

Exercise 3.15.2
Show that the following procedure defines a cryptosystem.

Let w be a string over $\{A,B,\ldots,Z\}$. Choose two Caesar cipher keys k_1 and k_2. Encrypt the elements of w having odd numbers with k_1 and those having even numbers with k_2. Then reverse the order of the encrypted string.

Determine the plaintext space, the ciphertext space, and the key space.

Exercise 3.15.3
Show that the encryption function of a cryptosystem is always injective.

Exercise 3.15.4
Determine the number of strings of length n over an alphabet Σ that do not change if they are reversed.

Exercise 3.15.5
Let Σ be an alphabet. Show that the set Σ^* together with concatenation is a monoid. Is this monoid a group?

Exercise 3.15.6
Determine the number of block ciphers over the alphabet $\{0.1\}$ whose ciphertexts have the same number of ones as the plain texts.

Exercise 3.15.7

Which of the following schemes is a cryptosystem? What is the plaintext space, the ciphertext space, and the key space? We always let $\Sigma = \mathbb{Z}_{26}$.

1. Each letter $\sigma \in \Sigma$ is replaced by $k\sigma \bmod 26$, $k \in \{1, 2, \ldots, 26\}$.
2. Each letter $\sigma \in \Sigma$ is replaced by $k\sigma \bmod 26$, $k \in \{1, 2, \ldots, 26\}$, $\gcd(k, 26) = 1$.

Exercise 3.15.8

Give an example for a cryptosystem with encryption functions that are injective but not surjective.

Exercise 3.15.9

Determine the number of bit permutations of the set $\{0, 1\}^n$, $n \in \mathbb{N}$ and the number of circular right shifts of $\{0, 1\}^n$.

Exercise 3.15.10

A *transposition* is a permutation that interchanges two elements and maps all other elements to themselves. Prove that every permutation can be obtained as a composition of transpositions.

Exercise 3.15.11

Find a permutation of $\{0, 1\}^n$ that is not a bit permutation.

Exercise 3.15.12

Find a permutation of $\{0, 1\}^n$ that is not affine linear.

Exercise 3.15.13

Let X be a set. Show that the set $S(X)$ of permutations of X is a group with respect to composition and that this group is, in general, not commutative.

Exercise 3.15.14

Decrypt the plaintext 111111111111 using ECB mode, CBC mode, CFB mode, and OFB mode. Use the permutation cipher with block length 3 and key

$$k = \begin{pmatrix} 1 & 2 & 3 \\ 2 & 3 & 1 \end{pmatrix}.$$

The initialization vector is 000. For the OFB and CFB modes, use $r = 2$.

Exercise 3.15.15
Encrypt the plaintext 101010101010 using ECB mode, CBC mode, CFB mode, and OFB mode. Use the permutation cipher with block length 3 and key

$$k = \begin{pmatrix} 1 & 2 & 3 \\ 2 & 1 & 3 \end{pmatrix}.$$

The initialization vector is 000. For OFB and CFB modes, use $r = 2$.

Exercise 3.15.16
Let $k = 1010101$, $c = 1110011$, $w = 1110001\ 1110001\ 1110001$. Encrypt w using the stream cipher from Section 3.9.

Exercise 3.15.17
Determine the determinant of the matrix

$$\begin{pmatrix} 1 & 2 & 3 \\ 2 & 3 & 1 \\ 3 & 1 & 2 \end{pmatrix}.$$

Exercise 3.15.18
Find a closed formula for the determinant of a 3×3 matrix.

Exercise 3.15.19
Find an injective affine linear map $(\mathbb{Z}/2\mathbb{Z})^3 \rightarrow (\mathbb{Z}/2\mathbb{Z})^3$ that sends $(1, 1, 1)$ to $(0, 0, 0)$.

Exercise 3.15.20
Determine the inverse of the matrix

$$\begin{pmatrix} 1 & 1 & 1 \\ 1 & 1 & 0 \\ 1 & 0 & 0 \end{pmatrix}$$

mod 2.

Exercise 3.15.21
Find a key for the affine linear cipher with alphabet {A,B,C,...,Z} and block length three that encrypts "RED" as "ONE".

Probability and Perfect Secrecy

CHAPTER 4

In the previous chapter, we have described a number of historical cryptosystems. It turned out that they were all affine linear and therefore insecure. Are there cryptosystems that are provably secure? In 1949, Claude Shannon was able to describe such systems. Unfortunately, those systems are not very efficient. In this chapter, we present Shannon's theory. At the same time, we will introduce a few notions and results of elementary probability theory.

4.1 Probability

Let S be a finite nonempty set. We call it the *sample space*. Its elements are called *elementary events*. The elementary events model outcomes of experiments.

Example 4.1.1
If we flip a coin, we either obtain heads H or tails T. The sample space is $S = \{H,T\}$.

If we throw a die, then we obtain a number in $\{1, 2, 3, 4, 5, 6\}$. Therefore, the sample space is $S = \{1, 2, 3, 4, 5, 6\}$.

An *event* (for S) is a subset of the sample space S. The *certain event* is the set S itself. The *null event* is the empty set $\emptyset$. We say that two events A and B are *mutually exclusive* if their intersection is empty. The set of all events is the *power set* $P(S)$ of S.

Example 4.1.2

An event is, for example, to obtain an even number when throwing a die. Formally, this event is $\{2, 4, 6\}$. It excludes the event $\{1, 3, 5\}$ to obtain an odd number.

A *probability distribution* on S is a map Pr that sends an event to a real number, namely

$$\text{Pr} : P(S) \to \mathbb{R},$$

and has the following properties:

1. $\text{Pr}(A) \geq 0$ for all events A,

2. $\text{Pr}(S) = 1$,

3. $\text{Pr}(A \cup B) = \text{Pr}(A) + \text{Pr}(B)$ for two events A and B, which are mutually exclusive.

If A is an event, then $\text{Pr}(A)$ is the *probability* of this event. The probability of an elementary event $a \in S$ is $\text{Pr}(a) = \text{Pr}(\{a\})$.

It is easy to see that $\text{Pr}(\emptyset) = 0$. Moreover, $A \subset B$ implies $\text{Pr}(A) \leq \text{Pr}(B)$. Therefore, $0 \leq \text{Pr}(A) \leq 1$ for all $A \in P(S)$. Moreover, $\text{Pr}(S \setminus A) = 1 - \text{Pr}(A)$. If $A_1, \ldots, A_n$ are pairwise mutually exclusive events, then $\text{Pr}(\cup_{i=1}^n A_i) = \sum_{i=1}^n \text{Pr}(A_i)$.

Since S is a finite set, it suffices to define the probability distribution on elementary events. In fact, if A is an event, then $\text{Pr}(A) = \sum_{a \in A} \text{Pr}(a)$.

Example 4.1.3

The probability distribution on the set $\{1, 2, 3, 4, 5, 6\}$, which models throwing a die, maps each elementary event to $1/6$. The probability of the event "even result" is $\text{Pr}(\{2, 4, 6\}) = \text{Pr}(2) + \text{Pr}(4) + \text{Pr}(6) = 1/6 + 1/6 + 1/6 = 1/2$.

The probability distribution that maps each elementary event $a \in S$ to the probability $P(a) = 1/|S|$ is called the *uniform distribution*.

4.2   Conditional Probability

Let S be a sample space, and let Pr be a probability distribution on S. We explain conditional probability in an example.

Example 4.2.1
Again, we model throwing a die. The sample space is $\{1, 2, 3, 4, 5, 6\}$, and Pr sends any elementary event to $1/6$. Suppose Claus has thrown one of the numbers $4, 5, 6$, so we know that the event $B = \{4, 5, 6\}$ has happened. Under this assumption, we want to determine the probability that Claus has thrown an even number. Each elementary event in B is equally probable. Therefore, each elementary event in B has probability $1/3$. Since two numbers in B are even, the probability that Claus has thrown an even number is $2/3$.

Definition 4.2.2
Let A and B be events and $\Pr(B) > 0$. The conditional probability of "A given that B" occurs is defined to be

$$\Pr(A|B) = \frac{\Pr(A \cap B)}{\Pr(B)}.$$

This definition can be understood as follows. We want to know the probability of A if B is certain to occur (i.e., the sum of the probabilities of all elementary events x in $A \cap B$). Such an elementary event has probability $\Pr(x)/\Pr(B)$ because $\Pr(B) = 1$. Therefore, the event $A \cap B$ has probability $\Pr(A \cap B)/\Pr(B)$.

Two events A and B are called *independent* if

$$\Pr(A \cap B) = \Pr(A)\Pr(B).$$

This condition is equivalent to

$$\Pr(A|B) = \Pr(A).$$

If the events are not independent, we call them *dependent*.

Example 4.2.3
If we flip two coins, then the probability of the event "the first coin comes up tails" is independent from the event "the second coin comes up tails". The probability that both events occur is $1/4$. The probability of each individual event is $1/2$.

If the coins are welded together such that they either both fall heads or both tails, then the probability of two tails is $1/2 \neq 1/2 * 1/2$. Hence, the events "the first coin comes up tails" and "the second coin comes up tails" are dependent.

We formulate and prove the theorem of Bayes.

Theorem 4.2.4
If A and B are events with $\Pr(A) > 0$ *and* $\Pr(B) > 0$, *then*

$$\Pr(B)\Pr(A|B) = \Pr(A)\Pr(B|A).$$

Proof. By definition, we have $\Pr(A|B)\Pr(B) = \Pr(A \cap B)$ and $\Pr(B|A)\Pr(A) = \Pr(A \cap B)$. This implies the assertion.   □

4.3   Birthday Paradox

A good example for reasoning in probability theory is the birthday paradox. The problem is the following. Suppose a group of people are in a room. What is the probability that two of them have the same birthday? This probability is astonishingly large.

We will make a slightly more general analysis. Suppose that there are n birthdays and that there are k people in the room. An elementary event is a tuple $(b_1, \ldots, b_k) \in \{1, 2, \ldots, n\}^k$. If it occurs, then the birthday of the ith person is b_i, $1 \leq i \leq k$, so we have n^k elementary events. We assume that those elementary events are equally probable. Then the probability of an elementary event is $1/n^k$.

We want to compute the probability that two people in the room have the same birthday. Denote this probability by p. Then with probability $q = 1 - p$ any two people have different birthdays. We estimate this probability. The event in which we are interested is the set E of all vectors $(g_1, \ldots, g_k) \in \{1, 2, \ldots, n\}^k$ whose entries are pairwise different. Since the probability of an elementary event is $1/n^k$, the probability of E is the number of elements in E divided by n^k. The number of elements in E is the number of vectors in $\{1, \ldots, n\}^k$ with pairwise different entries. This number is computed now. The first entry can be any of the n possibilities. If the first entry is fixed, then there are $n - 1$ possibilities for the second entry, and so on. Hence, we obtain

$$|E| = \prod_{i=0}^{k-1}(n-i)$$

and

$$q = \frac{1}{n^k}\prod_{i=0}^{k-1}(n-i) = \prod_{i=1}^{k-1}\left(1 - \frac{i}{n}\right). \qquad (4.1)$$

Now $1 + x \le e^x$ holds for all real numbers. Therefore, from (4.1) we obtain

$$q \le \prod_{i=1}^{k-1} e^{-i/n} = e^{-\sum_{i=1}^{k-1} i/n} = e^{-k(k-1)/(2n)}. \qquad (4.2)$$

If

$$k \ge (1 + \sqrt{1 + 8n\log 2})/2, \qquad (4.3)$$

then (4.2) implies that $q \le 1/2$. Hence the probability $p = 1 - q$ that two people have the same birthday is at least $1/2$. For $n = 365$, the choice $k = 23$ is sufficient for $q \le 1/2$. In other words, if 23 people are in a room, then the probability that two of them have the same birthday is at least $1/2$.

4.4 Perfect Secrecy

Following Shannon, we will now introduce perfect secrecy. We assume the following scenario. Alice uses a cryptosystem to send encrypted messages to Bob. If she sends such an encrypted message to Bob, the attacker, Oscar, can read the ciphertext. Oscar tries to obtain information concerning the plaintext from the ciphertext. A cryptosystem has perfect secrecy if Oscar learns nothing about the plaintext from the ciphertext. We want to formalize this property mathematically.

The cryptosystem has a finite plaintext space $\mathcal{P}$, a finite ciphertext space $\mathcal{C}$, and a finite key space $\mathcal{K}$. The encryption functions are E_k, $k \in \mathcal{K}$ and the decryption functions are D_k, $k \in \mathcal{K}$.

We assume that the probability of a plaintext p is $\Pr_{\mathcal{P}}(p)$. The function $\Pr_{\mathcal{P}}$ is a probability distribution on the plaintext space. It depends, for example, on the language that is used. For the encryption of a new plaintext, Alice chooses a new key which is independent of the plaintext to be encrypted. The probability for a key k is $\Pr_{\mathcal{K}}(k)$. The function $\Pr_{\mathcal{K}}$ is a probability distribution on the key space. The probability that a plaintext p occurs and is encrypted with key k is

$$\Pr(p, k) = \Pr_{\mathcal{P}}(p) \Pr_{\mathcal{K}}(k). \tag{4.4}$$

This defines a probability distribution $\Pr$ on the sample space $\mathcal{P} \times \mathcal{K}$. We will now consider this sample space only. If p is a plaintext, then we also denote by p the event $\{(p, k) : k \in \mathcal{K}\}$ that p is encrypted. Clearly, we have

$$\Pr(p) = \Pr_{\mathcal{P}}(p).$$

Also, for a key $k \in \mathcal{K}$ we denote by k the event $\{(p, k) : p \in \mathcal{P}\}$ that the key k is chosen for encryption. Clearly, we have

$$\Pr(k) = \Pr_{\mathcal{K}}(k).$$

By (4.4), the events p and k are independent. For a ciphertext $c \in \mathcal{C}$, we denote by c the event $\{(p, k) : E_k(p) = c\}$ that the result of the encryption is c.

Oscar knows the probability distribution $\Pr_{\mathcal{P}}$ on the plaintexts because he knows, for example, the language that Alice and Bob use. Now Oscar sees a ciphertext c. If the fact that c has occurred makes some plaintexts more likely than they are according to the probability distribution $\Pr_{\mathcal{P}}$ and others less likely, then Oscar learns something from observing c. Otherwise, if the probability for each plaintext remains the same, then Oscar learns nothing. This motivates Shannon's definition of perfect secrecy, which we present now.

Definition 4.4.1

The cryptosystem of this section has *perfect secrecy* if the events that a particular ciphertext occurs and that a particular plaintext has been encrypted are independent (i.e., $\Pr(p|c) = \Pr(p)$ for all plaintexts p and all ciphertexts c).

Example 4.4.2

Let $\mathcal{P} = \{0, 1\}$, $\Pr(0) = 1/4$, $\Pr(1) = 3/4$. Also, let $\mathcal{K} = \{A, B\}$, $\Pr(A) = 1/4$, $\Pr(B) = 3/4$. Finally, let $\mathcal{C} = \{a, b\}$. Then the probability that the plaintext 1 occurs and is encrypted with key B is $\Pr(1)\Pr(B) = 9/16$. The encryption function E_K works as follows:

$$E_A(0) = a, E_A(1) = b, E_B(0) = b, E_B(1) = a.$$

The probability of the ciphertext a is $\Pr(a) = \Pr(0, A) + \Pr(1, B) = 1/16 + 9/16 = 5/8$. The probability of the ciphertext b is $\Pr(b) = \Pr(1, A) + \Pr(0, B) = 3/16 + 3/16 = 3/8$.

We now compute the conditional probability $\Pr(p|c)$ for all plaintexts p and all ciphertexts c. It is $\Pr(0|a) = 1/10$, $\Pr(1|a) = 9/10$, $\Pr(0|b) = 1/2$, $\Pr(1|b) = 1/2$. Those results show that the cryptosystem described does not have perfect secrecy. If Oscar receives the ciphertext a he can be reasonably sure that the corresponding plaintext is 1.

We formulate and prove the famous theorem of Shannon.

Theorem 4.4.3

Let $|\mathcal{C}| = |\mathcal{K}|$ and $\Pr(p) > 0$ for any plaintext p. Our cryptosystem has perfect secrecy if and only if the probability distribution on the key space is the uniform distribution and if for any plaintext p and any ciphertext c there is exactly one key k with $E_k(p) = c$.

Proof. Suppose that the cryptosystem has perfect secrecy. Let p be a plaintext. If there is a ciphertext c for which there is no key k with $E_k(p) = c$, then $\Pr(p) \neq \Pr(p|c) = 0$ since $\Pr(p) > 0$ by assumption. This contradicts the perfect secrecy. Hence, for any ciphertext c there is a key k with $E_k(p) = c$. But the number of keys is equal to the number of ciphertexts. Therefore, for each ciphertext c there is exactly one key k with $E_k(p) = c$. This proves the second assertion. To prove the first assertion, we fix a ciphertext c. For a plaintext p, let $k(p)$ be the key with $E_{k(p)}(p) = c$. It follows from Theorem 4.2.4 that

$$\Pr(p|c) = \frac{\Pr(c|p)\Pr(p)}{\Pr(c)} = \frac{\Pr(k(p))\Pr(p)}{\Pr(c)} \qquad (4.5)$$

for each plaintext p. Since the cryptosystem has perfect secrecy, we have $\Pr(p|c) = \Pr(p)$. Also, (4.5) implies $\Pr(k(p)) = \Pr(c)$. Hence, the probability $\Pr(k(p))$ is the same for each plaintext p. But any key k is equal to $k(p)$ for some plaintext p. Therefore, the probability for all keys is the same, which means that the probability distribution on the key space is the uniform distribution.

Now we prove the converse. Assume that the probability distribution on the key space is the uniform distribution and that for any plaintext p and any ciphertext c there is exactly one key $k = k(p, c)$ with $E_k(p) = c$. Then

$$\Pr(p|c) = \frac{\Pr(p)\Pr(c|p)}{\Pr(c)} = \frac{\Pr(p)\Pr(k(p,c))}{\sum_{q \in \mathcal{P}} \Pr(q)\Pr(k(q,c))}. \qquad (4.6)$$

Now $\Pr(k(p,c)) = 1/|\mathcal{K}|$ since all keys are equally probable. Hence,

$$\sum_{q \in \mathcal{P}} \Pr(q)\Pr(k(q,c)) = \frac{\sum_{q \in \mathcal{P}}\Pr(q)}{|\mathcal{K}|} = \frac{1}{|\mathcal{K}|}.$$

If we use this equation in (4.6), then we obtain $\Pr(p|c) = \Pr(p)$, as asserted. □

Example 4.4.4

Theorem 4.4.3 implies that the cryptosystem from example 4.4.2 has perfect secrecy if we set $\Pr(A) = \Pr(B) = 1/2$.

4.5 Vernam One-Time Pad

The most famous cryptosystem that has perfect secrecy is the *Vernam one-time pad*, which is explained in this section. Let n be a positive integer. The Vernam one-time pad encrypts bitstrings of length n. Plaintext space, ciphertext space, and key space are $\mathcal{P} = \mathcal{C} = \mathcal{K} = \{0, 1\}^n$. The encryption function for key $k \in \{0, 1\}^n$ is

$$E_k : \{0, 1\}^n \to \{0, 1\}^n, \quad p \mapsto p \oplus k.$$

The decryption function for key k is the same.

To encrypt a plaintext $p \in \{0, 1\}^n$, Alice chooses a key k randomly with uniform distribution from the set $\{0, 1\}^n$. She computes the ciphertext $c = p \oplus k$. By Theorem 4.4.3, this cryptosystem has perfect secrecy because the uniform distribution is used on the key space and for each plaintext p and each ciphertext c there is exactly one key k with $c = p \oplus k$, namely $k = p \oplus c$.

This cryptosystem was invented and patented in 1917 by Gilbert Vernam. However, it was not until 1949 that Shannon proved that the Vernam one-time pad has perfect secrecy.

Unfortunately, the one-time pad is not very efficient. To secretly communicate a plaintext of length n, Alice and Bob must randomly generate and exchange a key of length n. This is the reason for the name "one-time pad". Each key can be used only once.

If a key is used to encrypt several plaintexts, the one-time pad loses its perfect secrecy. Oscar can determine the key in a known plaintext attack. Suppose he knows a plaintext p and the corresponding ciphertext c. Then the key can be determined as $m \oplus c = m \oplus m \oplus k = k$.

4.6 Random Numbers

If Alice and Bob want to use the Vernam one-time pad, then they need a source for uniformly distributed random bits. It is a philosophical question whether such a source can exist or whether anything that happens is predetermined. In practice, random-bit generators are used which are software or hardware-based. Such generators are devices that use, for example, the randomness of radioactive decay or the time between two keyboard strokes. An overview can be found in [1].

If random-bit generators are used in cryptography, then it is important that an attacker has no way of predicting the bits that it outputs. Therefore, those generators are typically secure hardware devices.

In the following, we assume that we are given a random-bit generator that generates random bits according to the uniform distribution. We explain how such a device is used to generate random numbers.

We want to generate uniformly distributed random numbers in the set $\{0, 1, \ldots, m\}$, $m \in \mathbb{N}$. We set $n = \text{size } m = \lfloor \log m \rfloor + 1$. Then we generate n random bits $b_1, \ldots, b_n$. If the number $a = \sum_{i=1}^{n} b_i 2^{n-i}$

is greater than m, then we forget it and generate a new one in the same way. Otherwise, a is the random number. It is easy to verify that the numbers a that are generated in this way are uniformly distributed random numbers in the set $\{0, 1, \ldots, m\}$.

If we want to generate uniformly distributed random n-bit numbers, $n \in \mathbb{N}$, then we generate $n - 1$ random bits $b_2, \ldots, b_n$ and set $b_1 = 1$ and output $a = \sum_{i=1}^{n} b_i 2^{n-i}$.

4.7 Pseudorandom Numbers

If it is too time-consuming to generate true random numbers, then pseudorandom number generators are used. A pseudorandom number generator is an algorithm that, given a short sequence of random bits, produces a long sequence of bits that "looks" random. This means that the output sequence cannot be distinguished in polynomial time from a true random sequence. A detailed description of the corresponding theory can be found in [14]. Pseudorandom number generators that are used in practice can be found in [24].

4.8 Exercises

Exercise 4.8.1
Let S be a finite set and Pr a probability distribution on S. Prove the following:
1. $\Pr(\emptyset) = 0$.
2. $A \subset B \subset S$ implies $\Pr(A) \leq \Pr(B)$.

Exercise 4.8.2
In an experiment, m is chosen with uniform distribution from $\{1, 2, \ldots, 1000\}$. Determine the following probabilities:
1. for choosing a square;
2. for choosing a number with i prime factors, $i \geq 1$.

Exercise 4.8.3

Find the sample space and probability distribution that model the experiment of flipping two coins. Describe the event "at least one coin comes up heads" formally and compute its probability.

Exercise 4.8.4

Determine the probability that a randomly chosen block cipher with alphabet $\{0, 1\}$ and block length 2 is affine linear.

Exercise 4.8.5

We throw two dice. Determine the probability that they both show different numbers under the condition that the sum of both numbers is even.

Exercise 4.8.6

Determine n such that the probability for two of n people having the same birthday is at least $9/10$.

Exercise 4.8.7

Suppose that four-digit PINs are randomly distributed. How many people must be in a room such that the probability that two of them have the same PIN is at least $1/2$?

Exercise 4.8.8

Prove that the Caesar cipher does not have perfect secrecy.

Exercise 4.8.9

Consider the linear block cipher with block length n and alphabet $\{0, 1\}^n$. On the key space of matrices $A \in \{0, 1\}^{(n,n)}$ with $\det(A) \equiv 1 \bmod 2$, choose the uniform distribution. Does this cryptosystem have perfect secrecy?

5

CHAPTER

DES

In Chapter 3, we defined cryptosystems and described some historical examples. All of the cryptosystems in Chapter 3 could be broken because they are affine linear. A cryptosystem with perfect secrecy, the Vernam one-time pad, was presented in Chapter 4, but it turned out to be very inefficient. In this chapter, we describe the Data Encryption Standard (DES). For many years, this cryptosystem was the encryption standard in the U.S. and was used worldwide. Today, DES is no longer secure. In October 2000 the US Secretary of Commerce announced the nation's proposed new Advanced Encryption Standard. He named the *Rijndael* data encryption formula as the winner of a three-year competition (see [28]). Nevertheless, there are secure variants of DES (see Section 3.7), and most of the suggested successors to DES are similar to DES. Therefore, DES is still an important cryptosystem and we describe it here.

5.1 Feistel Ciphers

The DES algorithm is a so-called *Feistel cipher*. In this section, we explain Feistel ciphers.

115

We use a block cipher with alphabet $\{0, 1\}$. Let t be its block length. Let f_K be the encryption function for the key K. The Feistel cipher that is constructed from these ingredients is a block cipher with block length $2t$ and alphabet $\{0, 1\}$. We fix a number $r \geq 1$ of rounds, a key space $\mathcal{K}$, and a method that, from any key $k \in \mathcal{K}$, generates a sequence $K_1, \ldots, K_r$ of round keys that belong to the key space of the underlying block cipher.

The encryption function E_k of the Feistel cipher for key $k \in \mathcal{K}$ works as follows. Let p be a plaintext of length $2t$. We split it into two halves of length t; that is, we write $p = (L_0, R_0)$, where L_0 is the left half and R_0 is the right half. Then the sequence

$$(L_i, R_i) = (R_{i-1}, L_{i-1} \oplus f_{K_i}(R_{i-1})), \quad 1 \leq i \leq r \qquad (5.1)$$

is constructed, and we set

$$E_k(L_0, R_0) = (R_r, L_r).$$

Clearly, the security of the Feistel cipher depends on the security of the internal block cipher. This security is increased by iterated application.

We explain the decryption of the Feistel cipher. From (5.1), we immediately obtain

$$(R_{i-1}, L_{i-1}) = (L_i, R_i \oplus f_{K_i}(L_i)), \quad 1 \leq i \leq r. \qquad (5.2)$$

Using this equation in r rounds with the reverse key sequence $(K_r, K_{r-1}, \ldots, K_1)$, the plaintext pair (R_0, L_0) is reconstructed from the ciphertext (R_r, L_r). Hence, for the Feistel cipher, encryption and decryption are the same except that the key sequence is reversed.

5.2   DES Algorithm

The DES cryptosystem is a slightly modified Feistel cipher with alphabet $\{0, 1\}$ and block length 64. In this section, we explain in detail how DES works.

TABLE 5.1 Valid DES key.

0	0	0	1	0	0	1	1
0	0	1	1	0	1	0	0
0	1	0	1	0	1	1	1
0	1	1	1	1	0	0	1
1	0	0	1	1	0	1	1
1	0	1	1	1	1	0	0
1	1	0	1	1	1	1	1
1	1	1	1	0	0	0	1

5.2.1   Plaintext and ciphertext space

The plaintext and ciphertext spaces of DES are $\mathcal{P} = \mathcal{C} = \{0, 1\}^{64}$. The DES keys are all bitstrings of length 64 with the following property. If a 64-bit DES key is divided into eight bytes, then the sum of the eight bits of each byte is odd. This means that seven of the eight bits determine the value of the eighth bit. Transmission errors of one bit can be corrected. Therefore, the key space is

$$\mathcal{K} = \{(b_1, \ldots, b_{64}) \in \{0, 1\}^{64} : \sum_{i=1}^{8} b_{8k+i} \equiv \mod 2, 0 \leq k \leq 7\}.$$

The number of DES keys is $2^{56} \sim 7.2 * 10^{16}$.

Example 5.2.1
A valid hexadecimal DES key is

133457799BBCDFF1.

Its binary expansion can be found in Table 5.1.

5.2.2   Initial permutation

Given a plaintext p, DES works in three steps.

Prior to the Feistel encryption, DES applies an *initial permutation* (IP) to p. This is a bit permutation on bit vectors of length 64 that is independent of the chosen key. The permutation IP and its inverse are shown in Table 5.2. Table 5.2 is read as follows: If $p \in \{0, 1\}^{64}$, $p = p_1 p_2 p_3 \ldots p_{64}$, then $\text{IP}(p) = p_{58} p_{50} p_{42} \ldots p_7$.

TABLE 5.2   The initial permutation, IP.

IP							
58	50	42	34	26	18	10	2
60	52	44	36	28	20	12	4
62	54	46	38	30	22	14	6
64	56	48	40	32	24	16	8
57	49	41	33	25	17	9	1
59	51	43	35	27	19	11	3
61	53	45	37	29	21	13	5
63	55	47	39	31	23	15	7

IP^{-1}							
40	8	48	16	56	24	64	32
39	7	47	15	55	23	63	31
38	6	46	14	54	22	62	30
37	5	45	13	53	21	61	29
36	4	44	12	52	20	60	28
35	3	43	11	51	19	59	27
34	2	42	10	50	18	58	26
33	1	41	9	49	17	57	25

A 16-round Feistel cipher is applied to the permuted plaintext. Finally, the ciphertext is constructed using the inverse permutation IP^{-1}:

$$c = \text{IP}^{-1}(R_{16}L_{16}).$$

5.2.3   Internal block cipher

We describe the block cipher on which the DES Feistel cipher is based. Its alphabet is $\{0, 1\}$, its block length is 32, and its key space is $\{0, 1\}^{48}$. We explain the encryption function $f_K : \{0, 1\}^{32} \to \{0, 1\}^{32}$ for a key $K \in \{0, 1\}^{48}$ (see Figure 5.1).

The argument $R \in \{0, 1\}^{32}$ is expanded by the expansion function $E : \{0, 1\}^{32} \to \{0, 1\}^{48}$. This function is shown in Table 5.3. If $R = R_1 R_2 \ldots R_{32}$, then $E(R) = R_{32} R_1 R_2 \ldots R_{32} R_1$.

Next, $E(R) \oplus K$ is computed, and the result is divided into eight blocks B_i, $1 \le i \le 8$ of length 6, namely,

$$E(R) \oplus K = B_1 B_2 B_3 B_4 B_5 B_6 B_7 B_8 \tag{5.3}$$

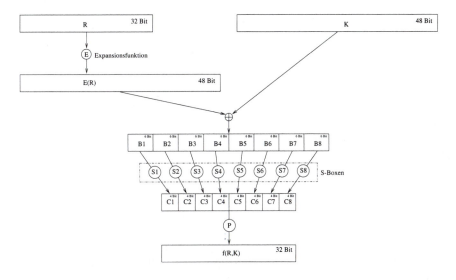

FIGURE 5.1   The f-function of DES.

is computed with $B_i \in \{0,1\}^6$, $1 \le i \le 8$. In the next step, functions

$$S_i : \{0,1\}^6 \to \{0,1\}^4, \quad 1 \le i \le 8$$

are used (the so-called S-boxes). They are described below. Using those functions, the string

$$C = C_1 C_2 C_3 C_4 C_5 C_6 C_7 C_8$$

is determined, where $C_i = S_i(B_i)$, $1 \le i \le 8$. It has length 32. The permutation P from Table 5.3 is applied to this string. The result is $f_K(R)$.

5.2.4   S-boxes

Now we describe the S-boxes S_i, $1 \le i \le 8$. They are the heart of DES because they are highly nonlinear (see Exercise 5.5.6). They are shown in Table 5.4. Each S-box is represented by a table with four rows and 16 columns. For each string $B = b_1 b_2 b_3 b_4 b_5 b_6$, the value $S_i(B)$ is computed as follows. The integer with binary expansion $b_1 b_6$ is used as the row index. The integer with binary expansion $b_2 b_3 b_4 b_5$ is used as the column index. The entry of the S-box in this row and

TABLE 5.3   The functions E and P.

E						P			
32	1	2	3	4	5	16	7	10	21
4	5	6	7	8	9	29	12	28	17
8	9	10	11	12	13	1	15	23	26
12	13	14	15	16	17	5	18	31	20
16	17	18	19	20	21	2	8	24	14
20	21	22	23	24	25	32	27	3	9
24	25	26	27	28	29	19	13	30	6
28	29	30	31	32	1	22	11	4	25

column is written in binary expansion. This expansion is padded with leading zeros such that its length is four. The result is $S_i(B)$.

Example 5.2.2
We compute $S_1(001011)$. The first bit is 0 and the last bit is 1. Therefore, the row index is the integer with binary expansion 01 (i.e., 1). The four middle bits are 0101. This is the binary expansion of 5. Therefore, the column index is 5. The entry in row 1 and column 5 of the first S-box is 2. The binary expansion of 2 is 10. Therefore, $S_1(001011) = 0010$.

5.2.5   Keys

Finally, we explain how the round keys are computed. Let $k \in \{0, 1\}^{64}$ be a DES key. We generate the round keys K_i, $1 \leq i \leq 16$, of length 48. We define the values v_i, $1 \leq i \leq 16$, as follows.

$$v_i = \begin{cases} 1 & \text{for } i \in \{1, 2, 9, 16\} \\ 2 & \text{otherwise.} \end{cases}$$

The round keys are computed by the following algorithm using the functions

$$\text{PC1} : \{0, 1\}^{64} \to \{0, 1\}^{28} \times \{0, 1\}^{28}, \quad \text{PC2} : \{0, 1\}^{28} \times \{0, 1\}^{28} \to \{0, 1\}^{48},$$

which are described later.

TABLE 5.4 S-boxes of DES.

Row	Column															
	[0]	[1]	[2]	[3]	[4]	[5]	[6]	[7]	[8]	[9]	[10]	[11]	[12]	[13]	[14]	[15]
S_1																
[0]	14	4	13	1	2	15	11	8	3	10	6	12	5	9	0	7
[1]	0	15	7	4	14	2	13	1	10	6	12	11	9	5	3	8
[2]	4	1	14	8	13	6	2	11	15	12	9	7	3	10	5	0
[3]	15	12	8	2	4	9	1	7	5	11	3	14	10	0	6	13
S_2																
[0]	15	1	8	14	6	11	3	4	9	7	2	13	12	0	5	10
[1]	3	13	4	7	15	2	8	14	12	0	1	10	6	9	11	5
[2]	0	14	7	11	10	4	13	1	5	8	12	6	9	3	2	15
[3]	13	8	10	1	3	15	4	2	11	6	7	12	0	5	14	9
S_3																
[0]	10	0	9	14	6	3	15	5	1	13	12	7	11	4	2	8
[1]	13	7	0	9	3	4	6	10	2	8	5	14	12	11	15	1
[2]	13	6	4	9	8	15	3	0	11	1	2	12	5	10	14	7
[3]	1	10	13	0	6	9	8	7	4	15	14	3	11	5	2	12
S_4																
[0]	7	13	14	3	0	6	9	10	1	2	8	5	11	12	4	15
[1]	13	8	11	5	6	15	0	3	4	7	2	12	1	10	14	9
[2]	10	6	9	0	12	11	7	13	15	1	3	14	5	2	8	4
[3]	3	15	0	6	10	1	13	8	9	4	5	11	12	7	2	14
S_5																
[0]	2	12	4	1	7	10	11	6	8	5	3	15	13	0	14	9
[1]	14	11	2	12	4	7	13	1	5	0	15	10	3	9	8	6
[2]	4	2	1	11	10	13	7	8	15	9	12	5	6	3	0	14
[3]	11	8	12	7	1	14	2	13	6	15	0	9	10	4	5	3
S_6																
[0]	12	1	10	15	9	2	6	8	0	13	3	4	14	7	5	11
[1]	10	15	4	2	7	12	9	5	6	1	13	14	0	11	3	8
[2]	9	14	15	5	2	8	12	3	7	0	4	10	1	13	11	6
[3]	4	3	2	12	9	5	15	10	11	14	1	7	6	0	8	13
S_7																
[0]	4	11	2	14	15	0	8	13	3	12	9	7	5	10	6	1
[1]	13	0	11	7	4	9	1	10	14	3	5	12	2	15	8	6
[2]	1	4	11	13	12	3	7	14	10	15	6	8	0	5	9	2
[3]	6	11	13	8	1	4	10	7	9	5	0	15	14	2	3	12
S_8																
[0]	13	2	8	4	6	15	11	1	10	9	3	14	5	0	12	7
[1]	1	15	13	8	10	3	7	4	12	5	6	11	0	14	9	2
[2]	7	11	4	1	9	12	14	2	0	6	10	13	15	3	5	8
[3]	2	1	14	7	4	10	8	13	15	12	9	0	3	5	6	11

TABLE 5.5   The functions PC1 and PC2.

PC1						
57	49	41	33	25	17	9
1	58	50	42	34	26	18
10	2	59	51	43	35	27
19	11	3	60	52	44	36
63	55	47	39	31	23	15
7	62	54	46	38	30	22
14	6	61	53	45	37	29
21	13	5	28	20	12	4

PC2					
14	17	11	24	1	5
3	28	15	6	21	10
23	19	12	4	26	8
16	7	27	20	13	2
41	52	31	37	47	55
30	40	51	45	33	48
44	49	39	56	34	53
46	42	50	36	29	32

1. Set $(C_0, D_0) = \mathrm{PC1}(k)$.

2. For $1 \le i \le 16$, do the following:

   (a) Let C_i be the string that is obtained from C_{i-1} by a circular left shift of v_i positions.

   (b) Let D_i be the string that is obtained from D_{i-1} by a circular left shift of v_i positions.

   (c) Determine $K_i = \mathrm{PC2}(C_i, D_i)$.

   The function PC1 maps a bitstring k of length 64 to two bitstrings C and D of length 28. This is done according to Table 5.5. The upper half of the table describes C. If $k = k_1 k_2 \ldots k_{64}$, then $C = k_{57} k_{49} \ldots k_{36}$. The lower half of the table represents D, so $D = k_{63} k_{55} \ldots k_4$. The function PC2 maps a pair (C, D) of bitstrings of length 28 (i.e., a bitstring of length 56) to a bitstring of length 48. The function is shown in Table 5.5. The value $\mathrm{PC2}(b_1 \ldots b_{56})$ is $b_{14} b_{17} \ldots b_{32}$.

   This concludes the description of the DES encryption algorithm.

5.2.6   Decryption

To decrypt a ciphertext, DES is applied with the reverse key sequence.

5.3 An Example

We illustrate the DES algorithm by way of an example.

We encrypt the plaintext $p = 0123456789ABCDEF$. Its binary expansion is

0	0	0	0	0	0	0	1
0	0	1	0	0	0	1	1
0	1	0	0	0	1	0	1
0	1	1	0	0	1	1	1
1	0	0	0	1	0	0	1
1	0	1	0	1	0	1	1
1	1	0	0	1	1	0	1
1	1	1	0	1	1	1	1

The application of IP yields

1	1	0	0	1	1	0	0
0	0	0	0	0	0	0	0
1	1	0	0	1	1	0	0
1	1	1	1	1	1	1	1
1	1	1	1	0	0	0	0
1	0	1	0	1	0	1	0
1	1	1	1	0	0	0	0
1	0	1	0	1	0	1	0

so we obtain

$$L_0 = 11001100000000001100110011111111,$$
$$R_0 = 11110000101010101111000010101010.$$

We use the DES key from Example 5.2.1,

$$133457799BBCDFF1,$$

whose binary expansion is

0	0	0	1	0	0	1	1
0	0	1	1	0	1	0	0
0	1	0	1	0	1	1	1
0	1	1	1	1	0	0	1
1	0	0	1	1	0	1	1
1	0	1	1	1	1	0	0
1	1	0	1	1	1	1	1
1	1	1	1	0	0	0	1

We compute the first round key. We have

$$C_0 = 1111000011001100101010101111,$$
$$D_0 = 0101010101100110011110001111$$
$$C_1 = 1110000110011001010101011111,$$
$$D_1 = 1010101011001100111100011110$$

and therefore

$$K_1 = 000110110000001011101111111111000111000001110010.$$

Using this key, we obtain

$$E(R_0) \oplus K_1 = 011000010001011110111010100001100110010100100111,$$

$$f(R_0, K_1) = 00000011010010111010100110111011,$$

and finally

$$R_1 = 11001111010010110110010101000100.$$

The other rounds are computed analogously.

5.4   Security of DES

Since its invention, the security of DES has been studied very intensively. Special techniques such as differential and linear crypt-analysis have been invented to attack DES (see [24] and [32]), but the most successful attack has been an exhaustive search of the key space. With special hardware or large networks of workstations, it is now possible to decrypt DES ciphertexts in a few days or even hours.

Today, DES can only be considered secure if triple encryption as described in Section 3.7 is used. In this context, it is important to know that DES is not a group. This means that for two DES keys k_1 and k_2 there is, in general, not a third DES key k_3 such that $\text{Des}_{k_1} \circ \text{Des}_{k_2} = \text{Des}_{k_3}$. If DES were a group, then multiple encryption would not lead to increased security. In fact, the subgroup that the DES encryption permutations generate in the permutation group $S_{64!}$ is at least of order 10^{2499} (see[24]).

5.5 Exercises

Exercise 5.5.1
Verify the example from Section 5.3 and compute the second round.

Exercise 5.5.2
Compute the third round of the encryption in Section 5.3.

Exercise 5.5.3
Prove that $\overline{\text{Des}\,(m,k)} = \text{Des}\,(\overline{m},\overline{k})$ holds for any $m, k \in \{0,1\}^{64}$.

Exercise 5.5.4
Show that C_{16} and D_{16} are obtained from C_1 and D_1 by a circular right shift of one position.

Exercise 5.5.5
1. Suppose that $K_1 = K_2 = \ldots = K_{16}$. Show that all bits in C_1 are equal as well as all bits of D_1.
2. Conclude that there are exactly four DES keys for which all round keys are the same. They are called *weak DES keys*.
3. Determine the four weak DES keys.

Exercise 5.5.6
Which of the functions IP, $E(R) \oplus K$, S_i, $1 \le i \le 8$, P, PC1, and PC2 are linear for a fixed key? Prove the linearity or give a counterexample.

6 Prime Number Generation

In many public-key cryptosystems, large random prime numbers are used. They are produced by generating random numbers of the right size and by testing whether those random numbers are prime. In this chapter, we explain how we can efficiently decide whether a given positive integer is a prime number. All algorithms that are presented in this chapter are implemented in the library LiDIA [22].

By small Roman letters we denote integers.

6.1 Trial Division

Let n be a positive integer. We want to know whether n is a prime number. A simple algorithm is based on the following theorem.

Theorem 6.1.1
If n is a composite positive integer, then n has a prime divisor p which is less than or equal to $\sqrt{n}$.

Proof. Since n is composite, we can write $n = ab$ with $a > 1$ and $b > 1$. Now we have $a \leq \sqrt{n}$ or $b \leq \sqrt{n}$, since otherwise $n = ab > \sqrt{n}\sqrt{n} = n$. Suppose that $a \leq \sqrt{n}$. By Theorem 1.11.2, a has a prime divisor p. That prime divisor also divides n and $p \leq a \leq n$. This proves the assertion. □

Theorem 6.1.1 suggests the following algorithm to test whether n is prime. The algorithm checks, for all prime numbers p that are less than or equal to $\sqrt{n}$, whether they divide n. If a prime divisor of n is found, then n is composite. Otherwise, n is prime. The prime numbers $p \leq \sqrt{n}$ can either be generated by the sieve of Eratosthenes (see[4]) or be obtained from a precomputed table. It is also possible to test whether n is divisible by any odd, positive integer $m \leq \sqrt{n}$. This procedure is called *trial division*.

Example 6.1.2
We use trial division to decide whether $n = 15413$ is prime. We have $\lfloor \sqrt{n} \rfloor = 124$. Hence, we must test whether one of the prime numbers $p \leq 124$ divides n. The odd primes $p \leq 124$ are 3, 5, 7, 11, 13, 17, 19, 23, 29, 31, 37, 41, 43, 47, 53, 59, 61, 67, 71, 73, 79, 83, 89, 97, 101, 103, 107, 109, 113. None of them divides n. Therefore, n is a prime number.

Trial division can also be used to find the prime factorization of n. If a prime factor p is found, then n is replaced by n/p and trial division is applied again. This is repeated until n is proven prime.

Example 6.1.3
We factor 476 by trial division. The first prime divisor that we find is 2 and $476/2 = 238$. The next prime factor is again 2 and $238/2 = 119$. The next prime factor is 7 and $119/7 = 17$. The number 17 is prime. Hence, the prime factorization of 476 is $476 = 2^2 * 7 * 17$.

If n is large, then trial division becomes very inefficient. In factoring algorithms, trial division is typically used to find all prime factors that are less than 10^6.

To estimate the running time of trial division, we need an estimate for the number of primes below a given bound. We use the following notation.

Definition 6.1.4
If x is a positive real number, then $\pi(x)$ denotes the number of primes that are less than or equal to x.

Example 6.1.5

We have $\pi(1) = 0$, $\pi(4) = 2$. As we have seen in Example 6.1.2, we also have $\pi(124) = 30$.

The following theorem is presented without proof. For the proof, see [29].

Theorem 6.1.6

1. *For $x \geq 17$, we have $\pi(x) > x/\log x$.*
2. *For $x > 1$, we have $\pi(x) < 1.25506(x/\log x)$.*

It follows from Theorem 6.1.6 that at least $\lceil \sqrt{n}/\log \sqrt{n} \rceil$ divisions are necessary to prove n prime by trial division. For the RSA cryptosystem, we need primes that are greater then 10^{75}. To prove the primality of such a number by trial division, more than $10^{75/2}/\log 10^{75/2} > 0.36 * 10^{36}$ divisions are necessary. This is impossible. In the following sections, we describe more efficient primality tests.

6.2   Fermat Test

It is expensive to prove that a given positive integer is prime. But there are very efficient algorithms that prove the primality of a positive integer with high probability. Such algorithms are called *primality tests*.

A first example of a primality test is the *Fermat test*. It is based on Fermat's theorem (2.11.1) in the following version.

Theorem 6.2.1 (Fermat's theorem)

If n is a prime number, then $a^{n-1} \equiv 1 \bmod n$ for all $a \in \mathbb{Z}$ with $\gcd(a, n) = 1$.

This theorem can be used to determine that a positive integer is composite. We choose a positive integer $a \in \{1, 2, \ldots, n-1\}$. We use fast exponentiation from Section 2.12 to compute $y = a^{n-1} \bmod n$. If $y \neq 1$, then n is composite by Theorem 6.2.1. If $y = 1$, then we do not know whether n is prime or composite, as the following example shows.

Example 6.2.2

Consider $n = 341 = 11 * 31$. We have

$$2^{340} \equiv 1 \bmod 341,$$

although n is composite. Therefore, if we use the Fermat test with $n = 341$ and $a = 2$, then we obtain $y = 1$, which proves nothing. On the other hand, we have

$$3^{340} \equiv 56 \bmod 341.$$

If we use the Fermat test with $n = 341$ and $a = 3$, then n is proven composite.

If the Fermat test proves that n is composite, it does not find a divisor of n. It only shows that n lacks a property that all prime numbers have. Therefore, the Fermat test cannot be used as a factoring algorithm.

The Fermat test is implemented in the LiDIA method `bool fermat(const bigint & a)`, which belongs to the class `bigint`.

6.3   Carmichael Numbers

The Fermat test can prove that a positive integer n is composite, but it cannot prove that n is prime. However, if the Fermat test was not able to find a proof for the compositeness of n for many bases a, then it seems likely that n is prime. Unfortunately, there are composite integers that cannot be proven composite by the Fermat test with any basis. They are called *Carmichael numbers* and we discuss them now.

We need two definitions. If n is an odd composite number and if a is an integer that satisfies

$$a^{n-1} \equiv 1 \bmod n,$$

then n is called a *pseudoprime* to the base a. If n is a pseudoprime to the base a for all integers a with $\gcd(a, n) = 1$, then n is called a *Carmichael number*. The smallest Carmichael number is $561 = 3 \cdot 11 \cdot 17$. It has been shown that there are infinitely many Carmichael numbers. Because of the existence of Carmichael numbers, the Fermat test is not optimal for practical use. A better choice is the Miller-Rabin test, which will be described shortly. For the analysis of the Miller-Rabin test, we need the following characterization of Carmichael numbers.

Theorem 6.3.1

An odd composite number $n \geq 3$ is a Carmichael number if and only if it is square free (i.e., it has no multiple prime divisors), and for each prime divisor p of n the integer $p - 1$ divides $n - 1$.

Proof.   Let $n \geq 3$ be a Carmichael number. Then

$$a^{n-1} \equiv 1 \bmod n \tag{6.1}$$

for any integer a that is prime to n. Let p be a prime divisor of n, and let a be a primitive root mod p that is prime to n. Such a primitive root can be constructed using the Chinese remainder theorem. Then(6.1) implies

$$a^{n-1} \equiv 1 \bmod p.$$

By Theorem 2.9.2, $p-1$, the order of a mod p, divides $n-1$. It remains to be shown that p^2 does not divide n. Suppose that p^2 divides n. Then $p(p-1)$ divides $\varphi(n)$. By Exercise 2.22.20, there is a subgroup of $(\mathbb{Z}/n\mathbb{Z})^*$ of order p and hence an integer a which is prime to n and whose order mod n is p. It follows from (6.1) and Theorem 2.9.2 that p divides $n - 1$ this is impossible since p divides n.

Conversely, let n be square-free and assume that $p - 1$ divides $n - 1$ for all prime divisors p of n. Let a be an integer that is prime to n and let p be a prime divisor of n. Then

$$a^{p-1} \equiv 1 \bmod p$$

by Fermat's little theorem, and therefore

$$a^{n-1} \equiv 1 \bmod p,$$

since $n - 1$ is a multiple of $p - 1$. This implies

$$a^{n-1} \equiv 1 \bmod n$$

because the prime divisors of n are pairwise distinct. $\square$

6.4   Miller-Rabin Test

In this section, we describe the Miller-Rabin test. Contrary to the Fermat test, the Miller-Rabin test can prove the compositeness of any composite positive integer. In other words, there is no analog of Carmichael numbers for the Miller-Rabin test.

The Miller-Rabin test is based on a modification of Fermat's little theorem. The situation is the following. Let n be an odd, positive integer and let

$$s = \max\{r \in \mathbb{N} : 2^r \text{ divides } n - 1\},$$

so 2^s is the largest power of 2 that divides $n - 1$. Set

$$d = (n - 1)/2^s.$$

Then d is odd.

Theorem 6.4.1
If n is a prime and if a is an integer that is prime to n, then with the previous notation we have either

$$a^d \equiv 1 \bmod n \tag{6.2}$$

or there exists r in the set $\{0, 1, \ldots, s - 1\}$ with

$$a^{2^r d} \equiv -1 \bmod n. \tag{6.3}$$

Proof.   Let a be an integer that is prime to n. The order of the multiplicative group of residues mod n is $n - 1 = 2^s d$ because n is a prime number. By Theorem 2.9.5, the order k of the residue class $a^d + n\mathbb{Z}$ is a power of 2. If this order is $k = 1 = 2^0$, then

$$a^d \equiv 1 \bmod d.$$

If $k > 1$, then $k = 2^l$ with $1 \leq l \leq s$. By Theorem 2.9.5, the residue class $a^{2^{l-1}d} + n\mathbb{Z}$ has order 2. By Exercise 2.22.20, the only element of order 2 in $(\mathbb{Z}/n\mathbb{Z})^*$ is $-1 + n\mathbb{Z}$. This implies

$$a^{2^r d} \equiv -1 \bmod n$$

for $r = l - 1$. Note that $0 \leq r < s$.   □

If n is a prime, then at least one of the conditions from Theorem 6.4.1 holds. Therefore, if we find an integer a that is prime to n and that satisfies neither (6.2) nor (6.3) for some $r \in \{0, \ldots, s-1\}$, then n is proven composite. Such an integer is called a *witness* for the compositeness of n.

Example 6.4.2
Let $n = 561$. Since n is a Carmichael number, the Fermat test cannot prove its compositeness. But $a = 2$ is a witness for the compositeness of n, as we will now show. We have $s = 4$, $d = 35$ and $2^{35} \equiv 263 \bmod 561$, $2^{2*35} \equiv 166 \bmod 561$, $2^{4*35} \equiv 67 \bmod 561$, $2^{8*35} \equiv 1 \bmod 561$. Therefore, Theorem 6.4.1 proves that 561 is composite.

For the efficiency of the Miller-Rabin test, it is important that there are sufficiently many witnesses for the compositeness of a composite number. This is shown in the next theorem.

Theorem 6.4.3
If $n \geq 3$ is an odd composite number, then the set $\{1, \ldots, n-1\}$ contains at most $(n-1)/4$ numbers that are prime to n and not witnesses for the compositeness of n.

Proof. Let $n \geq 3$ be an odd, composite positive integer.
We want to estimate the number of elements $a \in \{1, 2, \ldots, n-1\}$ with $\gcd(a, n) = 1$ and

$$a^d \equiv 1 \bmod n \tag{6.4}$$

or

$$a^{2^r d} \equiv -1 \bmod n \tag{6.5}$$

for some $r \in \{0, 1, \ldots, s-1\}$. If such an a does not exist, then we are finished. Suppose such a nonwitness a exists. Then there is one for which (6.5) holds. In fact, if a satisfies (6.4), $-a$ satisfies (6.5). Let k be the maximum value of r in $\{0, 1, \ldots, s-1\}$ for which there is an integer a that satisfies $\gcd(a, n) = 1$ and (6.5). We set

$$m = 2^k d.$$

Let

$$n = \prod_{p|n} p^{e(p)}$$

be the prime factorization of n. We define the following subgroups of $(\mathbb{Z}/n\mathbb{Z})^*$:

$$J = \{a + n\mathbb{Z} : \gcd(a, n) = 1, a^{n-1} \equiv 1 \bmod n\},$$
$$K = \{a + n\mathbb{Z} : \gcd(a, n) = 1, a^m \equiv \pm 1 \bmod p^{e(p)} \text{ for all } p|n\},$$
$$L = \{a + n\mathbb{Z} : \gcd(a, n) = 1, a^m \equiv \pm 1 \bmod n\},$$
$$M = \{a + n\mathbb{Z} : \gcd(a, n) = 1, a^m \equiv 1 \bmod n\}.$$

We have

$$M \subset L \subset K \subset J \subset (\mathbb{Z}/n\mathbb{Z})^*.$$

For each a that is prime to n and is not a witness for the compositeness of n, the residue class $a + n\mathbb{Z}$ belongs to L. We will prove the assertion of the theorem by proving that the index of L in $(\mathbb{Z}/n\mathbb{Z})^*$ is at least four.

The index of M in K is a power of 2 because the square of each element of K belongs to M. Therefore, the index of L in K is also a power of 2, say 2^j. If $j \geq 2$, then we are finished.

If $j = 1$, then n has two prime divisors. It follows from Exercise 6.6.5 that n is not a Carmichael number. This implies that J is a proper subgroup of $(\mathbb{Z}/n\mathbb{Z})^*$ and the index of J in $(\mathbb{Z}/n\mathbb{Z})^*$ is at least 2. By definition of m, the index of L in K is also 2. Therefore, the index of L in $(\mathbb{Z}/n\mathbb{Z})^*$ is at least 4.

Finally, let $j = 0$. Then n is a prime power. In this case, it can be verified that J has precisely $p - 1$ elements, namely the elements of the subgroup of order $p - 1$ of the cyclic group $(\mathbb{Z}/p^e\mathbb{Z})^*$. Therefore, the index of J in $(\mathbb{Z}/n\mathbb{Z})^*$ is at least 4 unless we have $n = 9$. For $n = 9$, the assertion can be verified directly.   □

Example 6.4.4

We determine all witnesses for the compositeness of $n = 15$. We have $n - 1 = 14 = 2 * 7$. Therefore, $s = 1$ and $d = 7$. An integer a, which is prime to 15, is a witness for the compositeness of n if and only if $a^7 \bmod 15 \neq 1$ and $a^7 \bmod 15 \neq -1$. The following table contains the corresponding residues:

a	1	2	4	7	8	11	13	14
$a^7 \bmod 15$	1	8	4	13	2	11	7	14

The only nonwitness is 1.

To apply the Miller-Rabin test to an odd, positive integer n, we choose a random number $a \in \{2, 3, \ldots, n-1\}$. If $\gcd(a, n) > 1$, then n is composite. Otherwise, we compute $a^d, a^{2d}, \ldots, a^{2^{s-1}d}$. If we find a witness for the compositeness of n, then we have proved that n is composite. By Theorem 6.4.3, the probability that n is composite and we do not find a witness is at most $1/4$. If we repeat the Miller-Rabin test t times and if n is composite, then the probability of not finding a witness is at most $(1/4)^t$. For $t = 10$, this probability is at most $1/2^{20} \sim 1/10^6$. This is very unlikely. A more detailed analysis of the Miller-Rabin test has shown that the error probability is in fact even smaller.

The Miller-Rabin test with n iterations is implemented in the LiDIA method `bool is_prime(const bigint & a, int n)` in the class `bigint`.

6.5 Random Primes

In many public-key systems, random primes of a fixed bit length are required. We describe the construction of such random primes.

We want to generate a random prime of bit length k. We generate a random odd k-bit number (see Section 4.6). For this purpose, we set the first and last bit of n to 1, and the remaining $k - 2$ bits are chosen randomly with uniform distribution. Then we test whether n is prime. First, we check whether n is divisible by a prime number below a predefined bound B, typically $B = 10^6$. If no prime divisor of n is found, then we apply the Miller-Rabin test t times. The choice $t = 3$ suffices to make the error probability less than $(1/2)^{80}$ if $k \geq 1000$. If this test finds no witness for the compositeness of n, then n is considered prime. If trial division is much more efficient than the Miller-Rabin test, then a larger B can be chosen.

6.6 Exercises

Exercise 6.6.1
Use the Fermat test to show that 1111 is not a prime number.

Exercise 6.6.2
Determine $\pi(100)$. Compare your result with the bounds from Theorem 6.1.6.

Exercise 6.6.3
Determine the smallest pseudoprime to the base 2.

Exercise 6.6.4
Use the Fermat test to prove that the fifth Fermat number $F_5 = 2^{2^5}+1$ is composite. Prove that any Fermat number is a pseudoprime to the base 2.

Exercise 6.6.5
Prove that a Carmichael number has at least three different prime factors.

Exercise 6.6.6
Use the Miller-Rabin test to prove that the fifth Fermat number $F_5 = 2^{2^5} + 1$ is composite. Compare the efficiency of the test with the efficiency of the Fermat test (see Exercise 6.6.4).

Exercise 6.6.7
Use the Miller-Rabin test to prove that the pseudoprime n from Exercise 6.6.3 is composite. Determine the smallest witness for the compositeness of n.

Exercise 6.6.8

Determine the number of Miller-Rabin witnesses for the composite-ness of 221 in $\{1, 2, \ldots, 220\}$. Compare your result with the bound in Theorem 6.4.3.

Exercise 6.6.9

Write a LiDIA program that implements the Miller-Rabin test and use it to determine the smallest 512-bit prime.

7

Public-Key Encryption

7.1   Idea

A key problem of the symmetric cryptosystems that we have described so far is key distribution and key management. When Alice and Bob use such a system, they must exchange a secret key before they can secretly communicate. For the key-exchange, they need, for example, a secure channel or a courier. The key-exchange problem becomes even more difficult if many people want to exchange encrypted messages, for example on the Internet. If a communication network has n users and any two of them exchange a key, then $n(n - 1)/2$ secret key exchanges are necessary and all those keys have to be stored securely. For $n = 1000$, there are $499, 500$ keys. Another possibility for organizing the key exchange is to use a key center, in which every user exchanges a secret key with this key center. If Alice wants to send a message to Bob, then she encrypts the message using her secret key and sends it to the key center. The center, knowing all secret keys, decrypts the message using Alice's key, encrypts it with Bob's key, and sends it to Bob. In this way, the number of key exchanges for n users is reduced to n. However, the key center gets to know all secret messages, and it must store all n keys securely.

In public-key systems, key-management is much simpler. Such systems have already been introduced in Section 3.2. In a public-key system, only the decryption keys must be kept secret. A decryption key is therefore called a *secret key* or a *private key*. The corresponding encryption key can be published. It is called a *public key*. Computing private keys from their corresponding public keys is infeasible. This is the key property of public-key cryptosystems. A simple key-management scheme works as follows. In a public directory, each user is listed with his or her public key. If Bob wants to send a message to Alice, he obtains Alice's public key from the key directory. Then he uses this public key to encrypt the message and sends the encrypted message to Alice. Alice is then able to decrypt the message with her private key.

Example 7.1.1

A directory of public keys may look like this:

Name	Public Key
Buchmann	131 21 311 23591 2753192375134123
Maurer	8422834964509823610263113 5768
Alice	546282919826246381 21025032510
⋮	⋮

In public-key systems, no key exchange between users is necessary. Encryption keys are listed in public directories. Although everybody may read those directories, they must be protected from unauthorized writing. If the attacker, Oscar, is able to replace Alice's public encryption key with his own, then he can decrypt the messages that are sent to Alice. This problem and its solution are discussed in Chapter 14.

Public-key cryptosystems not only simplify key management but can also be used to generate digital signatures. This will be shown in Chapter 11.

Unfortunately, the known public-key systems are not as efficient as many symmetric cryptosystems. Therefore, in practice, combinations of public-key systems and symmetric systems are used, for example as follows. Alice wants to send a message m in encrypted form to Bob. She generates a *session key* for an efficient symmetric cryptosystem. Then she encrypts the message m using that session key and the symmetric system, obtaining the ciphertext c. This encryption is fast because an efficient symmetric cryptosystem has been used. Alice also encrypts the session key with Bob's public key, which she obtains from a public directory. Since the session key is small, this encryption is also fast, although the encryption function of the public-key system may not be very efficient. Then Alice sends the ciphertext c and the encrypted session key to Bob. Bob decrypts the session key using his private key. Then he decrypts the ciphertext c with the session key, obtaining the original message m. Here, the public-key system is only used for the exchange of the session key. This combines the elegant key management of the public-key system with the efficiency of the symmetric cryptosystem.

In this chapter, we will describe some important public-key systems.

7.2 RSA Cryptosystem

The RSA system, named after its inventors Ron Rivest, Adi Shamir, and Len Adleman, was the first public-key cryptosystem and is still the most important. Its security is closely related to the difficulty of finding the factorization of a composite positive integer that is the product of two large primes. We first explain how the RSA system works and then we discuss its security and efficiency.

7.2.1 Key generation

We explain how Bob generates his private and public RSA keys.

Bob generates randomly and independently two large (odd) prime numbers p and q (see Section 6.5) and computes the product

$$n = pq.$$

Bob also chooses an integer e with

$$1 < e < \varphi(n) = (p-1)(q-1) \text{ and } \gcd(e, (p-1)(q-1)) = 1.$$

Note that e is always odd since $p-1$ is even. Bob computes an integer d with

$$1 < d < (p-1)(q-1) \text{ and } de \equiv 1 \bmod (p-1)(q-1). \quad (7.1)$$

Since gcd $(e, (p-1)(q-1)) = 1$, such a number d exists. It can be computed by the extended euclidean algorithm (see Section 2.6).

Bob's public key is the pair (n, e). His private key is d. The number n is called the *RSA modulus*, e is called the *encryption exponent*, and d is called the *decryption exponent*. Note that the secret key d can be computed from the encryption exponent e if the prime factors p and q of n are known. Therefore, if the attacker, Oscar, is able to find the prime factorization of n, then he can easily find Bob's secret key d. We will discuss in Section 7.2.4 how the factors p and q have to be chosen in order to make the factorization of n infeasible.

Example 7.2.1
Bob chooses the prime factors $p = 11$ and $q = 23$. Then $n = 253$ and $(p-1)(q-1) = 10 * 22 = 4 \cdot 5 \cdot 11$. The smallest possible e is $e = 3$ since $\gcd(3, 23) = 1$. The extended euclidean algorithm yields $d = 147$.

7.2.2　Encryption

We first explain how to encrypt numbers with the RSA system. Then we show how RSA can be used as a block cipher.

In the first variant, the plaintext space consists of all integers m with

$$0 \leq m < n.$$

A plaintext m is encrypted by computing

$$c = m^e \bmod n. \quad (7.2)$$

The ciphertext is c. If Alice knows the public key (n, e), she can encrypt. To make encryption efficient, Alice uses fast exponentiation (see Section 2.12).

Example 7.2.2

As in Example 7.2.1, let $n = 253$ and $e = 3$. Then the plaintext space is $\{0, 1, \ldots, 252\}$. Encrypting the integer $m = 165$, we obtain $165^3 \bmod 253 = 110$.

Now we show how to use RSA encryption as a block cipher. We use the alphabet $\Sigma = \mathbb{Z}_N = \{0, 1, \ldots, N-1\}$ for some positive integer N. We let

$$k = \lfloor \log_N n \rfloor. \tag{7.3}$$

A word $m_1 \ldots m_k \in \Sigma^k$ corresponds to the integer

$$m = \sum_{i=1}^{k} m_i N^{k-i}.$$

Note that the choice of k in (7.3) implies

$$0 \leq m \leq (N-1) \sum_{i=1}^{k} N^{k-i} = N^k - 1 < n.$$

We will identify the blocks in Σ^k with their corresponding integers. The block m is encrypted by computing $c = m^e \bmod n$. The integer c is written in base N. Since $0 \leq c < n < N^{k+1}$, the N-adic expansion of c has length at most $k + 1$. We can therefore write

$$c = \sum_{i=0}^{k} c_i N^{k-i}, \quad c_i \in \Sigma, 0 \leq i \leq k.$$

The ciphertext block is

$$c = c_0 c_1 \ldots c_k.$$

In this way, RSA maps blocks of length k injectively to blocks of length $k+1$. This is not a block cipher in the sense of Definition 3.6.1 because this definition requires the plaintext and ciphertext blocks to be of equal length. Nevertheless, the block version of RSA described here can be used to implement slightly modified versions of ECB mode and CBC mode (see Sections 3.8.1 and 3.8.2). It is, however, impossible to use CFB mode or OFB mode because they both use the block encryption function for both encryption and decryption. The block encryption function is public, so everybody would be able to decrypt.

Example 7.2.3

We continue Example 7.2.1. Let $\Sigma = \{0, a, b, c\}$ with the identification

0	a	b	c
0	1	2	3

With the RSA modulus $n = 253$, we obtain $k = \lfloor \log_4 253 \rfloor = 3$. This is the length of the plaintext blocks. The length of the ciphertext blocks is 4. We encrypt the block *abb*. It corresponds to the block 122, which, in turn, corresponds to the integer

$$m = 1 * 4^2 + 2 * 4^1 + 2 * 4^0 = 26.$$

This integer is encrypted as

$$c = 26^3 \bmod 253 = 119.$$

We write c in base 4 and obtain

$$c = 1 * 4^3 + 3 * 4^2 + 1 * 4 + 3 * 1.$$

The ciphertext block is

$$acac.$$

7.2.3 Decryption

The decryption of RSA is based on the following theorem.

Theorem 7.2.4

Let (n, e) be a public RSA key and d the corresponding private RSA key. Then

$$(m^e)^d \bmod n = m$$

for any integer m with $0 \le m < n$.

Proof.   Since $ed \equiv 1 \bmod (p-1)(q-1)$, there is an integer l with

$$ed = 1 + l(p-1)(q-1).$$

Therefore

$$(m^e)^d = m^{ed} = m^{1+l(p-1)(q-1)} = m(m^{(p-1)(q-1)})^l.$$

It follows that

$$(m^e)^d \equiv m(m^{(p-1)})^{(q-1)l} \equiv m \bmod p.$$

If p is not a divisor of m, then this congruence follows from Fermat's little theorem (Theorem 2.11.1). Otherwise, the assertion is trivial because both sides of the congruence are 0 mod p. Analogously, we see that

$$(m^e)^d \equiv m \bmod q.$$

Because p and q are distinct prime numbers, we obtain

$$(m^e)^d \equiv m \bmod n.$$

The assertion follows from the fact that $0 \leq m < n$. □

If the ciphertext c has been computed as in (7.2), then by Theorem 7.2.4 the plaintext m can be reconstructed as

$$m = c^d \bmod n.$$

This shows that the RSA system is, in fact, a cryptosystem. For each encryption function, there is a decryption function.

Example 7.2.5
We conclude Examples 7.2.1 and 7.2.3. There, we have chosen $n = 253$, $e = 3$, and $d = 147$. Moreover, we have computed the ciphertext $c = 119$. We obtain $119^{147} \bmod 253 = 26$, which is the original plaintext.

7.2.4 Security of the secret key

We have claimed that RSA is a public key system. Therefore, we must show that it is infeasible to compute the secret key d from the public key (n, e). In this section, we show that computing d from (n, e) is as difficult as finding the prime factors p and q of n. This does not prove the difficulty of computing the secret key directly, but it reduces this difficulty to that of a famous mathematical problem, the factoring problem for integers. This problem will be discussed in Chapter 8. There is no proof that factoring RSA modules is difficult. However, if the factors p and q of the RSA module n are sufficiently large, then nobody yet knows how to factor n.

There is another advantage to basing the security of a cryptosystem on a famous mathematical problem. Since many mathematicians work on this problem independently of its cryptographic relevance, significant progress in solving this problem may be difficult to keep secret. New discoveries are made in many places in the world and not only by the secret services. In this case, nobody can take advantage of RSA being broken. But this is clearly pure speculation and it may very well be that someone already knows an efficient factoring algorithm and that RSA is insecure.

Now we prove the equivalence of factoring and computing the secret RSA key from the public RSA key. Suppose that the attacker, Oscar, knows the prime factors p and q of the RSA modulus n. Then he can compute the secret RSA key d by solving the congruence $de \equiv 1 \bmod (p - 1)(q - 1)$, as we have explained in Section 7.2.1.

We show that the converse is also true (i.e., that it is possible to compute the prime factors p and q of n from n, e, d). Let

$$s = \max\{t \in \mathbb{N} : 2^t \text{ divides } ed - 1\}$$

and

$$k = (ed - 1)/2^s.$$

For computing the factorization of n, we need the following lemma.

Lemma 7.2.6
For all integers a that are prime to n, the order of the residue class $a^k + n\mathbb{Z}$ in the group $(\mathbb{Z}/n\mathbb{Z})^*$ is in $\{2^i : 0 \le i \le s\}$.

Proof.   Let a be an integer that is prime to n. By Theorem 7.2.4, we have $a^{ed-1} \equiv 1 \bmod n$. Since $ed - 1 = k2^s$, this implies $(a^k)^{2^s} \equiv 1 \bmod n$. Hence, by Theorem 2.9.2 the order of $a^k + n\mathbb{Z}$ is a divisor of 2^s.   □

The algorithm that factors n using e and d is based on the following theorem.

Theorem 7.2.7

Let a be an integer that is prime to n. If a has a different order mod *p and* mod *q, then* $1 < \gcd(a^{2^t k} - 1, n) < n$ *for some* $t \in \{0, 1, 2, \ldots, s - 1\}$.

Proof. By Lemma 7.2.6 and Theorem 2.9.2, the order of a^k mod p and a^k mod q is in $\{2^i : 0 \le i \le s\}$. Without loss of generality assume that the order of a^k mod p is greater than the order of a^k mod q. Let the order of a^k mod q be 2^t. Then $t < s$, $a^{2^t k} \equiv 1 \bmod q$ but $a^{2^t k} \not\equiv 1 \bmod p$. Therefore, $\gcd(a^{2^t k} - 1, n) = q$. $\square$

To factor n, we proceed as follows:

1. Choose at random an integer a in the set $\{1, \ldots, n - 1\}$.
2. Compute $g = \gcd(a, n)$.
3. If $g = 1$, then compute $g = \gcd(a^{2^t k} \bmod n, n)$ for $t = s - 1, s - 2, \ldots$ until $g > 1$ or $t = 0$.
4. If $g > 1$, then $g = p$ or $g = q$. Hence, the factorization of n is found and the algorithm terminates. Otherwise, the algorithm was unsuccessful with the chosen base a.

If the algorithm was not successful with the chosen a, then we run it again. We will now show that the probability of the algorithm being successful is at least $1/2$. Therefore, the probability of success after r iterations is at least $1 - 1/2^r$.

Theorem 7.2.8

The number of integers a prime to n in the set $\{1, 2, \ldots, n-1\}$ for which a^k has a different order mod p and mod q is at least $(p-1)(q-1)/2$.

Proof. Let g be a primitive root mod p and mod q. It exists by the Chinese remainder theorem 2.15.2.

First, we assume that the order of g^k mod p is greater than the order of g^k mod q. By Lemma 7.2.6, those orders are powers of 2. Let x be an odd integer in $\{1, \ldots, p - 1\}$ and let $y \in \{0, 1, \ldots, q - 2\}$. Let a be the least nonnegative solution of the simultaneous congruence

$$a \equiv g^x \bmod p, \quad a \equiv g^y \bmod q. \tag{7.4}$$

Then $a \in \{1, 2, \ldots, n - 1\}$. By Theorem 2.9.5, the order of a^k mod p is the same as the order of g^k mod p, since the order of g^k mod p is a power of 2 and x is odd. But the order of a^k mod q is at most the order of g^k mod q and hence smaller than the order of a^k mod p. Also, the solutions of (7.4) are pairwise distinct because g is a primitive root mod p and mod q. Therefore, we have found $(p-1)(q-1)/2$ integers a in $\{1, 2, \ldots, n-1\}$ that are pairwise distinct, prime to n, and for which the order of a^k mod p and mod q are distinct.

If the order of g^k mod q is greater than the order of g^k mod p, then the proof is analogous.

Finally, assume that the orders of g^k mod p and mod q are equal. Since $p-1$ and $q-1$ are both even, k is odd, and g is a primitive root mod p and mod q, this order is at least 2. We determine the required integers a as solutions of the simultaneous congruence (7.4). This time, the exponent pairs (x, y) consist of one even and one odd number. We leave it to the reader as an exercise that in this way we can find $(p-1)(q-1)/2$ solutions a with the desired properties.   □

Theorem 7.2.8 implies that the probability of success of our factoring algorithm is at least $1/2$.

Example 7.2.9
In Example 7.2.1, we have $n = 253$, $e = 3$, and $d = 147$. Hence, $ed - 1 = 440$. If we use $a = 2$, then we obtain $\gcd(2^{220} - 1, 253) = \gcd(2^{110} - 1, 253) = 253$. But $\gcd(2^{55} - 1, 253) = 23$.

7.2.5 RSA and factoring

In the previous section, we have shown that factoring the RSA modulus is as difficult as finding the secret RSA key. But finding the secret key is not the only possible goal of an attacker. He may also try to determine the plaintext that corresponds to a given ciphertext that was encrypted with Bob's public key. Clearly, he can do this if he knows Bob's secret key or the factorization of Bob's RSA modulus, but it is an open problem whether being able to decrypt individual RSA ciphertexts implies the ability to factor n efficiently. In other words, it is not known whether breaking RSA is as difficult as factoring integers.

But even if this were known, it would not mean that RSA is secure, since it is not known whether factoring is difficult. Therefore, it is very dangerous to implement public-key applications based only on RSA.

7.2.6 Choice of p and q

In order to make the factorization of the RSA modulus infeasible, its prime factors p and q must be chosen appropriately. Given the strength of the currently known factoring algorithms, p and q should both be of almost equal length and at least of binary length 512.

It is a common belief that p and q should be random primes of a given bit length. However, there are factoring algorithms that work better if the number n to be factored or one of its prime factors p is of a special form. For example, if $p - 1$ has only small prime factors, then the $p - 1$ factoring method is successful (see Chapter 8). The question is whether n and its prime factors p and q should be tested for those special properties. It seems that this is unnecessary. The probability of n or its random prime factors being of special form is negligible, at least for the known factoring algorithms. Hence, if the random choice works properly, n, p, or q will never have this form.

7.2.7 Choice of e and d

The public key e is chosen to be as small as possible to make encryption efficient. The choice $e = 2$ is impossible since $\varphi(n) = (p - 1)(q - 1)$ is even and we must have $\gcd(e, (p - 1)(q - 1)) = 1$. The least possible encryption exponent is $e = 3$. If this is used, then encryption requires one squaring and one multiplication mod n.

Example 7.2.10
Let $n = 253$, $e = 3$, and $m = 165$. To compute $m^e \bmod n$ we first determine $m^2 \bmod n = 154$ and then $m^3 \bmod n = ((m^2 \bmod n) * m) \bmod n = 154 * 165 \bmod 253 = 110$.

However, using small encryption exponents such as $e = 3$ may be dangerous because an attacker can use the *low-exponent attack*. This attack works if the same message m is encrypted e times with encryption exponent e and e pairwise coprime RSA moduli n_i, $1 \leq i \leq e$. The smaller e is, the more likely this is to happen. For example, a bank may send the same message to many of its customers using their different public keys. Because of their construction as products of large random primes, those different RSA moduli are pairwise coprime. We show how the attack works. Let $c_i = m^e \bmod n_i$, $1 \le i \le e$ be the corresponding RSA ciphertexts. Then the attacker uses the following algorithm:

1. Compute an integer c with $c \equiv c_i \bmod n_i$, $1 \le i \le e$ and $0 \le c < \prod_{i=1}^{e} n_i$ using the Chinese remainder theorem (see Section 2.15).

2. Determine the message m as the eth root of c in $\mathbb{Z}$.

The following theorem shows that this algorithm is correct.

Theorem 7.2.11
Let $e \in \mathbb{N}$, $n_1, n_2, \ldots, n_e \in \mathbb{N}$ be pairwise coprime and $m \in \mathbb{N}$ with $0 \le m < n_i$ for $1 \le i \le e$. Let $c \in \mathbb{N}$ with $c \equiv m^e \bmod n_i$, $1 \le i \le e$ and $0 \le c < \prod_{i=1}^{e} n_i$. Then $c = m^e$.

Proof. The integer $c' = m^e$ satisfies the simultaneous congruence $c' \equiv m^e \bmod n_i$, $1 \le i \le e$, and we have $0 \le c' < \prod_{i=1}^{e} n_i$ because $0 \le m < n_i$, $1 \le i \le e$. On the other hand, the integer c from the theorem satisfies the same congruence and also satisfies $0 \le c < \prod_{i=1}^{e} n_i$. By Theorem 2.15.2 (the Chinese remainder theorem), the solution of this congruence is uniquely determined mod $\prod_{i=1}^{e} n_i$. Therefore, we have $c = c' = m^e$. $\qquad\square$

The eth root of the eth power c can be determined very efficiently, for example by a cut and choose technique. Therefore, the low-exponent attack can be mounted efficiently.

Example 7.2.12
Let $e = 3$, $n_1 = 143$, $n_2 = 391$, $n_3 = 899$, $m = 135$. Then $c_1 = 60$, $c_2 = 203$, $c_3 = 711$. To use the Chinese remainder theorem, we compute integers x_1, x_2, x_3 with $x_1 n_2 n_3 \equiv 1 \bmod n_1$, $n_1 x_2 n_3 \equiv 1 \bmod n_2$ and $n_1 n_2 x_3 \equiv 1 \bmod n_3$. We obtain $x_1 = -19$, $x_2 = -62$, $x_3 = 262$. Then $c = (c_1 x_1 n_2 n_3 + c_2 n_1 x_2 n_3 + c_3 n_1 n_2 x_3) \bmod n_1 n_2 n_3 = 2460375$ and $m = 2460375^{1/3} = 135$.

The low-exponent attack cannot be mounted if the encrypted messages are pairwise different. This can be achieved by choosing a few bits in the plaintext blocks at random. We can also choose a larger encryption exponent; for example, $e = 2^{16} + 1$ is a popular choice (see Exercise 7.6.7).

7.2.8 Efficiency

RSA encryption requires one exponentiation modulo n. The smaller the encryption exponent, is the more efficiently encryption works. As we have explained in the previous section, however, small encryption exponents open the possibility of a low-exponent attack, and special countermeasures are necessary.

RSA decryption also requires one exponentiation mod n, but the decryption exponent must be as large as n. Small decryption exponents d can be efficiently computed from the corresponding public key (e, d). Suppose that the RSA modulus n is a k-bit number. Then, typically, d is also a k-bit number and $k/2$ bits are 1. Hence, using the fast exponentiation technique from Section 2.12, decryption requires k squarings and $k/2$ multiplications mod n. If the RSA modulus is a 1024-bit number, these are 1024 squarings and 512 multiplications mod n. Compared to DES decryption, this is very slow, in particular if a smart card is used for decryption.

RSA decryption can be hastened if the Chinese remainder theorem is used. This works as follows. Alice wants to decrypt the ciphertext c. Her private RSA key is d. She computes

$$m_p = c^{d \bmod p-1} \bmod p, \quad m_q = c^{d \bmod q-1} \bmod q.$$

She computes an integer $m \in \{0, 1, \ldots, n-1\}$ such that

$$m \equiv m_p \bmod p, \quad m \equiv m_q \bmod q.$$

This m is the plaintext that was encrypted. To find m, she uses the extended euclidean algorithm to find integers y_p and y_q with

$$y_p p + y_q q = 1.$$

Then

$$m = (m_p y_q q + m_q y_p p) \bmod n.$$

Note that the coefficients $y_p p \bmod n$ and $y_q q \bmod n$ are independent of the ciphertext. They can be precomputed.

Example 7.2.13
To hasten the decryption in Example 7.2.5, Alice computes

$$m_p = 119^7 \bmod 11 = 4, \quad m_q = 119^{15} \bmod 23 = 3,$$

and $y_p = -2$, $y_q = 1$. Then

$$m = (4 * 23 - 3 * 2 * 11) \bmod 253 = 26.$$

We show that RSA decryption with the Chinese remainder theorem is more efficient than the standard decryption method. Suppose that the RSA modulus is a k-bit number and so is d. Its prime factors p and q are $k/2$-bit numbers. The multiplication of two integers of binary length $\leq r$ takes time $\leq Cr^2$, where C is a constant. Likewise, the division with remainder of an integer of length $\leq r$ by another integer of length $\leq r$ requires time $\leq Cr^2$. The computation of $m = c^d \bmod n$ takes time $\leq 2Ck^3$. The computation of m_p and m_q requires time $Ck^3/2$. We ignore the time for the precomputation of $y_p p \bmod n$ and $y_q q \bmod n$ since it requires only one application of the extended euclidean algorithm, which has quadratic running time. The computation $m = m_p y_q q + m_q y_p p \bmod m$ requires only two multiplications and one addition mod n, so decryption with the Chinese remainder theorem is almost four times as fast as standard decryption.

7.2.9   Multiplicativity

Let (n, e) be a a public RSA key. If two messages m_1 and m_2 are encrypted under this key, then we obtain

$$c_1 = m_1^e \bmod n, \quad c_2 = m_2^e \bmod n.$$

The product of the ciphertexts is

$$c = c_1 c_2 \bmod n = (m_1 m_2)^e \bmod n.$$

Anyone who knows the ciphertexts c_1 and c_2 can compute the encryption of $m = m_1 m_2$ without knowing this plaintext. This is a form of *existential forgery*.

In order for the receiver to notice the forgery, the plaintext space must be reduced. Only plaintexts of a certain form are accepted. For example, one can require the first and last bytes in the plaintext to be identical. It is then extremely unlikely that the product $m_1 m_2$ of two legal plaintexts has this property. Therefore, if Alice receives the encryption of $m = m_1 m_2$, then she rejects the plaintext m.

7.2.10 Generalization

We explain how the RSA cryptosystem can be generalized. The public key consists of a finite group G and an encryption exponent e, which is prime to the order o of G. In the case of RSA, this group is $(\mathbb{Z}/n\mathbb{Z})^*$, where n is an RSA modulus. The secret key is an integer d with $ed \equiv 1 \bmod o$. Clearly, the order o of the group G must also be kept secret since otherwise the secret key d can be determined by solving the congruence $ed \equiv 1 \bmod o$. Messages must be embedded into the group G. The encryption of $m \in G$ is $c = m^e$. Since $de \equiv 1 \bmod o$, it follows from Corollary 2.11.3 that $c^d = m^{ed} = m$. This shows that decryption works by raising c to the dth power.

Finding groups G of which the order can be kept secret although everyone can compute in G seems to be difficult. Variants of RSA are known, but they all become insecure if factoring integers turns out to be easy. Hence, the factoring problem for integers is so far the only mathematical problem on which RSA-type cryptosystems are based. It is an interesting question whether there are alternatives.

7.3 Rabin Encryption

It is considered advantageous if the security of a cryptosystem is based on the difficulty of a mathematical problem that is also of interest outside of cryptography. The security of the RSA system, for example, is related to the difficulty of factoring integers. It is, however, not known if breaking RSA is as difficult as factoring integers (i.e., if being able to break RSA implies the ability of factoring integers; see Section 7.2.4).

The security of the Rabin system, which is explained in this section, is also based on the difficulty of factoring integers. But in contrast to RSA, it can be shown that anyone who can break the Rabin system efficiently can also efficiently factor integers.

7.3.1   Key generation

Alice chooses randomly two large prime numbers p and q with $p \equiv q \equiv 3 \bmod 4$. The prime generation works as explained in Section 7.2.6, except for the additional congruence property. This property makes decryption more efficient. But, as we will see below, the Rabin system also works without it. Alice computes $n = pq$. Her public key is n. Her private key is the pair (p, q).

7.3.2   Encryption

As in the RSA system, the plaintext space is the set $\{0, \ldots, n-1\}$. To encrypt the plaintext $m \in \{0, \ldots, n-1\}$, Bob uses the public key n of Alice and computes

$$c = m^2 \bmod n.$$

The ciphertext is c.

    Like RSA, the Rabin system can be used to implement a kind of block cipher. This works as explained in Section 7.2.2.

7.3.3   Decryption

Alice computes the plaintext m from the ciphertext c by extracting square roots. She proceeds as follows. She computes

$$m_p = c^{(p+1)/4} \bmod p, \quad m_q = c^{(q+1)/4} \bmod q.$$

Then $\pm m_p + p\mathbb{Z}$ are the two square roots of $c + p\mathbb{Z}$ in $\mathbb{Z}/p\mathbb{Z}$, and $\pm m_q + q\mathbb{Z}$ are the two square roots of $c + q\mathbb{Z}$ in $\mathbb{Z}/q\mathbb{Z}$ (see Exercise 2.22.21). This method of computing the square roots of $c \bmod p$ and q only works because p and q are both congruent to 3 mod 4. If this is not true, then computing those square roots is more difficult, although still possible in polynomial time. Now Alice can compute the four square roots of $c + n\mathbb{Z}$ in $\mathbb{Z}/n\mathbb{Z}$ using the Chinese remainder theorem. This is analogous to the RSA decryption using the Chinese remainder theorem as explained in Section 7.2.8. Using the extended euclidean algorithm, Alice determines coefficients $y_p, y_q \in \mathbb{Z}$ with

$$y_p p + y_q q = 1.$$

Then she computes

$$r = (y_p p m_q + y_q q m_p) \bmod n, \quad s = (y_p p m_q - y_q q m_p) \bmod n.$$

It is easy to verify that $\pm r, \pm s$ are the four square roots of c mod n in the set $\{0, 1, \ldots, n-1\}$. One of those square roots must be the original message m.

Example 7.3.1
Alice uses the prime numbers $p = 11$ and $q = 23$. Then $n = 253$. Bob encrypts the message $m = 158$. He computes

$$c = m^2 \bmod n = 170.$$

Alice determines $y_p = -2$ and $y_q = 1$ as in Example 7.2.13. She obtains the square roots

$$m_p = c^{(p+1)/4} \bmod p = c^3 \bmod p = 4,$$
$$m_q = c^{(q+1)/4} \bmod q = c^6 \bmod q = 3.$$

She determines

$$r = (y_p p m_q + y_q q m_p) \bmod n = -2 * 11 * 3 + 23 * 4 \bmod n = 26,$$

and

$$s = (y_p p m_q - y_q q m_p) \bmod n = -2 * 11 * 3 - 23 * 4 \bmod n = 95.$$

The square roots of 170 mod 253 in $\{1, \ldots, 252\}$ are $26, 95, 158, 227$. One of those square roots is the original plaintext.

There are various methods of choosing the original plaintext from the four square roots of c mod n. Alice can choose the message that looks most meaningful, but this might not always work; for example, if an encryption key for a symmetric system is the encrypted message. It is also possible to encrypt only messages of a special form. For example, messages are only encrypted if the first and the last 64 bits are equal. Then it is very unlikely that more than one of the square roots of the ciphertext has this form, so Alice can choose this particular plaintext. If this method is chosen for making the plaintext recoverable, however, the proof of the equivalence between factoring and breaking the Rabin system no longer works.

7.3.4   Efficiency

In the Rabin system, encryption only requires one squaring, so Rabin encryption is more efficient than RSA encryption, even with the smallest possible RSA encryption exponent 3. Decryption in the Rabin system is as expensive as RSA decryption with the Chinese remainder theorem. It requires one exponentiation mod p, one mod q, and one application of the Chinese remainder theorem.

7.3.5   Security

We show that breaking the Rabin system is as difficult as factoring the Rabin modulus. Clearly, everyone who can factor the Rabin modulus can also break the Rabin system. We prove that the converse is also true.

Suppose the attacker, Oscar, can break the Rabin system. Let n be the public RSA modulus and let p, q be its prime factors. Let R be the algorithm that breaks the Rabin system. Given $c \in \{0, 1, \ldots, n-1\}$ such that $c + n\mathbb{Z}$ is a square in $(\mathbb{Z}/n\mathbb{Z})^*$, it computes $m = R(c) \in \{0, 1, \ldots, n-1\}$, which is the original plaintext. The residue class $m + n\mathbb{Z}$ is a square root of $c + n\mathbb{Z}$. In other words, given a square c mod n the algorithm R determines a square root m of c mod n. We explain how the algorithm R can be used to factor n. Oscar chooses at random an integer $x \in \{1, \ldots, n-1\}$. If $\gcd(x, n) \neq 1$, then this gcd is equal to one of the prime factors of n. Hence, the factorization of n is found. Otherwise, Oscar computes

$$c = x^2 \bmod n \text{ and } m = R(c).$$

The residue class $m + n\mathbb{Z}$ is a square root of $c + n\mathbb{Z}$. It is not necessarily equal to $x + n\mathbb{Z}$, but m satisfies one of the following pairs of congruences:

$$m \equiv x \bmod p \text{ and } m \equiv x \bmod q, \tag{7.5}$$

$$m \equiv -x \bmod p \text{ and } m \equiv -x \bmod q, \tag{7.6}$$

$$m \equiv x \bmod p \text{ and } m \equiv -x \bmod q, \tag{7.7}$$

$$m \equiv -x \bmod p \text{ and } m \equiv x \bmod q. \tag{7.8}$$

In case (7.5), we have $m = x$, and hence $\gcd(m - x, n) = n$. In case (7.6), we have $m = n - x$, and hence $\gcd(m - x, n) = 1$. In case (7.7), we have $\gcd(m - x, n) = p$. In case (7.8), we have $\gcd(m - x, n) = q$. Since x has been chosen at random with equidistribution, each of those cases has the same probability. Therefore, this procedure factors n with probability $1/2$. After k applications of this procedure, n is factored with probability $1 - (1/2)^k$.

Example 7.3.2
As in Example 7.3.1, we let $n = 253$. Suppose Oscar is able to compute square roots modulo 253 with algorithm R. He chooses $x = 17$ and obtains $\gcd(17, 253) = 1$. Then he computes $c = 17^2 \bmod 253 = 36$. The square roots of 36 mod 253 are 6, 17, 236, 247. Now $\gcd(6 - 17, n) = 11$ and $\gcd(247 - 17, 253) = 23$. If R yields one of those square roots, then Oscar has found the factorization of n.

In the factoring algorithm just described, we have assumed that the plaintext space consists of all numbers in the set $\{0, 1, \ldots, n-1\}$. Now suppose that we use only plaintexts of a special form. As explained in Section 7.3.3, this helps avoid the ambiguity in Rabin decryption, but then the factoring algorithm no longer works. The decryption algorithm R can only decrypt ciphertexts that are encryptions of plaintexts of the special form. Hence, when Oscar wants to use this decryption algorithm to factor n as just described, he must make sure that one of the square roots of $c = x^2 \bmod n$ is of the special form. But it is unclear how this can be done unless x itself is of the special form. Then no other square root is likely to be of the special form and R will always return the square root x, which does not lead to a factorization.

7.3.6   A chosen ciphertext attack

We have seen that Oscar can factor n if he can break the Rabin system. This seems to be advantageous for the security of the Rabin system. On the other hand, a chosen ciphertext attack can be based on this fact.

Suppose that Oscar can decrypt ciphertexts of his choice. Then he can factor the Rabin modulus as described in the previous section and can determine the secret key.

To make this attack impossible, the plaintext space can be reduced to plaintexts of a special form, as described in Section 7.3.3. But then, as we have seen in Section 7.3.5, the equivalence between breaking the Rabin system and factoring the RSA modulus is lost.

Some attacks on the RSA system can be modified such that they work for the Rabin system; for example, the low-exponent attack and the attack that uses the multiplicativity of RSA (see Exercise 7.6.17).

7.4   Diffie-Hellman Key Exchange

In this section, we describe the protocol of Diffie and Hellman for exchanging secret keys over insecure channels. This protocol itself is not a public-key cryptosystem, but it is the basis for the ElGamal system, which is described in the next section.

The situation is the following. Alice and Bob wish to use a symmetric encryption system to keep their communication over an insecure channel secret. Initially, Alice and Bob must exchange a secret key. The Diffie Hellman key-exchange system enables Alice and Bob to use their insecure channel for this key exchange. Everybody can listen to the key exchange but the information obtained cannot be used to construct the secret key. The protocol of Diffie and Hellman is a milestone in public-key cryptography.

The security of the Diffie-Hellman key exchange is not based on the factoring problem for integers but on the discrete logarithm problem (DLP), which is introduced in the next section.

7.4.1 Discrete logarithms

Let p be a prime number. We know from Corollary 2.21.1 that the group $(\mathbb{Z}/p\mathbb{Z})^*$ is cyclic of order $p - 1$. Let g be a primitive root mod p. Then for any integer $A \in \{1, 2, \ldots, p - 1\}$ there is an exponent $a \in \{0, 1, 2, \ldots, p - 2\}$ with

$$A \equiv g^a \bmod p.$$

This exponent a is called the *discrete logarithm* of A to the base g. We write $a = \mathrm{dlog}_g A$. The computation of discrete logarithms is considered to be difficult. No efficient algorithm for solving this problem is known. But on the other hand, there is no proof that this problem is in fact difficult. Algorithms for solving the discrete logarithm problem are discussed in Chapter 9.

Example 7.4.1
Let $p = 13$. A primitive root modulo 13 is 2. In the following table, the discrete logarithms of all integers in $\{1, 2, \ldots, 12\}$ to the base 2 are listed.

A	1	2	3	4	5	6	7	8	9	10	11	12
$\mathrm{dlog}_2 A$	0	1	4	2	9	5	11	3	8	10	7	6

Discrete logarithms can be defined in arbitrary cyclic groups. Let G be a cyclic group of order n with generator g, and let A be a group element. Then there is an exponent $a \in \{0, 1, \ldots, n - 1\}$ with

$$A = g^a.$$

This exponent a is called the *discrete logarithm* of A to the base g. We will see in Section 7.5.8 that the Diffie-Hellman key exchange can be implemented in all cyclic groups in which the discrete logarithm problem is difficult.

Example 7.4.2
Consider the additive group $\mathbb{Z}/n\mathbb{Z}$ for a positive integer n. It is cyclic of order n. A generator of this group is the residue class $1 + n\mathbb{Z}$. Let $A \in \{0, 1, \ldots, n - 1\}$. The discrete logarithm a of $A + n\mathbb{Z}$ to the base $1 + n\mathbb{Z}$ satisfies the congruence

$$A \equiv a \bmod n.$$

Hence, $a = A$. The other generators of $\mathbb{Z}/n\mathbb{Z}$ are the residue classes $g + n\mathbb{Z}$ with $\gcd(g, n) = 1$. The discrete logarithm a of $A + n\mathbb{Z}$ to the base $g + n\mathbb{Z}$ satisfies the congruence

$$A \equiv ga \bmod n.$$

This congruence can be solved with the extended euclidean algorithm. Therefore, in $\mathbb{Z}/n\mathbb{Z}$, discrete logarithms can be computed very efficiently. This group cannot be used for implementing a secure Diffie-Hellman key-exchange protocol.

7.4.2 Key exchange

The Diffie-Hellman protocol works as follows. Alice and Bob wish to agree on a common secret key. They can communicate only over an insecure channel. First, they agree on a large prime number p and a primitive root g mod p with $2 \leq g \leq p - 2$ (see Section 2.21). The prime p and the primitive root g can be publicly known. Hence, Bob and Alice can use their insecure communication channel for this agreement.

Now Alice chooses an integer $a \in \{0, 1, \ldots, p-2\}$ randomly. She computes

$$A = g^a \bmod p$$

and sends the result A to Bob, but she keeps the exponent a secret. Bob chooses an integer $b \in \{0, 1, \ldots, p-2\}$ randomly. He computes

$$B = g^b \bmod p$$

and sends the result to Alice. He also keeps his exponent b secret. To obtain the common secret key, Alice computes

$$B^a \bmod p = g^{ab} \bmod p$$

and Bob computes

$$A^b \bmod p = g^{ab} \bmod p.$$

Then the common key is

$$K = g^{ab} \bmod p.$$

Example 7.4.3
Let $p = 17$ and $g = 3$. Alice chooses $a = 7$, computes $g^a \bmod p = 11$, and sends the result $A = 11$ to Bob. Bob chooses $b = 4$, computes $g^b \bmod p = 13$, and sends the result $B = 13$ to Alice. Alice computes $B^a \bmod p = 4$. Bob computes $A^b \bmod p = 4$. The common key is 4.

7.4.3 Security

The eavesdropper, Oscar, learns the integers p, g, A, and B but not the discrete logarithm a of A and b of B to the base g. He wants to determine the secret key $K = g^{ab} \bmod p$ from p, g, A, and B. This is called the *Diffie-Hellman problem*. If Oscar can compute discrete logarithms mod p, he can also solve the Diffie-Hellman problem. He determines the discrete logarithm b of B to the base g and computes the key $K = A^b$. This is the only known method for breaking the Diffie-Hellman protocol. So far, nobody has been able to prove that if Oscar can break the Diffie-Hellman problem he can also efficiently compute discrete logarithms mod p. It is an important open problem of public-key cryptography to find such a proof.

As long as the Diffie-Hellman problem is difficult to solve, no eavesdropper can determine the secret key from the publicly known information. But this is not the only possible attack on the Diffie-Hellman protocol.

In the *man in the middle attack*, Oscar exploits the fact that Alice cannot verify that the messages that she receives really come from Bob, and the same is true for Bob. Oscar intercepts all messages between Alice and Bob. He impersonates Bob and exchanges a key with Alice. He also impersonates Alice and exchanges a key with Bob. Whenever Bob sends an encrypted message to Alice, he uses the key that he has previously exchanged with Oscar. But he thinks that this is the key for the communication with Alice. Oscar intercepts that message and decrypts it. Then he changes the message and sends it to Alice.

To prevent this attack, digital signatures can be used. They are described in Chapter 11.

7.4.4 Other groups

A secure and efficient Diffie-Hellman key-exchange protocol can be implemented in all cyclic groups in which the Diffie-Hellman problem is difficult to solve and for which the group operations can be efficiently implemented. In Chapter 12, we will discuss examples for such groups. Here we only describe how the implementation of the Diffie-Hellman protocol in such groups works in principle.

Alice and Bob agree on a finite cyclic group G and a generator g of G. Let n be the order of G. Alice chooses randomly an integer $a \in \{1, 2, \ldots, n-1\}$. She computes

$$A = g^a$$

and sends the result A to Bob. Bob chooses randomly an integer $b \in \{1, 2, \ldots, n-1\}$. He computes

$$B = g^b$$

and sends the result to Alice. Alice determines

$$B^a = g^{ab}$$

and Bob determines

$$A^b = g^{ab}.$$

The common secret key is

$$K = g^{ab}.$$

7.5 ElGamal Encryption

The ElGamal cryptosystem is closely connected to the Diffie-Hellman key exchange. Its security is also based on the difficulty of solving the Diffie-Hellman problem in $(\mathbb{Z}/p\mathbb{Z})^*$.

7.5.1 Key generation

Alice chooses a prime number p and, as explained in Section 2.21, a primitive root g mod p. Then she chooses a random exponent $a \in \{0, \ldots, p-2\}$ and computes

$$A = g^a \bmod p.$$

The public key of Alice is (p, g, A). Her secret key is the exponent a. The integer A is Alice's key part from the Diffie-Hellman protocol. This key part is fixed in the ElGamal cryptosystem.

7.5.2 Encryption

The plaintext space is the set $\{0, 1, \ldots, p-1\}$. To encrypt a plaintext m, Bob gets the authentic public key (p, g, A) of Alice. He chooses a random exponent $b \in \{1, \ldots, p-2\}$ and computes

$$B = g^b \bmod p.$$

The number B is Bob's key part from the Diffie-Hellman system. Bob determines

$$c = A^b m \bmod p.$$

In other words, Bob encrypts the message m by multiplying it mod p by the Diffie-Hellman key. The complete ElGamal ciphertext is the pair (B, c).

7.5.3 Decryption

Alice has obtained the ciphertext (B, c). She knows her secret key a. To reconstruct the plaintext m, she divides c by the Diffie-Hellman key $B^a \bmod p$. In order to avoid inversions mod p, she determines the exponent $x = p - 1 - a$. Since $1 \leq a \leq p - 2$, we have $1 \leq x \leq p - 2$. Then she computes $m = B^x c \bmod p$. This is, in fact, the original plaintext, as the following computation shows:

$$B^x c \equiv g^{b(p-1-a)} A^b m \equiv (g^{p-1})^b (g^a)^{-b} A^b m \equiv A^{-b} A^b m \equiv m \bmod p.$$

Example 7.5.1

Alice chooses $p = 23, g = 7, a = 6$, and computes $A = g^a \bmod p = 4$. Her public key is $(p = 23, g = 7, A = 4)$. Her secret key is $a = 6$. Bob encrypts $m = 7$. He chooses $b = 3$, and computes $B = g^b \bmod p = 21$ and $c = A^b m \bmod p = 11$. The ciphertext is $(B, c) = (21, 11)$. Alice recovers m by computing $B^{p-1-6} c \bmod p = 7 = m$.

7.5.4   Efficiency

ElGamal decryption like RSA decryption, requires one modular exponentiation. We will see that the moduli must be of equal size in both systems. The Chinese remainder theorem, however, does not speed up ElGamal decryption.

ElGamal encryption requires two modular exponentiations: the computation of $A^b \bmod p$ and $B = g^b \bmod p$. RSA encryption requires only one modular exponentiation. But the exponentiations for the ElGamal encryption are independent of the plaintext that is actually encrypted. Therefore, those exponentiations can be carried out as precomputations. Then the actual encryption requires only one modular multiplication and is therefore much more efficient than RSA encryption. But the precomputed values must be kept secret, and must be securely stored, such as on a smart card.

Example 7.5.2

As in Example 7.5.1, the public key of Alice is $(p = 23, g = 7, A = 4)$. Her secret key is $a = 6$. As a precomputation, Bob chooses $b = 3$ and computes $B = g^b \bmod p = 21$ and $K = A^b \bmod p = 18$. Later, Bob encrypts $m = 7$. Then he simply computes $c = K * m \bmod 23 = 11$. The ciphertext is $(B, c) = (21, 11)$. Again, Alice recovers the plaintext by computing $B^{p-1-6} c \bmod p = 7 = m$.

In the ElGamal cryptosystem, the ciphertext is twice as long as the plaintext. This is called *message expansion* and is a disadvantage of this cryptosystem. On the other hand, the ElGamal system is a randomized cryptosystem, which can be regarded as an advantage (see Section 7.5.7).

The length of the public key in the ElGamal cryptosystem can be reduced if the same prime number p is used in all public keys. However, if it turns out that computing discrete logarithms modulo this specific prime number p is easy, then the whole system is insecure.

7.5.5 ElGamal and Diffie-Hellman

If the attacker, Oscar, can compute discrete logarithms mod p, then he can break the ElGamal system. He just determines Alice's secret key a as the discrete logarithm of A to the base g. Then he computes the plaintext by the formula $m = B^{p-1-a}c \bmod p$. It is, however, not known whether being able to break ElGamal implies the ability to compute efficiently discrete logarithms mod p.

We will now show, however, that breaking the ElGamal cryptosystem and breaking the Diffie-Hellman key-exchange protocol are equally difficult. Suppose Oscar can break the Diffie-Hellman key-exchange system (i.e., he can construct the secret key $g^{ab} \bmod p$ from p, g, A, and B). Oscar wants to decrypt an ElGamal ciphertext (B, c). He also knows the corresponding public key (p, g, A). Since he can break the Diffie-Hellman system, he can determine the key $K = g^{ab} \bmod p$ and can reconstruct the message $m = K^{-1}c \bmod p$.

Conversely, assume that Oscar can break the ElGamal cryptosystem. Then he can recover any encrypted plaintext m from p, g, A, B, and c. Suppose Oscar wants to determine the Diffie-Hellman key g^{ab} from p, g, A, B. He applies the decryption algorithm with input $p, g, A, B, c = 1$ and obtains a plaintext m. He knows that $1 = g^{ab}m \bmod p$. Therefore, he can determine the Diffie-Hellman key as $g^{ab} \equiv m^{-1} \bmod p$.

7.5.6 Choice of parameters

To prevent the application of the known DL algorithms (see Chapter 9), the prime number p must be at least of binary length 768. Furthermore, to prevent the application of DL algorithms such as the Pohlig-Hellman algorithm or the number field sieve, which work efficiently for prime numbers of a special form, such primes must be avoided. It appears best to choose the prime p randomly with equidistribution from all primes of a certain length.

For each new ElGamal encryption, a new exponent b must be chosen. If Bob chooses the same exponent b for the encryption of the plaintexts m and m', then he obtains

$$c = A^b m \bmod p \text{ and } c' = A^b m' \bmod p.$$

Therefore,

$$c' c^{-1} \equiv m' m^{-1} \bmod p.$$

An attacker who knows the plaintext m can recover the plaintext m' using the formula

$$m' = c' c^{-1} m \bmod p.$$

7.5.7   ElGamal as a randomized cryptosystem

ElGamal encryption is randomized by the random choice of the exponent b. This means the following. If the plaintext m is encrypted twice, then two different random exponents b and b' are chosen. Hence, the two ciphertexts are $(B = g^b \bmod p, c = A^b m \bmod p)$ and $(B' = g^{b'} \bmod p, c' = A^{b'} m \bmod p)$. Since the exponent b is a random number, the ciphertexts (B, c) are random numbers in $\{0, \ldots, p-2\}$, and the ciphertexts (B, c) are random pairs in $\{0, \ldots, p-1\}^2$ provided that A is a primitive root mod p (i.e., $\gcd(a, p-1) = 1$). This randomization makes cryptanalysis, in particular the application of statistical methods, much more difficult.

7.5.8   Generalization

An important advantage of the ElGamal system is the fact that it can be implemented in any cyclic group. The only requirements are that computation in that group be efficient and that the Diffie-Hellman problem be difficult. In particular, computing discrete logarithms in that group must be infeasible since otherwise the Diffie-Hellman problem would be easy to solve.

Examples of groups in which a secure ElGamal cryptosystem can be implemented are given in Chapter 12. It is very important that the

ElGamal system can also be implemented in other groups because nobody knows whether the discrete logarithm problem in $(\mathbb{Z}/p\mathbb{Z})^*$ is difficult. If someone finds an efficient DL algorithm for $(\mathbb{Z}/p\mathbb{Z})^*$, then one can switch to another group in which the DL problem is still infeasible.

7.6 Exercises

Exercise 7.6.1
Show that in the RSA cryptosystem the decryption exponent d can be chosen such that $de \equiv 1 \mod \operatorname{lcm}(p-1, q-1)$.

Exercise 7.6.2
Determine all possible encryption exponents for the RSA modulus $n = 437$. Also, give a formula for the number of possible encryption exponents for a given RSA modulus $n = pq$.

Exercise 7.6.3
Generate two 8-bit prime numbers p and q such that the RSA modulus $n = pq$ is a 16-bit number and the public RSA key $e = 5$ can be used. Compute the corresponding private key d. Encrypt the string 110100110110111 with the public exponent 5.

Exercise 7.6.4
Alice encrypts a message m with Bob's public RSA key $(899, 11)$. The ciphertext is 468. Determine the plaintext.

Exercise 7.6.5
Describe a polynomial time algorithm which given positive integers c and e decides whether c is an eth power in $\mathbb{Z}$ and extracts the eth root of c if this is the case. Prove that the algorithm has polynomial running time.

Exercise 7.6.6
Implement the algorithm from Exercise 7.6.5.

Exercise 7.6.7
How many operations are required for an RSA encryption with encryption exponent $e = 2^{16} + 1$?

Exercise 7.6.8

The same message m is encrypted by the RSA system using the public keys $(391, 3)$, $(55, 3)$, and $(87, 3)$. The ciphertexts are 208, 38, and 32. Use the low-exponent attack to find m.

Exercise 7.6.9 (Common modulus attack)

If a plaintext is encrypted twice with the RSA system using two public RSA keys (n, e) and (n, f) and if $\gcd(e, f) = 1$, then the plaintext m can be recovered from the two ciphertexts $c_e = m^e \bmod n$ and $c_f = m^f \bmod n$. How?

Exercise 7.6.10

The message m is encrypted by the RSA system using the public keys $(493, 3)$ and $(493, 5)$. The ciphertexts are 293 and 421. Use the common modulus attack to find m.

Exercise 7.6.11

Let $n = 1591$. Alice's public RSA key is (n, e) with minimal e. Alice receives the encrypted message $c = 1292$. Decrypt this message using the Chinese remainder theorem.

Exercise 7.6.12

Suppose that the RSA modulus is $n = 493$, the encryption exponent is $e = 11$, and the decryption exponent is $d = 163$. Use the method of Section 7.2.4 to factor n.

Exercise 7.6.13 (Cycling attack)

Let (n, e) be a public RSA key. For a plaintext $m \in \{0, 1, \ldots, n - 1\}$, let $c = m^e \bmod n$ be the corresponding ciphertext. Prove that there is a positive integer k with

$$m^{e^k} \equiv m \bmod n.$$

For such an integer k, prove that

$$c^{e^{k-1}} \equiv m \bmod n.$$

Is this dangerous for RSA?

Exercise 7.6.14

Let $n = 493$ and $e = 3$. Determine the smallest value of k for which the cycling attack from Exercise 7.6.13 works.

Exercise 7.6.15
Bob uses the Rabin cryptosystem with the same parameters as in Example 7.3.1 to send encrypted messages to Alice. The plaintexts are blocks in $\{0, 1\}^8$ in which the first and the last two bits are equal. Can Alice uniquely decrypt all possible plaintexts?

Exercise 7.6.16
Let $n = 713$ be a Rabin modulus and let $c = 289$ be a ciphertext that is obtained by Rabin encryption using this modulus. Determine all possible plaintexts.

Exercise 7.6.17
Explain the low-exponent attack and the multiplicativity attack for the Rabin system. How can those attacks be prevented?

Exercise 7.6.18
Let $n = 713$ be the public Rabin key and let $c = 200$ be a ciphertext that was obtained by Rabin encryption with this key. Determine the corresponding plaintext.

Exercise 7.6.19
How can two ElGamal ciphertexts be used to generate a third ElGamal ciphertext of an unknown plaintext? How can this attack be prevented?

Exercise 7.6.20
Alice receives the ElGamal ciphertext $(B = 30, c = 7)$. Her public key is $(p = 43, g = 3)$. Determine the corresponding plaintext.

Exercise 7.6.21
Let $p = 53$, $g = 2$, $A = 30$ be Bob's public ElGamal key. Alice uses it to generate the ciphertext $(24, 37)$. Determine the corresponding plaintext.

8

CHAPTER

Factoring

We have seen that the security of the RSA system and the Rabin system is closely connected to the difficulty of factoring a positive integer into primes. But it is not known whether the integer factoring problem is in fact difficult to solve. On the contrary, over the years many efficient integer factoring algorithms have been invented, and the number of digits required for secure RSA moduli has been increased from 512 to 1024 bits.

In this chapter, we describe some important factoring algorithms. We let n be a positive integer that is known to be composite. This can be detected with the Fermat test or with the Miller-Rabin test (see Sections 6.2 and 6.4). However, those tests do not determine a divisor of n. For a more detailed overview of factoring algorithms, we refer the reader to [18] and [8]. The algorithms that we describe here are implemented in the LiDIA library [22].

8.1 Trial Division

To find small prime factors of n, a precomputed table of all prime numbers below a fixed bound B is computed. This can be done using the sieve of Eratosthenes (see Exercise 1.12.24 and [4]). Then for each prime number p in this table, the maximum exponent $e(p)$ is determined such that $p^{e(p)}$ divides n. A typical bound is $B = 10^6$.

Example 8.1.1

We want to factor $n = 3^{21} + 1 = 10460353204$. Trial division with all primes ≤ 50 yields the factors 2^2, 7^2, and 43. If we divide n by those factors, then we obtain $m = 1241143$. Since $2^{m-1} \equiv 793958 \bmod m$, Fermat's little theorem implies the compositeness of m.

8.2 $p - 1$ Method

There are factoring algorithms that work particularly well for composite integers with certain properties. Those integers must be avoided as RSA or Rabin moduli. As an example of such factoring algorithms, we describe the $p - 1$ method of John Pollard.

The $(p - 1)$ method works best for composite integers with a prime factor p such that $p - 1$ has only small prime divisors. Then it is possible to determine a multiple k of $p - 1$ without knowing $p - 1$ as the product of powers of small prime numbers. The details are described below. Then Fermat's little theorem implies

$$a^k \equiv 1 \bmod p$$

for all integers a that are not divisible by p. This means that p divides $a^k - 1$. If $a^k - 1$ is not divisible by n, then $\gcd(a^k - 1, n)$ is a proper divisor of n, so a factor of n is found.

As candidates for k, the $p - 1$ method uses the product of all prime powers below a given bound B; namely,

$$k = \prod_{q \in \mathbb{P}, q^e \leq B} q^e.$$

If the prime powers that divide $p - 1$ are all less than B, then k is a multiple of $p - 1$. The algorithm computes $g = \gcd(a^k - 1, n)$ for an appropriate basis a. If no divisor of n is found, then a new bound B is used.

Example 8.2.1

In Example 8.1.1, the composite number $n = 1241143$ remained to be factored. We use $B = 13$. Then $k = 8 * 9 * 5 * 7 * 11 * 13$ and

$$\gcd(2^k - 1, n) = 547.$$

Hence, $p = 547$ is a divisor of n. The cofactor is $q = 2269$. Both 547 and 2269 are prime numbers.

8.3 Quadratic Sieve

One of the most efficient factoring algorithms is the quadratic sieve (QS), which we describe in this section.

8.3.1 Idea

We try to factor the odd composite positive integer. We describe how one proper divisor of n is found. This is sufficient for breaking the RSA system because RSA moduli are the product of two large primes. In general, a recursive application of QS factors n completely.

The quadratic sieve finds integers x and y such that

$$x^2 \equiv y^2 \bmod n \tag{8.1}$$

and

$$x \not\equiv \pm y \bmod n. \tag{8.2}$$

Then n is a divisor of $x^2 - y^2 = (x - y)(x + y)$, but of neither $x - y$ nor of $x + y$. Hence, $g = \gcd(x - y, n)$ is a proper divisor of n.

Example 8.3.1

Let $n = 7429$, $x = 227$, $y = 210$. Then $x^2 - y^2 = n$, $x - y = 17$, $x + y = 437$. Therefore, $\gcd(x - y, n) = 17$. This is a proper divisor of n.

8.3.2   Determination of x and y

The idea from the previous section is also used in other factoring algorithms, such as the number field sieve (NFS) (see [20]), but those algorithms have different ways of finding x and y. We describe how x and y are found in the quadratic sieve.

Let

$$m = \lfloor \sqrt{n} \rfloor$$

and

$$f(X) = (X + m)^2 - n.$$

We first explain the procedure in an example.

Example 8.3.2

As in Example 8.3.1, let $n = 7429$. Then $m = 86$ and $f(X) = (X + 86)^2 - 7429$. We have

$$
\begin{array}{llllll}
f(-3) & = & 83^2 - 7429 & = & -540 & = & -1 * 2^2 * 3^3 * 5 \\
f(1) & = & 87^2 - 7429 & = & 140 & = & 2^2 * 5 * 7 \\
f(2) & = & 88^2 - 7429 & = & 315 & = & 3^2 * 5 * 7.
\end{array}
$$

This implies

$$
\begin{array}{llll}
83^2 & \equiv & -1 * 2^2 * 3^3 * 5 & \mathrm{mod}\ 7429 \\
87^2 & \equiv & 2^2 * 5 * 7 & \mathrm{mod}\ 7429 \\
88^2 & \equiv & 3^2 * 5 * 7 & \mathrm{mod}\ 7429.
\end{array}
$$

If the last two congruences are multiplied, then we obtain

$$(87 * 88)^2 \equiv (2 * 3 * 5 * 7)^2 \ \mathrm{mod}\ n.$$

Therefore, we can set

$$x = 87 * 88 \ \mathrm{mod}\ n = 227, \quad y = 2 * 3 * 5 * 7 \ \mathrm{mod}\ n = 210.$$

Those are the values for x and y from Example 8.3.1.

In Example 8.3.2, we have presented numbers s for which the value $f(s)$ has only small prime factors. Then we use the congruence

$$(s + m)^2 \equiv f(s) \ \mathrm{mod}\ n. \tag{8.3}$$

From those congruences, we select a subset whose product yields squares on the left- and the right-hand sides. The left-hand side of each congruence is a square anyway. Also, we know the prime factorization of each right-hand side. The product of a number of right-hand sides is a square if the exponents of -1 and all prime factors are even. In the next section, we explain how an appropriate subset of congruences is chosen.

8.3.3 Choosing appropriate congruences

In Example 8.3.2, it is obvious which congruences must be multiplied such that the product of the right-hand sides is a square. If n is large, many more prime factors and congruences must be considered. The selection process uses linear algebra. We will illustrate this in the next example.

Example 8.3.3
We show how we can choose appropriate congruences in Example 8.3.2 by solving a linear system. We can choose from three congruences. The goal is that the product of the right-hand sides of the chosen congruences be a square. The selection process is controlled by coefficients $\lambda_i \in \{0, 1\}$, $1 \leq i \leq 3$. If $\lambda_i = 1$, then congruence i is chosen; otherwise it is not. The product of the right-hand sides of the chosen congruences is

$$(-1 * 2^2 * 3^3 * 5)^{\lambda_1} * (2^2 * 5 * 7)^{\lambda_2} * (3^2 * 5 * 7)^{\lambda_3} =$$
$$(-1)^{\lambda_1} * 2^{2\lambda_1 + 2\lambda_2} * 3^{3\lambda_1 + 2\lambda_3} * 5^{\lambda_1 + \lambda_2 + \lambda_3} * 7^{\lambda_2 + \lambda_3}.$$

We want this number to be a square. It is a square if and only if the exponents of -1 and of all prime numbers are even. This leads to the following linear system:

$$\lambda_1 \equiv 0 \bmod 2$$
$$2\lambda_1 + 2\lambda_2 \equiv 0 \bmod 2$$
$$3\lambda_1 + 2\lambda_3 \equiv 0 \bmod 2$$
$$\lambda_1 + \lambda_2 + \lambda_3 \equiv 0 \bmod 2$$
$$\lambda_2 + \lambda_3 \equiv 0 \bmod 2.$$

The coefficients of the λ_i are reduced mod 2, so we obtain the simplified system

$$\lambda_1 \equiv 0 \bmod 2$$
$$\lambda_1 + \lambda_2 + \lambda_3 \equiv 0 \bmod 2$$
$$\lambda_2 + \lambda_3 \equiv 0 \bmod 2.$$

A solution is

$$\lambda_1 = 0, \quad \lambda_2 = \lambda_3 = 1.$$

The product of the right-hand sides of the second and third congruences is a square.

We sketch how the quadratic sieve chooses the appropriate congruences in general. We choose a positive integer B. Then we look for integers s such that $f(s)$ has only prime factors that belong to the *factor base*

$$F(B) = \{p \in \mathbb{P} : p \leq B\} \cup \{-1\}.$$

Such values $f(s)$ are called B-smooth. Table 8.1 gives an impression of the factor base sizes required. If we have found as many values for s as the factor base has elements, then we try to solve the corresponding linear system. Because the linear system is a system over the field $\mathbb{Z}/2\mathbb{Z}$, the Gauss algorithm can be used to solve it. However, for large n more efficient algorithms are used, which are not described here.

8.3.4   Sieving

It remains to be shown how the values of s are found for which $f(s)$ is B-smooth. One possibility is to compute the value $f(s)$ for $s = 0, \pm 1, \pm 2, \pm 3, \ldots$, and to test by trial division whether $f(s)$ is B-smooth. Unfortunately, those values typically are not B-smooth. To detect this, trial division by each element of the factor base is needed. This is very inefficient because the factor base is large for large n, as Table 8.1 shows. A more efficient method is to use sieving techniques, which are described as follows.

TABLE 8.1   Size of factor base and sieving interval.

# decimal digits of n	50	60	70	80	90	100	110	120
# factor base *1000	3	4	7	15	30	51	120	245
# sieving interval in million	0.2	2	5	6	8	14	16	26

We explain a simplified version that shows the main idea. We fix a *sieving interval*

$$S = \{-C, -C + 1, \ldots, 0, 1, \ldots, C\}.$$

We want to find all $s \in S$ such that $f(s)$ is B-smooth. First, we compute $f(s)$ for all $s \in S$. For each prime number p in the factor base, we divide the values $f(s)$ by the highest possible power of p. The B-smooth values $f(s)$ are exactly those for which 1 or -1 remains.

To find out which of the values $f(s) = (s+m)^2 - n$ is divisible by a prime number p in the factor base, we first determine all integers $s \in \{0, 1, \ldots, p-1\}$ for which $f(s)$ is divisible by p. By Corollary 2.19.7, the polynomial $f(X)$ can have at most two zeros modulo p. For small prime numbers, the zeros can be found by trying all possibilities. If p is large, then more sophisticated methods must be used (see [4]).

Now suppose that we know the zeros of $f(X)$ modulo a prime number p in $\{0, 1, \ldots, p-1\}$ (i.e., the arguments $s \in \{0, 1, \ldots, p-1\}$ for which $f(s)$ is divisible by p). The other values s for which $f(s)$ is divisible by p are obtained from the zeros that we already know by adding integer multiples of p. Starting at the zeros that we know, we walk in steps of length p in both directions through the sieving interval. After each step, we divide the corresponding $f(s)$ by p. This is called *sieving with p*. No unsuccessful trial divisions by p are necessary. Prime powers can be treated similarly.

Example 8.3.4
As in Examples 8.3.1 and 8.3.2, let $n = 7429$, $m = 86$, and $f(X) = (X+86)^2 - 7429$. The factor base is the set $\{2, 3, 5, 7\} \cup \{-1\}$. As sieving interval, we use the set $\{-3, -2, \ldots, 3\}$. The sieve is shown in Table 8.2.

The sieve can be made more efficient. This is described in [27].

TABLE 8.2   The sieve.

s	-3	-2	-1	0	1	2	3
$(s+m)^2 - n$	-540	-373	-204	-33	140	315	492
Sieve with 2	-135		-51		35		123
Sieve with 3	-5		-17	-11		35	41
Sieve with 5	-1				7	7	
Sieve with 7					1	1	

8.4   Analysis of the Quadratic Sieve

In this section, we sketch the analysis of the quadratic sieve to give an impression why the quadratic sieve is more efficient than, for example, trial division. Some techniques used in this analysis are beyond the scope of this book. Therefore, we only mention them briefly. For a deeper introduction into the subject, we refer the reader to [19].

Let n, u, v be real numbers and let n be greater than the Euler constant $e = 2.718\ldots$. Then we write

$$L_n[u, v] = e^{v(\log n)^u (\log \log n)^{1-u}}. \qquad (8.4)$$

This function is used to describe the running time of factoring algorithms. We first explain its meaning. We have

$$L_n[0, v] = e^{v(\log n)^0 (\log \log n)^1} = (\log n)^v \qquad (8.5)$$

and

$$L_n[1, v] = e^{v(\log n)^1 (\log \log n)^0} = e^{v \log n}. \qquad (8.6)$$

An algorithm that factors the positive integer n receives as input n. The binary length of n is $\lfloor \log_2 n \rfloor + 1$. If an algorithm has running time $L_n[0, v]$, then it is a polynomial time algorithm. Its complexity is bounded by a polynomial in the size of the input. The algorithm is considered efficient, although its real efficiency depends on the degree v of the polynomial. If the algorithm has running time $L_n[1, v]$, then it is exponential. Its complexity is bounded by an exponential function in the length of the input. The algorithm is considered inefficient. If the algorithm has running time $L_n[u, v]$ with $0 < u < 1$, then it is *subexponential*. The algorithm is slower than polynomial but faster than exponential. The fastest integer factoring algorithms are subexponential. Trial division is an exponential algorithm.

So far, nobody has been able to analyze completely the running time of the quadratic sieve. Under certain plausible assumptions, however, it can be shown that this running time is $L_n[1/2, 1 + o(1)]$. Here $o(1)$ stands for a function that converges to zero as n approaches infinity. Thus, the complexity of the quadratic sieve can be considered to be in the middle between polynomial and exponential.

We will now try to give an impression of the analysis of the quadratic sieve. As we have seen, in the QS we choose bounds B and C and search for the integers s in the sieving interval $S = \{-C, -C + 1, \ldots, C\}$ for which the value

$$f(s) = (s + m)^2 - n = s^2 + 2ms + m^2 - n \qquad (8.7)$$

is B-smooth. The bounds B and C must be chosen such that the number of successful integers s and the number of elements of the factor base are approximately equal.

Since $m = \lfloor\sqrt{n}\rfloor$, it follows that $m^2 - n$ is very small. Therefore, (8.7) implies that for small s the value $f(s)$ is of the same magnitude as $\sqrt{n}$. Assume that the fraction of B-smooth values $f(s)$, $s \in S$ is the same as the fraction of B-smooth integers $\leq \sqrt{n}$. This assumption is unproven, but experiments indicate that it is probably correct. It also makes the analysis of the quadratic sieve possible.

Denote the number of B-smooth integers below a bound x by $\psi(x, B)$. This number is estimated in the following theorem, the proof of which can be found in [13].

Theorem 8.4.1

Let ε be a positive real number. Then for all real numbers $x \geq 10$ and $w \leq (\log x)^{1-\varepsilon}$, we have

$$\psi(x, x^{1/w}) = xw^{-w+f(x,w)}$$

with a function f that satisfies $f(x, w)/w \to 0$ for $w \to \infty$ and all x.

Theorem 8.4.1 means that the fraction of $x^{1/w}$-smooth numbers $\leq x$ is approximately w^{-w}.

From this theorem, we can deduce the following result.

Corollary 8.4.2

Let a, u, v be positive real numbers. Then for $n \to \infty$ we have

$$\psi(n^a, L_n[u, v]) = n^a L_n[1 - u, -(a/v)(1 - u) + o(1)].$$

Proof.   We have

$$L_n[u, v] = (e^{(\log n)^u (\log \log n)^{1-u}})^v = n^{v((\log \log n)/\log n)^{1-u}}.$$

If we set

$$w = (a/v)((\log n)/(\log \log n))^{1-u}$$

and apply Theorem 8.4.1, then we obtain

$$\psi(n^a, L_n[u, v]) = n^a w^{-w(1+o(1))}.$$

Now

$$w^{-w(1+o(1))}$$
$$= (e^{(1-u)(\log(a/v)+\log \log n - \log \log \log n)(-(a/v)((\log n)/(\log \log n))^{1-u}(1+o(1)))})^{1-u}.$$

In this formula, we use

$$\log(a/v) + \log \log n - \log \log \log n = \log \log n(1 + o(1)).$$

Then we find

$$w^{-w(1+o(1))}$$
$$= e^{(\log n)^{1-u}(\log \log n)^u (-(a/v)(1-u)+o(1))}$$
$$= L_n[1 - u, -(a/v)(1 - u) + o(1)].$$

This proves the assertion.   □

In the quadratic sieve, we generate numbers $f(s)$ which are approximately $n^{1/2}$. We assume that with respect to smoothness the values $f(s)$ behave as random numbers $\leq n^{1/2}$. In Corollary 8.4.2, we therefore set $a = 1/2$. Then we find that the probability of such a value $f(s)$ being $L_n[u, v]$-smooth is $L_n[1 - u, (-1/(2v))(1 - u) + o(1)]$. This means that on average we must try $L_n[1 - u, (1/(2v))(1 - u) + o(1)]$ integers s in the factor base before we find one for which $f(s)$ is $L_n[u, v]$-smooth. The number of elements in the factor base is approximately $L_n[u, v]$, so we need to find $L_n[u, v]$ successful values s in order for the linear system to have a solution. Therefore, the time for finding the values of s is some multiple of

$L_n[u, v]L_n[1 - u, (1/(2v))(1 - u) + o(1)]$. To make this value as small as possible, we choose $u = 1/2$.

For the further computation, we need a few simple rules. If x and y are real numbers, then

$$L_n[1/2, x]L_n[1/2, y] = L_n[1/2, x + y]. \qquad (8.8)$$

Also, if $p \in \mathbb{Z}[X]$ is a polynomial and if x is a real number, then

$$p(\log n)L_n[1/2, x] = L_n[1/2, x + o(1)]. \qquad (8.9)$$

This means that polynomial factors in $\log n$ are swallowed by $L_n[1/2, x]$.

Now the factor base contains all prime numbers p with $p \leq B = L_n[1/2, v]$. For each successful s, we need $L_n[1/2, 1/(4v)]$ elements in the sieving interval, as we have just seen. Since we need $L_n[1/2, v]$ values of s, the sieving interval is of size $L_n[1/2, v]L_n[1/2, 1/(4v)] = L_n[1/2, v + 1/(4v)]$.

The optimal value for v will be found later. First, we collect the running times for the different steps of the algorithm.

Computing the zeros of $f(X)$ modulo p for a prime number p in the factor base is possible in polynomial time in $\log n$. Hence, (8.9) implies that all zeros can be computed in time $L_n[1/2, v + o(1)]$.

The sieving time for a prime p is $O(L_n[1/2, v + 1/(4v) + o(1)]/p)$, since we walk in steps of width p through the sieving interval. It can be deduced from this formula that the total sieving time, including the precomputation, is $L_n[1/2, v + 1/(4v) + o(1)]$.

The Wiedemann algorithm for solving sparse linear systems takes time $L_n[1/2, 2v + o(1)]$. This algorithm takes advantage of the special structure of the system. The value $v = 1/2$ minimizes the sieving time. Hence, the total running time is $L_n[1/2, 1 + o(1)]$.

8.5 Efficiency of Other Factoring Algorithms

The analysis that was presented in the previous section raises two questions. Are there faster algorithms? Are there algorithms for which the running time can be rigorously proved?

The most efficient algorithm for which the running time can be rigorously proved uses quadratic forms. It is a probabilistic algorithm with expected running time $L_n[1/2, 1+o(1)]$. This is the same as the running time of the quadratic sieve and is proved in [21]. In practice, however, the quadratic sieve is much more efficient.

The elliptic curve method (ECM) is also a probabilistic algorithm. It is similar to the $p - 1$ method and has expected running time $L_p[1/2, \sqrt{1/2}]$, where p is the smallest prime factor of n. This is a major difference from the quadratic sieve. While the running time of QS depends mainly on the size of n, ECM is faster if n has a small prime factor. Therefore, ECM is used to find prime factors that are considerably smaller than $\sqrt{n}$. For prime factors that are of size $\sqrt{n}$, however, the running time of ECM is $L_n[1/2, 1]$, the same as the running time of QS, but ECM is less efficient in practice.

Until 1988, the fastest integer factoring algorithms had running time $L_n[1/2, 1]$. Some people even thought that there were no faster integer factoring algorithms. But in 1988, John Pollard invented the number field sieve (NFS). Under appropriate assumptions, it can be shown that the running time of NFS is $L_n[1/3, (64/9)^{1/3}]$. Hence, NFS is much closer to a polynomial time algorithm than QS. A collection of papers concerning NFS can be found in [20].

Since the 1980s, there has been dramatic progress in the field of factoring algorithms. It is therefore very possible that one day a polynomial time factoring algorithm will be found.

8.6   Exercises

Exercise 8.6.1 (Fermat's factoring method)
Fermat factored a positive integer n by writing it as $n = x^2 - y^2 = (x - y)(x + y)$. Factor $n = 13199$ by this method. Is this a general factoring algorithm that works for all composite integers? What is the running time of the algorithm?

Exercise 8.6.2
Factor 831802500 using trial division.

Exercise 8.6.3
Use the $p - 1$ method to factor $n = 138277151$.

Exercise 8.6.4
Use the $p - 1$ method to factor $n = 18533588383$.

Exercise 8.6.5
Estimate the running time of the $p - 1$ method.

Exercise 8.6.6
The *random square method* of Dixon is similar to the quadratic sieve factoring method. The major difference is that the relations are found by factoring x^2 mod n, where n is a random number in $\{1, \ldots, n - 1\}$. Use the random square method to factor n with the smallest possible factor base.

Exercise 8.6.7
Factor 11111 using the quadratic sieve.

Exercise 8.6.8
Draw the function $f(k) = L_{2^k}[1/2, 1]$ for $k \in \{1, 2, \ldots, 2048\}$.

9

Discrete Logarithms

CHAPTER

In this chapter, we discuss the difficulty of the discrete logarithm problem (DL problem). The security of many public-key cryptosystems is based on the difficulty of this problem. An example is the ElGamal cryptosystem (see Section 7.5).

First, we describe generic algorithms that work in any cyclic group. Then we explain special algorithms that work in the group $(\mathbb{Z}/p\mathbb{Z})^*$ for a prime number p.

9.1 DL Problem

In this chapter, G is a finite cyclic group of order n, γ is a generator of this group, and 1 is the neutral element in G. We assume that the group order n is known. Many algorithms for computing discrete logarithms, however, also work with an upper bound on the group order. Moreover, we let α be a group element. The goal is to find the smallest nonnegative integer x with

$$\alpha = \gamma^x. \tag{9.1}$$

185

It is called the *discrete logarithm* of α to the base γ. When we talk about the DL problem, we mean the problem of finding this integer x.

There is a more general version of the DL problem. In a group H, which is not necessarily cyclic, two elements α and γ are given. The problem is to decide whether there is an integer x such that (9.1) is satisfied, and if such an x exists to find the smallest nonnegative x. In cryptographic applications, the existence of x is typically guaranteed. The attacker's only problem is to find it. Therefore, our version of the DL problem is sufficient for the cryptographic context.

9.2   Enumeration

The simplest method for computing the discrete logarithm x from (9.1) is to test whether $x = 0, 1, 2, 3, \ldots$ satisfy (9.1). As soon as the answer is "yes", the discrete logarithm is found. This is called *enumeration*. Enumeration requires $x - 1$ multiplications and x comparisons in G. Only the elements α, γ and γ^x need to be stored. Hence, enumeration only requires space for three group elements.

Example 9.2.1
We determine the discrete logarithm of 3 to the base 5 in $(\mathbb{Z}/2017\mathbb{Z})^*$. Enumeration yields $x = 1030$ using 1029 multiplications modulo 2017.

In cryptographic applications, we have $x \geq 2^{160}$. Therefore, enumeration is infeasible because it would require at least $2^{160} - 1$ group operations.

9.3   Shanks Baby-Step Giant-Step Algorithm

A considerable improvement of the enumeration algorithm is the *baby-step giant-step algorithm* of D. Shanks. This algorithm requires fewer group operations but more storage. We describe this algorithm as follows.

We set

$$m = \lceil \sqrt{n} \rceil$$

and write the unknown discrete logarithm x as

$$x = qm + r, \quad 0 \leq r < m.$$

Hence, r is the remainder and q is the quotient of the division of x by m. The baby-step giant-step algorithm computes q and r. This works as follows.

We have

$$\gamma^{qm+r} = \gamma^x = \alpha.$$

This implies

$$(\gamma^m)^q = \alpha\gamma^{-r}.$$

First, we compute the set of *baby-steps*

$$B = \{(\alpha\gamma^{-r}, r) : 0 \leq r < m\}.$$

If in this set we find a pair $(1, r)$, then $\alpha\gamma^{-r} = 1$ (i.e., $\alpha = \gamma^r$). Hence, we can set $x = r$ with the smallest such x. If we do not find such a pair, we determine

$$\delta = \gamma^m.$$

Then we test for $q = 1, 2, 3, \ldots$ whether the group element δ^q is the first component of an element in B (i.e., whether there is a pair (δ^q, r) in B). As soon as this is true, we have

$$\alpha\gamma^{-r} = \delta^q = \gamma^{qm}$$

which implies

$$\alpha = \gamma^{qm+r}.$$

Therefore, the discrete logarithm is

$$x = qm + r.$$

The elements δ^q, $q = 1, 2, 3 \ldots$ are called *giant-steps*. We must compare each δ^q with all first components of the baby-step set B. To make this comparison efficient, the elements of B are stored in a hash table where the key is the first element (see [12], Chapter 12).

Example 9.3.1

We determine the discrete logarithm of 3 to the base 5 in $(\mathbb{Z}/2017\mathbb{Z})^*$. We have $\gamma = 5 + 2017\mathbb{Z}$, $\alpha = 3 + 2017\mathbb{Z}$, $m = \lceil\sqrt{2017}\rceil = 45$. The baby-step set is

$$B = \{(3, 0), (404, 1), (1291, 2), (1065, 3), (213, 4), (446, 5), (896, 6),$$
$$(986, 7), (1004, 8), (1411, 9), (1089, 10), (1428, 11), (689, 12),$$
$$(1348, 13), (673, 14), (538, 15), (511, 16), (909, 17), (1392, 18),$$
$$(1892, 19), (1992, 20), (2012, 21), (2016, 22), (1210, 23), (242, 24),$$
$$(1662, 25), (1946, 26), (1196, 27), (1046, 28), (1016, 29), (1010, 30),$$
$$(202, 31), (1654, 32), (1541, 33), (1115, 34), (223, 35), (448, 36),$$
$$(493, 37), (502, 38), (1714, 39), (1553, 40), (714, 41), 1353, 42),$$
$$(674, 43), (1345, 44)\}.$$

Here, the residue classes are represented by their least nonnegative representatives.

Next, we compute $\delta = \gamma^m = 45 + 2017\mathbb{Z}$. The giant-steps are

$$45, 8, 360, 64, 863, 512, 853, 62, 773, 496, 133, 1951,$$
$$1064, 1489, 444, 1827, 1535, 497, 178, 1959, 1424, 1553.$$

We find $(1553, 40)$ in the baby-step set. Therefore, $\alpha\gamma^{-40} = 1553 + 2017\mathbb{Z}$. Since 1553 has been found as the twenty-second giant-step, we obtain

$$\gamma^{22*45} = \alpha\gamma^{-40}.$$

Hence

$$\gamma^{22*45+40} = \alpha.$$

The solution of the DL problem is $x = 22 * 45 + 40 = 1030$. To compute the baby-step set, 45 multiplications mod 2017 were necessary. To compute the giant-steps, 21 multiplications mod 2017 were necessary. Enumeration requires many more multiplications, namely 1029. On the other hand, a baby-step set with 45 elements had to be stored, whereas enumeration only requires the storage of three elements.

If we use a hash table, then a constant number of comparisons are sufficient to check whether a group element computed as a giant-step is a first component of a baby-step. Therefore, the following result is easy to verify.

Theorem 9.3.2
The baby-step giant-step algorithm requires $O(\sqrt{|G|})$ multiplications and comparisons in G. It needs storage for $O(\sqrt{|G|})$ elements of G.

Time and space requirements of the baby-step giant-step algorithm are approximately $\sqrt{|G|}$. If $|G| > 2^{160}$, then computing discrete logarithms with the baby-step giant-step algorithm is still infeasible.

9.4 Pollard ρ-Algorithm

The algorithm of Pollard described in this section has the same running time as the baby-step giant-step algorithm, namely $O(\sqrt{|G|})$. However, it only requires constant storage, while the baby-step giant-step algorithm needs to store roughly $\sqrt{|G|}$ group elements.

Again, we want to solve the DL problem (9.1). We need three pairwise disjoint subsets G_1, G_2, G_3 of G such that $G_1 \cup G_2 \cup G_3 = G$. Let $f : G \to G$ be defined by

$$f(\beta) = \begin{cases} \gamma\beta & \text{if } \beta \in G_1, \\ \beta^2 & \text{if } \beta \in G_2, \\ \alpha\beta & \text{if } \beta \in G_3. \end{cases}$$

We choose a random number x_0 in the set $\{1, \ldots, n\}$ and compute the group element $\beta_0 = \gamma^{x_0}$. Then, we compute the sequence (β_i) by the recursion

$$\beta_{i+1} = f(\beta_i).$$

The elements of this sequence can be written as

$$\beta_i = \gamma^{x_i}\alpha^{y_i}, \quad i \geq 0.$$

Here, x_0 is the initial random number, $y_0 = 0$, and we have

$$x_{i+1} = \begin{cases} x_i + 1 \bmod n & \text{if } \beta_i \in G_1, \\ 2x_i \bmod n & \text{if } \beta_i \in G_2, \\ x_i & \text{if } \beta_i \in G_3, \end{cases}$$

and

$$y_{i+1} = \begin{cases} y_i & \text{if } \beta_i \in G_1, \\ 2y_i \bmod n & \text{if } \beta_i \in G_2, \\ y_i + 1 \bmod n & \text{if } \beta_i \in G_3. \end{cases}$$

Since we are working in a finite group, two elements in the sequence (β_i) must be equal (i.e., there is $i \geq 0$ and $k \geq 1$ with $\beta_{i+k} = \beta_i$). This implies

$$\gamma^{x_i} \alpha^{y_i} = \gamma^{x_{i+k}} \alpha^{y_{i+k}}$$

and therefore

$$\gamma^{x_i - x_{i+k}} = \alpha^{y_{i+k} - y_i}.$$

Hence, by Corollary 2.9.3, the discrete logarithm x of α to the base γ satisfies

$$(x_i - x_{i+k}) \equiv x(y_{i+k} - y_i) \bmod n.$$

We solve this congruence. The solution is unique mod n if $y_{i+k} - y_i$ is invertible mod n. If the solution is not unique, then the discrete logarithm can be found by testing the different possibilities mod n. If there are too many possibilities, then the algorithm is applied again with a different initial x_0.

We estimate the number of elements β_i that must be computed before a *match* is found (i.e., a pair $(i, i+k)$ of indices for which $\beta_{i+k} = \beta_i$). For this purpose, we use the birthday paradox (see Section 4.3). The possible birthdays are the group elements. We assume that the elements of the sequence $(\beta_i)_{i \geq 0}$ are random group elements. This is obviously not true, but the construction of the sequence makes it very similar to a random sequence. As we have shown in Section 4.3, $O(\sqrt{|G|})$ sequence elements are sufficient to make the probability for a match greater than $1/2$.

Thus far, our algorithm must store all triplets (β_i, x_i, y_i). As we have seen, the number of elements of the sequence is of the order of magnitude $\sqrt{|G|}$, as in Shanks' baby-step giant-step algorithm. But we will now show that it suffices to store a single triplet. Therefore, the Pollard ρ-algorithm is much more space efficient than the baby-step giant-step algorithm.

Initially, (β_0, x_0, y_0) is stored. Now suppose that at a certain point in the algorithm (β_i, x_i, y_i) is stored. Then (β_j, x_j, y_j) is computed for $j = i+1, i+2, \ldots$ until either a match is found or $j = 2i$. In the latter case, we delete β_i and store β_{2i}. Hence, we only store the triplets (β_i, x_i, y_i) with $i = 2^k$. Before we show that in this way a match is found, we give an example.

Example 9.4.1

With the Pollard ρ-algorithm, we solve the discrete logarithm problem

$$5^x \equiv 3 \bmod 2017.$$

All residue classes are represented by their smallest nonnegative representatives. We set

$$G_1 = \{1, \ldots, 672\}, G_2 = \{673, \ldots, 1344\}, G_3 = \{1345, \ldots, 2016\}.$$

As our starting value, we use $x_0 = 1023$.

Here are the stored triplets and the final triplet, which is a match and allows us to compute the discrete logarithm.

j	β_j	x_j	y_j
0	986	1023	0
1	2	30	0
2	10	31	0
4	250	33	0
8	1366	136	1
16	1490	277	8
32	613	447	155
64	1476	1766	1000
98	1476	966	1128

We see that

$$5^{800} \equiv 3^{128} \bmod 2017.$$

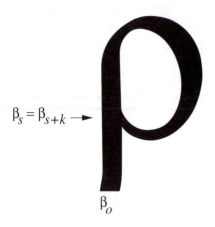

$\beta_s = \beta_{s+k} \longrightarrow$

β_o

FIGURE 9.1   The Pollard ρ-algorithm.

To compute x, we must solve the congruence

$$128x \equiv 800 \bmod 2016.$$

Since $\gcd(128, 2016) = 32$ divides 800, this congruence has a solution that is unique modulo 63. To find x, we solve the congruence

$$4z \equiv 25 \bmod 63.$$

We obtain the solution $z = 22$. Therefore, the discrete logarithm is one of the values $x = 22 + k * 63$, $0 \le k < 32$. For $k = 16$, we find the discrete logarithm $x = 1030$.

Now we prove that the preceding algorithm will eventually find a match.

First, we show that the sequence $(\beta_i)_{i \geq 0}$ is periodic after a match occurs. Let $(s, s+k)$ be the first match, which is not necessarily found in the algorithm because the wrong elements are stored. Then $k > 0$ and $\beta_{s+k} = \beta_s$. Moreover, $\beta_{s+k+l} = \beta_{s+l}$ for $l \geq 0$ since the construction of the next group element only depends on the previous group element in the sequence, so the sequence (β_i) is in fact periodic. We can draw it as the Greek letter ρ (see Figure 9.1). The *preperiod* is the sequence $\beta_0, \beta_1, \ldots, \beta_{s-1}$. It has length s. The *period* is $\beta_s, \beta_{s+1}, \ldots, \beta_{s+k-1}$ and has length k.

Now we explain how a match is found if only one triplet is stored. Denote by i the index of the triplet that is currently stored. If $i = 2^j \geq$

s, then β_i is in the period. In addition, if $2^j \geq k$, then the sequence

$$\beta_{2^j+1}, \beta_{2^j+2}, \ldots, \beta_{2^{j+1}}$$

is at least as long as the period. One of its elements is equal to β_{2^j}. But this is exactly the sequence that is computed after b_{2^j} has been stored. All of its elements are compared with β_{2^j}. Hence, one of these comparisons will reveal a match. Because the sum of the lengths of the preperiod and the period is $O(\sqrt{|G|})$, it follows that the number of sequence elements that must be computed before a match is found is $O(\sqrt{|G|})$. Therefore, the algorithm has running time $O(\sqrt{|G|})$ and needs space for $O(1)$ triplets. This is much more space efficient than the baby-step giant-step algorithm.

The algorithm is even more efficient if eight triplets are stored. This works as follows. Initially, all eight triplets are equal to (β_0, x_0, y_0). Then those triplets are successively replaced. Let i be the index of the last stored triplet. Initially, we have $i = 0$. For $j = 1, 2, \ldots$ we compute (β_j, x_j, y_j) and do the following:

1. If β_j is equal to one of the stored group elements, then a match is found and the computation of the sequence terminates.

2. If $j \geq 3i$, then the first of the eight triplets is deleted and (β_j, x_j, y_j) is the new last triplet.

This modification does not change the asymptotic time or space complexity.

9.5 Pohlig-Hellman Algorithm

We now show that the problem of computing the discrete logarithm in our group G can be reduced to a discrete logarithm problem in a cyclic group of prime order if we know the factorization

$$n = |G| = \prod_{p|n} p^{e(p)}$$

of the group order $n = |G|$ of our cyclic group.

9.5.1   Reduction to prime powers

For each prime divisor p of n, we set

$$n_p = n/p^{e(p)}, \quad \gamma_p = \gamma^{n_p}, \quad \alpha_p = \alpha^{n_p}.$$

Then the order of γ_p is exactly $p^{e(p)}$ and

$$\gamma_p^x = \alpha_p.$$

The group element α_p belongs to the cyclic group generated by γ_p. Therefore, the discrete logarithm $x(p)$ of α_p to the base γ_p exists. The following theorem describes how the discrete logarithm x can be computed from all the $x(p)$.

Theorem 9.5.1

For a prime divisor p of n, let $x(p)$ be the discrete logarithm of α_p to the base γ_p. Moreover, let $x \in \{0, 1, \dots, n-1\}$ be a solution of the simultaneous congruence $x \equiv x(p) \bmod p^{e(p)}$ for all prime divisors p of n. Then x is the discrete logarithm of α to the base γ.

Proof.   We have

$$(\gamma^{-x}\alpha)^{n_p} = \gamma_p^{-x(p)}\alpha_p = 1$$

for all prime divisors p of n. Therefore, the order of the element $\gamma^{-x}\alpha$ is a divisor of n_p for all prime divisors p of n and therefore a divisor of the gcd of all n_p. But this gcd is 1. Hence, the order is 1 and this shows that $\alpha = \gamma^x$. $\square$

We have seen that the discrete logarithm x can be computed by first determining all $x(p)$ and then applying the Chinese remainder theorem. The baby-step giant-step algorithm takes time $O(\sqrt{p^{e(p)}})$ for computing $x(p)$. If n has more than one prime divisor, then this modification is already considerably faster than the application of the baby-step giant-step algorithm in the full group. The computing time for the application of the Chinese remainder theorem is negligible.

Example 9.5.2

As in Example 9.3.1, let G be the multiplicative group of residues mod 2017. Its order is

$$2016 = 2^5 * 3^2 * 7.$$

We compute the discrete logarithm $x(2)$ in a subgroup of order $2^5 = 32$, $x(3)$ in a subgroup of order 9, and $x(7)$ in a subgroup of order 7. For those computations, we could use the baby-step giant-step algorithm. A more efficient variant is described in the next section.

9.5.2   Reduction to prime orders

In the previous section, we have seen that the computation of discrete logarithms in the cyclic group G can be reduced to the computation of discrete logarithms in subgroups of prime power order. Now we will show that the computation of discrete logarithms in cyclic groups of prime power order can be reduced to the computation of discrete logarithms in subgroups of prime order.

Let $|G| = n = p^e$ for a prime number p and a positive integer e. We want to solve the congruence (9.1) in this group. We know that $x < p^e$. By Theorem 1.3.3, we can write

$$x = x_0 + x_1 p + \ldots + x_{e-1} p^{e-1}, \quad 0 \le x_i < p, \quad 0 \le i \le e-1. \quad (9.2)$$

We show that the coefficient x_i, $0 \le i \le e-1$ is a discrete logarithm in a group of order p.

Raise the equation $\gamma^x = \alpha$ to the power p^{e-1}. Then

$$\gamma^{p^{e-1}x} = \alpha^{p^{e-1}}. \quad (9.3)$$

Now we obtain from (9.2)

$$p^{e-1}x = x_0 p^{e-1} + p^e(x_1 + x_2 p + \ldots x_{e-1} p^{e-1}). \quad (9.4)$$

From Fermat's little theorem (see Theorem 2.11.1), (9.4), and (9.3) we obtain

$$(\gamma^{p^{e-1}})^{x_0} = \alpha^{p^{e-1}}. \quad (9.5)$$

By (9.5), the coefficient x_0 is a discrete logarithm in a group of order p because $\gamma^{p^{e-1}}$ is of order p. The other coefficients are determined recursively. Suppose that $x_0, x_1, \ldots, x_{i-1}$ have been determined. Then

$$\gamma^{x_i p^i + \ldots + x_{e-1} p^{e-1}} = \alpha \gamma^{-(x_0 + x_1 p + \ldots + x_{i-1} p^{i-1})}.$$

Denote the group element on the right-hand side by α_i. If we raise this equation to the power p^{e-i-1}, then we obtain

$$(\gamma^{p^{e-1}})^{x_i} = \alpha_i^{p^{e-i-1}}, \quad 0 \leq i \leq e-1. \tag{9.6}$$

This is a discrete logarithm problem with solution x_i. Hence, in order to compute $x(p)$ we must solve e DL problems in groups of order p.

Example 9.5.3

As in Example 9.3.1, we solve

$$5^x \equiv 3 \bmod 2017.$$

The order of the multiplicative group of residues mod 2017 is

$$n = 2016 = 2^5 * 3^2 * 7.$$

First, we determine $x(2) = x \bmod 2^5$. We obtain $x(2)$ as a solution of the congruence

$$(5^{3^2*7})^{x(2)} \equiv 3^{3^2*7} \bmod 2017.$$

This means that

$$500^{x(2)} \equiv 913 \bmod 2017.$$

To solve this congruence, we write

$$x(2) = x_0(2) + x_1(2) * 2 + x_2(2) * 2^2 + x_3(2) * 2^3 + x_4(2) * 2^4.$$

According to (9.6), the coefficient $x_0(2)$ is a solution of

$$2016^{x_0(2)} \equiv 1 \bmod 2017.$$

We obtain $x_0(2) = 0$ and $\alpha_1 = \alpha_0 = 913 + 2017\mathbb{Z}$. Hence, $x_1(2)$ is the solution of

$$2016^{x_1(2)} \equiv 2016 \bmod 2017.$$

We obtain $x_1(2) = 1$ and $\alpha_2 = 1579 + 2017\mathbb{Z}$. Hence, $x_2(2)$ is the solution of

$$2016^{x_2(2)} \equiv 2016 \bmod 2017.$$

We obtain $x_2(2) = 1$ and $\alpha_3 = 1 + 2017\mathbb{Z}$, so $x_3(2) = x_4(2) = 0$. Concluding those computations, we obtain

$$x(2) = 6.$$

Now we compute

$$x(3) = x_0(3) + x_1(3) * 3.$$

We obtain $x_0(5)$ as the solution of

$$294^{x_0(3)} \equiv 294 \bmod 2017,$$

so $x_0(3) = 1$ and $\alpha_1 = 294 + 2017\mathbb{Z}$. Hence, $x_1(3) = 1$ and

$$x(3) = 4.$$

Finally, we compute $x(7)$ as the solution of the congruence

$$1879^{x(7)} \equiv 1879 \bmod 2017,$$

so $x(7) = 1$. We obtain x as the solution of the simultaneous congruence

$$x \equiv 6 \bmod 32, \quad x \equiv 4 \bmod 9, \quad x \equiv 1 \bmod 7.$$

The solution is $x = 1030$.

9.5.3   Complete algorithm and analysis

We describe the complete Pohlig-Hellman algorithm and analyze it. First, the group elements $\gamma_p = \gamma^{n_p}$ and $\alpha_p = \alpha^{n_p}$ are computed for all prime divisors p of n. Then the coefficients $x_i(p)$ are computed for all prime divisors p of n and $0 \leq i \leq e(p) - 1$ using the Pollard ρ-algorithm or Shanks' baby-step giant-step algorithm. Finally, the Chinese remainder theorem is used to compute the discrete logarithm. The complexity of the algorithm is estimated in the following theorem.

Theorem 9.5.4
The Pohlig-Hellman algorithm finds discrete logarithms in the cyclic group G using $O(\sum_{p||G|}(e(p)(\log |G| + \sqrt{p})))$ group operations.

Proof.   We use the notation introduced in the previous section. The computation of the powers γ_p and α_p for a prime divisor p of $n = |G|$ requires $O(\log n)$ group operations. The computation of each digit in $x(p)$ for a prime divisor p of n requires $O(\log n)$ group operations for computing the powers and $O(\sqrt{p})$ group operations for the baby-step giant-step algorithm. The number of digits is $e(p)$. For the Chinese remaindering step no group operations are necessary.   □

Note that by Theorem 2.15.3 the time for the Chinese remaindering step is $O((\log |G|)^2)$.

Theorem 9.5.3 shows that the time for computing discrete logarithms with the Pohlig-Hellman algorithm is dominated by the square root of the largest prime divisor of $|G|$. If this prime divisor is small, then it is easy to compute discrete logarithms in G.

Example 9.5.5

The integer $p = 2 * 3 * 5^{278} + 1$ is a prime number. Its binary length is 649. The order of the multiplicative group of residues mod p is $p - 1 = 2 * 3 * 5^{278}$. The computation of discrete logarithms in this group is very easy because the largest prime divisor of the group order is 5. Therefore, this prime cannot be used in the ElGamal cryptosystem.

9.6   Index Calculus

For the multiplicative group of residues modulo prime numbers or, more generally, for the unit group of a finite field, there are more efficient DL algorithms, the *index calculus algorithms*. They are closely related to integer factoring algorithms such as the quadratic sieve and the number field sieve. In this section, we describe a simple index calculus algorithm.

9.6.1   Idea

Let p be a prime number, g a primitive root mod p, and $a \in \{1, \ldots, p-1\}$. We want to solve the discrete logarithm problem

$$g^x \equiv a \bmod p. \tag{9.7}$$

We choose a bound B and determine the set

$$F(B) = \{q \in \mathbb{P} : q \leq B\}.$$

This is the *factor base*. An integer b is called B-smooth if it has only prime factors in $F(B)$.

Example 9.6.1

Let $B = 15$. Then $F(B) = \{2, 3, 5, 7, 11, 13\}$. The number 990 is 15-smooth. Its prime factorization is $990 = 2 * 3^2 * 5 * 11$.

We proceed in two steps. First, we compute the discrete logarithms of the factor base elements; that is, we solve

$$g^{x(q)} \equiv q \bmod p \qquad (9.8)$$

for all $q \in F(B)$. Then we determine an exponent $y \in \{1, 2, \ldots, p-1\}$ such that $ag^y \bmod p$ is B-smooth. We obtain

$$ag^y \equiv \prod_{q \in F(B)} q^{e(q)} \bmod p \qquad (9.9)$$

with nonnegative exponents $e(q)$, $q \in F(B)$. Equations (9.8) and (9.9) imply

$$ag^y \equiv \prod_{q \in F(B)} q^{e(q)} \equiv \prod_{q \in F(B)} g^{x(q)e(q)} \equiv g^{\sum_{q \in F(B)} x(q)e(q)} \bmod p,$$

and hence

$$a \equiv g^{\sum_{q \in F(B)} x(q)e(q) - y} \bmod p.$$

Therefore,

$$x = \left(\sum_{q \in F(B)} x(q)e(q) - y \right) \bmod (p-1) \qquad (9.10)$$

is the discrete logarithm for which we were looking.

9.6.2 Discrete logarithms of the factor base elements

To compute the discrete logarithms of the factor base elements, we choose random numbers $z \in \{1, \ldots, p-1\}$ and compute $g^z \bmod p$. We check whether those numbers are B-smooth. If they are, we compute the decomposition

$$g^z \bmod p = \prod_{q\in F(B)} q^{f(q,z)}.$$

Each exponent vector $(f(q,z))_{q\in F(B)}$ is called a *relation*.

Example 9.6.2
We choose $p = 2027$, $g = 2$ and determine relations for the factor base $\{2,3,5,7,11\}$. We obtain

$$
\begin{array}{rclcll}
3*11 & = & 33 & \equiv & 2^{1593} & \bmod 2027 \\
5*7*11 & = & 385 & \equiv & 2^{983} & \bmod 2027 \\
2^7*11 & = & 1408 & \equiv & 2^{1318} & \bmod 2027 \\
3^2*7 & = & 63 & \equiv & 2^{293} & \bmod 2027 \\
2^6*5^2 & = & 1600 & \equiv & 2^{1918} & \bmod 2027.
\end{array}
$$

If we have found as many relations as there are factor base elements, then we try to find the discrete logarithms by solving a linear system. Using (9.8), we obtain

$$g^z \equiv \prod_{q\in F(B)} q^{f(q,z)} \equiv \prod_{q\in F(B)} g^{x(q)f(q,z)} \equiv g^{\sum_{q\in F(B)} x(q)f(q,z)} \bmod p.$$

This implies

$$z \equiv \sum_{q\in F(B)} x(q)f(q,z) \bmod (p-1) \tag{9.11}$$

for all z, so each relation yields one linear congruence. We can solve this linear system by applying the Gauss algorithm modulo each prime power l^e of $p-1$. If $e = 1$, then the standard Gauss algorithm over a field can be applied. If $e > 1$, then the linear algebra is slightly more complicated. Finally, the $x(q)$ are computed using the Chinese remainder theorem.

Example 9.6.3
We continue Example 9.6.2. If we write

$$q \equiv g^{x(q)} \bmod 2027, \quad q = 2,3,5,7,11$$

and use the relations from Example 9.6.2, then we obtain the linear system

$$x(3) + x(11) \equiv 1593 \bmod 2026$$
$$x(5) + x(7) + x(11) \equiv 983 \bmod 2026$$
$$7x(2) + x(11) \equiv 1318 \bmod 2026 \qquad (9.12)$$
$$2x(3) + x(7) \equiv 293 \bmod 2026$$
$$6x(2) + 2x(5) \equiv 1918 \bmod 2026.$$

Because $2026 = 2*1013$ and 1013 is prime, we solve this system mod 2 and mod 1013. We obtain

$$x(3) + x(11) \equiv 1 \bmod 2$$
$$x(5) + x(7) + x(11) \equiv 1 \bmod 2 \qquad (9.13)$$
$$x(2) + x(11) \equiv 0 \bmod 2$$
$$x(7) \equiv 1 \bmod 2.$$

We know that $x(2) = 1$ because the primitive root $g = 2$ is used, so we find

$$x(2) \equiv x(5) \equiv x(7) \equiv x(11) \equiv 1 \bmod 2, \quad x(3) \equiv 0 \bmod 2. \quad (9.14)$$

Next, we compute the discrete logarithms of the factor base elements mod 1013. Again, we have $x(2) = 1$. From (9.12), we get

$$x(3) + x(11) \equiv 580 \bmod 1013$$
$$x(5) + x(7) + x(11) \equiv 983 \bmod 1013$$
$$x(11) \equiv 298 \bmod 1013 \qquad (9.15)$$
$$2x(3) + x(7) \equiv 293 \bmod 1013$$
$$2x(5) \equiv 899 \bmod 1013.$$

This implies $x(11) \equiv 298 \bmod 1013$. To compute $x(5)$, we invert 2 mod 1013. The result is $2*507 \equiv 1 \bmod 1013$. Hence, $x(5) \equiv 956 \bmod 1013$. From the second congruence, we obtain $x(7) \equiv 742 \bmod 1013$. From the first congruence, we obtain $x(3) \equiv 282 \bmod 1013$. Using (9.14), we finally obtain

$$x(2) = 1, x(3) = 282, x(5) = 1969, x(7) = 1755, x(11) = 1311.$$

It is easy to verify that this result is correct.

9.6.3   Individual logarithms

When the discrete logarithms of the factor base elements are computed, then the discrete logarithm of a to the base g is determined. We choose a random $y \in \{1, \dots, p-1\}$. If $ag^y \bmod p$ is B-smooth, then (9.10) is applied. Otherwise, we choose a new y.

Example 9.6.4
We solve

$$2^x \equiv 13 \bmod 2027.$$

We choose a random $y \in \{1, \dots, 2026\}$ until all prime factors of $13 * 2^y \bmod 2027$ are in the factor base $\{2, 3, 5, 7, 11\}$. We find

$$2 * 5 * 11 = 110 \equiv 13 * 2^{1397} \bmod 2027.$$

Using (9.10), we obtain $x = (1+1969+1311-1397) \bmod 2026 = 1884$.

9.6.4   Analysis

It can be shown that the index calculus algorithm that was described in the previous sections has subexponential running time $L_p[1/2, c+o(1)]$ (see Section 8.4), where the constant c depends on the technical realization of the algorithm; for example, on the complexity of the algorithm for solving the linear system. The analysis is similar to the analysis of the quadratic sieve in Section 8.4. Since all of the generic algorithms described earlier have exponential running time, index calculus algorithms are asymptotically much more efficient and also much faster in practice.

9.7   Other Algorithms

There are more efficient variants of the index calculus algorithm. Currently, the fastest index calculus algorithm is the number field sieve (see [31]). It has running time $L_p[1/3, (64/9)^{1/3}]$ and was invented shortly after the discovery of the number field sieve factoring algorithm. Other efficient integer factoring algorithms also have DL variants. This shows that the integer factoring problem and the DL problem in finite fields are closely related. Therefore, cryptosystems based on the discrete logarithm problem in finite fields cannot really be considered to be an alternative to systems that are based on the difficulty of factoring integers. Real alternatives are the DL problem on elliptic curves or in algebraic number fields.

9.8 Generalization of the Index Calculus Algorithm

Although the baby-step giant-step algorithm and the Pollard ρ-algorithm work in any cyclic group, we have explained the index calculus algorithm only in multiplicative group of residues modulo a prime number. But in principle, the index calculus algorithm also works in any group. Some factor base of group elements is fixed. Relations for this factor base are computed. The discrete logarithms are computed by linear algebra techniques. However, the factor base must be chosen such that relations can be found efficiently. Unfortunately, for some groups, such as for elliptic curves over finite fields, it is not known how to choose the factor base and how to compute relations. Therefore, the index calculus algorithm is not applicable in those groups.

9.9 Exercises

Exercise 9.9.1
Solve the DL problem $3^x \equiv 693 \bmod 1823$ using the baby-step giant-step algorithm.

Exercise 9.9.2
Use the baby-step giant-step algorithm to compute the discrete logarithm of 15 to the base 2 mod 239.

Exercise 9.9.3

Solve the DL problem $g^x \equiv 507 \bmod 1117$ for the smallest primitive root $g \bmod 1117$ with the Pohlig-Hellman algorithm.

Exercise 9.9.4

Use the Pohlig-Hellman algorithm to compute the discrete logarithm of 2 to the base 3 mod 65537.

Exercise 9.9.5

Use the Pollard ρ-algorithm to solve the DL problem $g^x \equiv 15 \bmod 3167$ for the smallest primitive root $g \bmod 3167$.

Exercise 9.9.6

Use the variant of the Pollard ρ-algorithm that stores eight triplets (β, x, y) to solve the DL problem $g^x \equiv 15 \bmod 3167$ for the smallest primitive root $g \bmod 3167$. Compare the efficiency of this computation with the efficiency of the simple Pollard ρ-algorithm (Exercise 9.9.5).

Exercise 9.9.7

Use the index calculus algorithm with the factor base $\{2, 3, 5, 7, 11\}$ to solve $7^x \equiv 13 \bmod 2039$.

Exercise 9.9.8

Determine the smallest factor base that can be used in the index calculus algorithm to solve $7^x \equiv 13 \bmod 2039$.

10 CHAPTER | Cryptographic Hash Functions

In this chapter, we discuss cryptographic hash functions. They are used, for example, in digital signatures. Throughout this chapter, we assume that Σ is an alphabet.

10.1 Hash Functions and Compression Functions

By a *hash function*, we mean a map

$$h : \Sigma^* \to \Sigma^n, \quad n \in \mathbb{N}.$$

Thus, hash functions map arbitrarily long strings to strings of fixed length. They are never injective.

Example 10.1.1
The map that sends $b_1 b_2 \ldots b_k$ in $\{0, 1\}^*$ to $b_1 \oplus b_2 \oplus b_3 \oplus \cdots \oplus b_k$ is a hash function. It maps, for example, 01101 to 1. In general, it sends a string b to 1 if the number of ones in b is odd and to 0 otherwise.

Hash functions can be generated using *compression functions*. A compression function is a map

$$h : \Sigma^m \to \Sigma^n, \quad n, m \in \mathbb{N}, \quad m > n.$$

It maps strings of fixed length to strings of shorter length.

Example 10.1.2
The map that sends the word $b_1 b_2 \ldots b_m \in \{0, 1\}^m$ to $b_1 \oplus b_2 \oplus b_3 \oplus \cdots \oplus b_m$ is a compression function if $m > 1$.

Hash functions and compression functions are used in many contexts (e.g., for making dictionaries). In cryptography, they also play an important role. Cryptographic hash and compression functions must have properties that guarantee their security. We now describe these properties informally. Let $h : \Sigma^* \to \Sigma^n$ be a hash function or $h : \Sigma^m \to \Sigma^n$ a compression function. We denote the set Σ^* or Σ^m of arguments of h by D. If h is a hash function, then $D = \Sigma^*$. If h is a compression function, then $D = \Sigma^m$.

If h is used in cryptography, then $h(x)$ must be easy to compute for all $x \in D$. We will assume that this is the case.

The function h is called a *one-way function* if it is infeasible to invert h; that is, to compute an inverse image x such that $h(x) = s$ for a given image s. What does "infeasible" mean? It is complicated to describe this in a precise mathematical way. To do so, we would need the language of complexity theory (see [6]), which is beyond the scope of this book. Therefore, we only give an intuitive description. Any algorithm that on input of $s \in \Sigma^n$ tries to compute x with $h(x) = s$ almost always fails because it uses too much space or time. It is not known whether one-way functions exist. There are functions, however, that are easy to evaluate but for which no efficient inversion algorithms are known and that therefore can be used as one-way functions.

Example 10.1.3
If p is a randomly chosen 1024-bit prime and g is a primitive root mod p, then the function $f : \{0, 2, \ldots, p - 2\} \to \{1, 2, \ldots, p - 1\}$, $x \mapsto g^x$ mod p is easy to compute by fast exponentiation, but an efficient inversion function is not known because it is difficult to

compute discrete logarithms (see Chapter 9). Therefore, f can be used as a one-way function.

A *collision* of h is a pair $(x, x') \in D^2$ for which $x \neq x'$ and $h(x) = h(x')$. There are collisions of all hash functions and compression functions because they are not injective.

Example 10.1.4

A collision of the hash function from Example 10.1.1 is a pair of distinct strings, both of which have an odd number of ones, such as $(111, 101)$.

The function h is called *weak collision resistant* if it is infeasible to compute a collision (x, x') for a given $x \in D$. The following example shows where weak collision resistant functions are necessary.

Example 10.1.5

Alice wants to protect an encryption algorithm x on her hard disk from unauthorized changes. She uses a hash function $h : \Sigma^* \to \Sigma^n$ to compute the hash value $y = h(x)$ of the program x, and she stores this hash value y on her personal smart card. After work, Alice goes home and takes her smart card with her. On the next morning, Alice goes to her office. Before she uses the encryption program again, she checks whether the program is unchanged that is, whether the hash value of the program is the same as the hash value stored on her smart card.

This test is only secure if the hash function h is weak collision resistant. If not, then an adversary can compute another preimage x' of the hash value $h(x)$ and can change the program x to x' without Alice noticing.

Example 10.1.5 shows a typical use of collision resistant hash functions. They permit reducing the integrity of a document to the integrity of a much smaller string, which, for example, can be stored on a smart card.

The function h is called *(strong) collision resistant* if it is infeasible to compute any collision (x, x') of h. In some applications, it is even necessary to use strong collision resistant hash functions (e.g., for electronic signatures, which are discussed in the next chapter). It can be shown that collision resistant hash functions are one-way functions. The idea is the following. Suppose that there is an inversion algorithm for h. Then one randomly chooses a string x'. Using the inversion algorithm, an inverse image x of $y = h(x')$ is computed. Then (x, x') is a collision of h, unless $x = x'$.

10.2   Birthday Attack ·

In this section, we describe a simple attack on hash functions

$$h : \Sigma^* \to \Sigma^n$$

called the *birthday attack*. It attacks the strong collision resistance of h. The attack is based on the birthday paradox.

In the birthday attack, we compute as many hash values as time and space permit. Those values are stored together with their inverse images and sorted. Then we look for a collision. Using the birthday paradox (see Section 4.3), we can analyze this procedure. The hash values correspond to birthdays. We assume that strings from Σ^* can be chosen such that the distribution on the corresponding hash values is the uniform distribution. In Section 4.3, we have shown the following: If k strings in $x \in \Sigma^*$ are chosen, where

$$k \geq (1 + \sqrt{1 + (8 \ln 2)|\Sigma|^n})/2,$$

then the probability of two hash values being equal exceeds $1/2$. For simplicity, we assume that $\Sigma = \{0, 1\}$. Then

$$k \geq f(n) = (1 + \sqrt{1 + (8 \ln 2)2^n})/2$$

is sufficient. The following table shows $\log_2(f(n))$ for typical sizes of n.

n	50	100	150	200
$\log_2(f(n))$	25.24	50.24	75.24	100.24

Hence, if we compute a little more than $2^{n/2}$ hash values, then the birthday attack finds a collision with probability $> 1/2$. To prevent the birthday attack, n has to be chosen such that the computation of $2^{n/2}$ hash values is infeasible. Today, $n \geq 128$ or sometimes even $n \geq 160$ is required.

10.3 Compression Functions from Encryption Functions

It is unknown whether collision resistant hash functions exist. It is also not known whether secure and efficient encryption schemes exist. It is, however, possible to construct a hash function from an encryption function that appears to be collision resistant as long as the encryption scheme is secure. We will describe this now.

We use a cryptosystem with plaintext space, ciphertext space, and key space $\{0, 1\}^n$. The encryption functions are $e_k : \{0, 1\}^n \to \{0, 1\}^n$, $k \in \{0, 1\}^n$. The hash values have length n. To prevent the birthday attack, we chose $n \geq 128$. Therefore, DES cannot be used.

The hash function

$$h : \{0, 1\}^n \times \{0, 1\}^n \to \{0, 1\}^n$$

can be defined as follows:

$$h(k, x) = e_k(x) \oplus x$$
$$h(k, x) = e_k(x) \oplus x \oplus k$$
$$h(k, x) = e_k(x \oplus k) \oplus x$$
$$h(k, x) = e_k(x \oplus k) \oplus x \oplus k.$$

As long as the cryptosystem is secure, those hash functions appear to be collision resistant. Unfortunately, no proof for this statement is known.

10.4 Hash Functions from Compression Functions

Collision resistant compression functions can be used to construct collision resistant hash functions. This was shown by R. Merkle, and we now describe his idea.

Let

$$g : \{0, 1\}^m \to \{0, 1\}^n$$

be a compression function and let

$$r = m - n.$$

Since g is a compression function, we have $r > 0$. A typical choice for n and r is $n = 128$ and $r = 512$. From g, we want to construct a hash function

$$h : \{0, 1\}^* \to \{0, 1\}^n.$$

Let $x \in \{0, 1\}^*$. We explain the computation of $h(x)$ in the case $r > 1$. The case $r = 1$ is left to the reader as an exercise. We append a minimum number of zeros to x such that the length of the new string is divisible by r. To this string we append r zeros. Now we determine the binary representation of the original string x. We append zeros to that representation such that its length is divisible by $r - 1$. In front of the normalized representation string and in front of each $(r - 1)j$th, $j = 1, 2, 3, \ldots$, symbol of that string we insert a one. The resulting representation string is appended to the previously normalized string. The complete string is written as a sequence

$$x = x_1 x_2 \ldots x_t, \quad x_i \in \{0, 1\}^r, \quad 1 \leq i \leq t$$

of words of length r. Note that each word in the part which represents the length of the original x starts with the symbol 1.

Example 10.4.1

Let $r = 4$, $x = 111011$. First, we transform x into 0011 1011. Then we append 0000 to that string. We obtain 0011 1011 0000. The length of the original x is 6. The binary expansion of 6 is 110. It is written as 1110. So we finally obtain the string 0011 1011 0000 1110.

The hash value $h(x)$ is computed iteratively. We set

$$H_0 = 0^n.$$

This string consists of n zeros. Then we determine

$$H_i = g(H_{i-1} \circ x_i), \quad 1 \leq i \leq t.$$

Finally, we set

$$h(x) = H_t.$$

We show that h is collision resistant if g is collision resistant by proving that from a collision of h we can determine a collision of g.

Let (x, x') be a collision of h. Moreover, let $x_1, \ldots, x_t, x'_1, \ldots, x'_{t'}$ be the block sequences for x and x' as above and let $H_0, \ldots, H_t$, $H'_0, \ldots, H'_{t'}$ be the corresponding sequences of hash values. Assume that $t \leq t'$. Then

$$H_t = H'_{t'}$$

since (x, x') is a collision of h. First, we assume that there is an index i with $0 \leq i < t$ such that

$$H_{t-i} = H'_{t'-i}$$

and

$$H_{t-i-1} \neq H'_{t'-i-1}.$$

Then

$$H_{t-i-1} \circ x_{t-i} \neq H'_{t'-i-1} \circ x'_{t'-i}$$

and

$$g(H_{t-i-1} \circ x_{t-i}) = H_{t-i} = H'_{t'-i} = g(H'_{t'-i-1} \circ x'_{t'-i}).$$

This is a collision of g. Now assume that

$$H_{t-i} = H'_{t'-i}, \quad 0 \leq i \leq t.$$

Below we show that there is an index i with $0 \leq i \leq t - 1$ and

$$x_{t-i} \neq x'_{t'-i}.$$

This implies

$$H_{t-i-1} \circ x_{t-i} \neq H'_{t'-i-1} \circ x'_{t'-i}$$

and

$$g(H_{t-i-1} \circ x_{t-i}) = H_{t-i} = H'_{t'-i} = g(H'_{t'-i-1} \circ x'_{t'-i}).$$

Hence, we have found a collision of g.

We show that there is an index i with $0 \leq i < t$ such that

$$x_{t-i} \neq x'_{t'-i}.$$

TABLE 10.1   Parameter for special hash functions.

hash function	block length	relative speed
MD4	128	1.00
MD5	128	0.68
RIPEMD-128	128	0.39
SHA-1	160	0.28
RIPEMD-160	160	0.24

If the number of words required to represent the length of x is smaller than the number of words required to represent the length of x', then there is an index i such that x_{t-i} (the string between x and the representation of its length) is the zero string but $x'_{t'-i}$ is non-zero since it starts with 1 (because all words in the representation of the length of x' start with 1).

If the number of words required to represent the length of x is the same as the number of words required to represent the length of x' but the length of x is different from the length of x' then the representations of the lengths contain a different word with the same index.

10.5   Efficient Hash Functions

The hash functions that are used in practice are constructed as in Section 10.4. Modifications of this construction hasten the evaluation. Table 10.1 contains technical data of some practically used hash functions.

All of the hash functions in the table are very efficient.

The hash function MD4 can no longer be considered as collision resistant because by computing 2^{20} hash values a collision can be found. However, the construction principle of MD4 is used in all other hash functions in this table. Also, MD5 is no longer totally secure since a collision of its compression function has been found.

10.6 An Arithmetic Compression Function

As we have mentioned earlier, there are no provably collision resistant compression functions. There is, however, a compression function that can be proven to be collision resistant if computing discrete logarithms in $(\mathbb{Z}/p\mathbb{Z})^*$ is infeasible. It was invented by Chaum, van Heijst, and Pfitzmann, and we will explain how it works.

Let p be a prime number, $q = (p-1)/2$ also a prime number, a a primitive root mod p, and b randomly chosen in $\{1, 2, \ldots, p-1\}$. Consider the following map:

$$h : \{0, 1, \ldots, q-1\}^2 \to \{1, \ldots, p-1\}, \quad (x_1, x_2) \mapsto a^{x_1} b^{x_2} \bmod p.$$

$$(10.1)$$

This is not a compression function as defined in Section 10.1. However, since $q = (p-1)/2$, it maps bitstrings (x_1, x_2), whose binary length is approximately twice the binary length of p, to strings whose binary length is at most that of p. It is not difficult to modify this function in such a way that it is a compression function in the sense of Section 10.1.

Example 10.6.1
Let $q = 11$, $p = 23$, $a = 5$, $b = 4$. Then $h(5, 10) = 5^5 \cdot 4^{10} \bmod 23 = 20 \cdot 6 \bmod 23 = 5$.

A collision of h is a pair $(x, x') \in \{0, 1, \ldots, q-1\}^2 \times \{0, 1, \ldots, q-1\}^2$ with $x \neq x'$ and $h(x) = h(x')$. We show that being able to find a collision of h implies the ability of computing the discrete logarithm of b for base a mod p.

Let (x, x') be a collision of h, $x = (x_1, x_2)$, $x' = (x_3, x_4)$, $x_i \in \{0, 1, \ldots, q-1\}$, $1 \leq i \leq 4$. Then

$$a^{x_1} b^{x_2} \equiv a^{x_3} b^{x_4} \bmod p,$$

which implies

$$a^{x_1 - x_3} \equiv b^{x_4 - x_2} \bmod p.$$

Denote by y the discrete logarithm of b for base a modulo p. Then

$$a^{x_1 - x_3} \equiv a^{y(x_4 - x_2)} \bmod p.$$

Since a is a primitive root modulo p, this implies the congruence

$$x_1 - x_3 \equiv y(x_4 - x_2) \mod (p - 1) = 2q. \qquad (10.2)$$

This congruence has a solution y, namely the discrete logarithm of b for base a. This is only possible if $d = \gcd(x_4 - x_2, p - 1)$ divides $x_1 - x_3$ (see Exercise 2.22.11). Because of the choice of x_2 and x_4, we have $|x_4 - x_2| < q$. Since $p - 1 = 2q$, this implies

$$d \in \{1, 2\}.$$

If $d = 1$, then (10.2) has a unique solution modulo $p - 1$. The discrete logarithm y can be determined as the smallest nonnegative solution of this congruence. If $d = 2$, then the congruence has two different solutions mod $p - 1$ and the discrete logarithm can be found by trying both.

We have seen that the compression function from (10.1) is collision resistant as long as the computation of discrete logarithms is difficult. Therefore, collision resistance has been reduced to a well-studied problem of number theory. Unfortunately, the evaluation of this compression function is not very efficient, since it requires modular exponentiations. Therefore, this hash function is only of theoretical interest.

10.7   Message Authentication Codes

Cryptographic hash functions can be used to check whether a file has been changed. The hash value of the file is stored separately. The integrity of the file is checked by computing the hash value of the actual file and comparing it with the stored hash value. If the two hash values are the same, then the file is unchanged.

If not only the integrity of a document but also the authenticity is to be proven, then parameterized hash functions can be used.

Definition 10.7.1
A *parameterized hash function* is a family $\{h_k : k \in \mathcal{K}\}$ of hash functions. Here, $\mathcal{K}$ is a set. It is called the *key space* of h.

A parameterized hash function is also called a *message authentication code* or MAC.

Example 10.7.2
Consider a hash function

$$g : \{0, 1\}^* \to \{0, 1\}^4.$$

It can be transformed into the MAC

$$h_k : \{0, 1\}^* \to \{0, 1\}^4, \quad x \mapsto g(x) \oplus k$$

with key space $\{0, 1\}^4$.

The following example shows how MACs can be used.

Example 10.7.3
Professor Alice sends a list with the names of all students who have passed the cryptography class via email to the college office. It is important that the college office be convinced that this email is authentic. For the proof of authenticity, a MAC $\{h_k : k \in \mathcal{K}\}$ is used. Alice and the college office exchange a secret key $k \in \mathcal{K}$. Together with her list x, Alice also sends the hash value $y = h_k(x)$ to the college office. Bob, the secretary, can also compute the hash value $y' = h_k(x')$ of the received message x'. He accepts x' if $y = y'$.

The protocol from Example 10.7.3 only proves the authenticity if without the knowledge of k it is infeasible to compute a pair $(x', h_k(x'))$ from the pair $(x, h_k(x))$ with $x \neq x'$.

A MAC can, for example, be constructed as follows. We use a block cipher with the CBC mode and throw away all blocks of the ciphertext except for the last one, which is the hash value. We give no further details but refer the reader to [24].

10.8   Exercises

Exercise 10.8.1
Construct a one-way function that is secure if factoring integers is difficult.

Exercise 10.8.2

For a permutation π in S_3, let e_π be the bit permutation of bitstrings of length 3. For each $\pi \in S_3$, determine the number of collisions of the compression function $h_\pi : \{0,1\}^3 \times \{0,1\}^3 \to \{0,1\}^3$, $(x_1, x_2) \mapsto e_\pi(x_1) \oplus x_2$.

Exercise 10.8.3

Consider the hash function $h : \{0,1\}^* \to \{0,1\}^*$, $k \mapsto \lfloor 10000(k(1 + \sqrt{5})/2) \bmod 1) \rfloor$, where the strings are identified with the integers they represent and $r \bmod 1 = r - \lfloor r \rfloor$ for a nonnegative real number r.

1. Determine the maximal length of the images.
2. Find a collision for this hash function.

Exercise 10.8.4

We consider the hash function h obtained from the compression function e_π from Exercise 10.8.2 with $\pi = \begin{pmatrix} 1 & 2 & 3 \\ 3 & 2 & 1 \end{pmatrix}$ as described in Section 10.4. Determine $h(0101010101011)$.

11
C H A P T E R

Digital Signatures

11.1 Idea

Digital signatures are used to sign electronic documents. Such signatures have properties similar to handwritten signatures. We will briefly describe those properties here.

If Alice signs a document with her handwritten signature, then everybody who sees the document and who knows Alice's signature can verify that Alice has in fact signed the document. For example, the signature can be used in a trial as proof that Alice has knowledge of the document and has agreed to its contents.

In many situations, electronic documents also must be signed. For example, electronic contracts, electronic bank transactions, and binding electronic mails must be signed.

In principle, digital signatures work as follows. Suppose that Alice wants to sign the document m. She uses a secret key d and computes the signature $s(d, m)$. Using the corresponding public key e, Bob can verify that $s(d, m)$ is in fact the signature of m.

Such a signature scheme is secure if nobody can produce the signature $s(d, m)$ without the knowledge of the secret d. In the following sections, we describe some of the known signature schemes. By Σ we denote an alphabet.

A Signatures

we have described the oldest public-key system, the ~~~~tem. This system can also be used to generate digital signatures. The idea is very simple. Alice signs the document m by computing the signature $s = s(d, m) = m^d \bmod n$. Here d is Alice's secret exponent and n is the public RSA modulus. Bob verifies the signature by computing $s^e \bmod n = m^{ed} \equiv m \bmod n$. The verification congruence follows from Theorem 7.2.4.

Why is this a signature? By raising the randomly looking number s to the power e, Bob can recover the document m. Therefore, s can be considered to be the eth root of the document m, and currently computing eth roots of an integer $m \bmod n$ without the knowledge of d is infeasible. But Alice is the only person who knows d, so Alice must have computed s and thereby signed m.

11.2.1   Key generation

The key generation for RSA signatures is the same as the key generation for RSA encryption. Alice chooses independently two large random primes p and q and an exponent e with $1 < e < (p-1)(q-1)$ and $\gcd(e, (p-1)(q-1)) = 1$. She computes $n = pq$ and $d \in \mathbb{Z}$ with $1 < d < (p-1)(q-1)$ and $de \equiv 1 \bmod (p-1)(q-1)$. Her public key is (n, e) and her secret key is d.

11.2.2   Signature generation

We explain how Alice signs $m \in \{0, 1, \ldots, n-1\}$. The integer m can be a short document or message or the hash value of a long message (see Section 11.2.6). To sign m, Alice computes

$$s = m^d \bmod n. \tag{11.1}$$

The signature is s. This signing method has its problems, as we will see later. But for the moment, we are only interested in the principle.

11.2.3 Verification

Bob wants to verify the signature s. He gets Alice's public key (n, e) from some public directory and recovers the signed message by computing

$$m = s^e \bmod n. \tag{11.2}$$

This equation follows from Theorem 7.2.4. Which information has Bob obtained by computing m? He now knows the signed message m. Since he has computed m from s, he knows that s is the signature of m. He does not need to know m in advance. But he is sure that Alice has generated s. Given his present knowledge, s cannot be computed without d, and d is Alice's secret.

Anyone who knows Alice's public key, for example a judge, can verify this signature.

Example 11.2.1
Alice chooses $p = 11$, $q = 23$, $e = 3$. She obtains $n = 253$, $d = 147$. Alice's public key is $(253, 3)$. Her private key is 147.

Alice wants to obtain \$ 111 from an automated teller machine. She signs 111. She computes $s = 111^{147} \bmod 253 = 89$. The cash dispenser computes $m = s^3 \bmod 253 = 111$. The machine knows that Alice wants to withdraw \$ 111 and it can also prove it to third parties.

11.2.4 Attacks

If the RSA signature is implemented as described thus far, then there are a number of possible attacks.

In order to verify a signature from Alice, Bob gets Alice's public key. If the attacker, Oscar, is able to replace Alice's public key with his own public key without Bob noticing this, then he can sign in Alice's name. Therefore, it is important that Bob be able to convince himself that he has Alice's authentic public key. This is the reason for using a trust center (see Chapter 14).

Another attack works as follows. Oscar chooses an integer $s \in \{0, \ldots, n - 1\}$. Then he claims that s is an RSA signature of Alice. Bob wants to verify this signature. He computes $m = s^e \bmod n$ and believes that Alice has signed m. If m is a meaningful text, then Oscar was able to fake a signature of Alice. This is called an *existential forgery*.

Example 11.2.2

As in Example 11.2.1, Alice chooses $p = 11$, $q = 23$, $e = 3$. She obtains $n = 253$, $d = 147$. Alice's public key is $(253, 3)$. Her private key is 147.

Oscar wants to withdraw money from Alice's account. He sends the signature $s = 123$ to the cash dispenser. The cash dispenser computes $m = 123^{147} \bmod 253 = 117$. It believes that Alice wants to withdraw \$ 117, but this is not true. Alice has never signed the \$ 117. She was the victim of an existential forgery.

Another danger comes from the fact that RSA is multiplicative. If $m_1, m_2 \in \{0, \dots, n-1\}$ and $s_1 = m_1^d \bmod n$ and $s_2 = m_2^d \bmod n$ are the signatures of m_1 and m_2, then

$$s = s_1 s_2 \bmod n = (m_1 m_2)^d \bmod n$$

is the signature of $m = m_1 m_2$. From two valid RSA signatures, a third one can be computed.

In the following section, we explain how the attacks from this section can be prevented.

11.2.5   Signature with redundancy

Two of the attacks of the previous section are impossible if only integers $m \in \{0, 1, \dots, n-1\}$ having a binary expansion of the form wow with $w \in \{0, 1\}^*$ can be signed. Thus, the binary expansion has two identical halves. The text that is really signed is, of course, w, but the string wow is technically signed. When verifying a signature, Bob computes $m = s^e \bmod n$. He checks whether the binary expansion of m is of the form $w \circ w$. If not, then the signature is rejected.

If only documents of the form $w \circ w$ are signed, then the existential forgery of the previous section no longer works. Oscar would need to come up with a false signature $s \in \{0, 1, \dots, n-1\}$ such that the binary expansion of $m = s^e \bmod n$ is of the form $w \circ w$. It is not known how such an s can be constructed without the knowledge of the private key. The multiplicativity of RSA can no longer be used because it is extremely unlikely that $m = m_1 m_2 \bmod n$ is a binary expansion of the form $w \circ w$ if this is true for the two factors.

The function

$$R : \{0, 1\}^* \to \{0, 1\}^*, w \mapsto R(w) = w \circ w,$$

which is used for the generation of the special structure of the documents that can be signed, is called a *redundancy function*. Clearly, other redundancy functions can also be used.

11.2.6   Signature with hash functions

Thus far, we have explained how documents m that are integers in $\{0, 1, \ldots, n - 1\}$ are signed. By verifying the signature, Bob also obtains the document that has been signed.

If Alice wants to sign an arbitrarily long document x, then she uses a publicly known collision resistant hash function

$$h : \{0, 1\}^* \to \{0, \ldots, n - 1\}.$$

Since h is collision resistant, h is also a one-way function (see Section 10.1). In practice, h is constructed using a standard collision resistant hash function whose values are, for example, 160 bitstrings. They are expanded by a method that is described in the standard PKCS #1 (see [24]).

The signature of the document x is

$$s = h(x)^d \bmod n.$$

From this signature, only the hash value $h(x)$ but not the document x can be reconstructed. Therefore, Bob can only verify the signature of x if he also knows the document x. After Alice computes the signature s of x, she sends s together with the document x to Bob. Bob computes $m = s^e \bmod n$ and compares this number with the hash value of x. Since the hash function is public, Bob can compute this hash value. If m and $h(x)$ are equal, Bob accepts the signature. Otherwise, he rejects it.

This procedure makes the existential forgery from Section 11.2.4 impossible. Suppose that Oscar chooses the signature s. Because he must send a document x together with s to Bob, he must come up with x such that $h(x) = s^e \bmod n$. This is exactly what Bob checks when he tries to verify the signature, so x is an inverse image of $m = s^e \bmod n$ under h. Because the hash function h is one way, Bob cannot compute such an x.

The multiplicativity attack from Section 11.2.4 can no longer be applied. Since h is one way, it is impossible to find x such that $h(x) = m = m_1 m_2 \bmod n$.

Finally, Oscar cannot replace the document x signed by Alice by another document x' since the pair (x, x') is a collision of h and h is collision resistant.

11.2.7   Choice of p and q

If Oscar can factor the RSA modulus, then he can determine Alice's secret key d and can sign documents in Alice's name. Therefore, p and q must be chosen such that n cannot be factored. For the RSA cryptosystem, the choice of p and q has already been described in Section 7.2.6.

11.3   Signatures from Public-Key Systems

Consider another public-key cryptosystem. For a pair (e, d) of public key and corresponding private key, let E_e be the encryption function and let D_d be the decryption function. Suppose that for any such pair (e, d) and any plaintext m, we have

$$m = E(D(m, d), e). \tag{11.3}$$

Then a signature scheme can be constructed from this public-key system. The signature of the document x is $s = D(h(x), d)$, where h is a publicly known collision resistant hash function. This signature is verified by computing $h(x) = E(s, e)$. The verification works because of (11.3). It is also possible to use a redundancy function instead of the hash function. The details are explained in the standard ISO/IEC 9796 [2].

Note that RSA satisfies (11.3) since

$$(m^d)^e \equiv (m^e)^d \equiv m \bmod n$$

for any public RSA key (n, e) with corresponding private key d. The Rabin cryptosystem can also be transformed into a signature scheme (see Exercise 11.6.3).

11.4   ElGamal Signature

The ElGamal signature scheme is similar to the ElGamal cryptosystem (see Section 7.5), although it is not constructed from it by the method described in Section 11.3. Its security is based on the difficulty of computing discrete logarithms in $(\mathbb{Z}/p\mathbb{Z})^*$, where p is a prime number.

11.4.1   Key generation

Key generation is the same as for the ElGamal encryption system (see Section 7.5.1). Alice generates a large random prime p and a primitive root $g \bmod p$. She also chooses a randomly in the set $\{1, 2, \ldots, p - 2\}$ and computes $A = g^a \bmod p$. Her private key is a. Her public key is (p, g, A).

11.4.2   Signature generation

Alice signs a document $x \in \{0, 1\}^*$. She uses the publicly known collision resistant hash function

$$h : \{0, 1\}^* \to \{1, 2, \ldots, p - 2\}.$$

Alice also chooses a random number $k \in \{1, 2, \ldots, p - 2\}$ which is prime to $p - 1$. She computes

$$r = g^k \bmod p, \quad s = k^{-1}(h(x) - ar) \bmod (p - 1). \qquad (11.4)$$

where k^{-1} is the inverse of k modulo $p-1$. The signature of x is the pair (r, s). Since a hash function has been used, the verifier cannot recover the document x from the signature. Alice has to give it to him.

11.4.3   Verification

Bob, the verifier, uses Alice's public key (p, g, A). As in the RSA signature scheme, he has to convince himself of the authenticity of this public key. He verifies that

$$1 \leq r \leq p - 1.$$

If this condition is not satisfied, then he rejects the signature; otherwise, he checks the congruence

$$A^r r^s \equiv g^{h(x)} \bmod p. \tag{11.5}$$

He accepts the signature if this congruence holds; otherwise, he rejects it.

We show that the verification works. If s is computed according to (11.4), then

$$A^r r^s \equiv g^{ar} g^{kk^{-1}(h(x)-ar)} \equiv g^{h(x)} \bmod p \tag{11.6}$$

as asserted. Conversely, if (11.5) is satisfied for a pair (r, s), and if k is the discrete logarithm of r to the base g then,

$$g^{ar+ks} \equiv g^{h(x)} \bmod p.$$

Since g is a primitive root mod p, Corollary 2.9.3 implies

$$ar + ks \equiv h(x) \bmod p - 1.$$

If k and $p-1$ are coprime, this implies (11.4). There is no other way to construct the signature.

Example 11.4.1
As in Example 7.5.1, Alice chooses $p = 23$, $g = 7$, $a = 6$ and computes $A = g^a \bmod p = 4$. Her public key is $(p = 23, g = 7, A = 4)$. Her private key is $a = 6$.

Alice wants to sign the document x, which has value $h(x) = 7$. She chooses $k = 5$ and obtains $r = 17$. The inverse of k mod $(p - 1 = 22)$ is $k^{-1} = 9$. Therefore, $s = k^{-1}(h(x) - ar) \bmod (p - 1) = 9 * (7 - 6 * 17) \bmod 22 = 3$. The signature is $(17, 3)$.

Bob wants to verify this signature. He computes $A^r r^s \bmod p = 4^{17} * 17^3 \bmod 23 = 5$. He also computes $g^{h(x)} \bmod p = 7^7 \bmod 23 = 5$, so the signature is verified.

11.4.4 Choice of p

If the attacker, Oscar, can compute discrete logarithms mod p, then he can determine Alice's secret key and can generate signatures in Alice's name. This remains the only known general method of generating ElGamal signatures. Therefore, p must be chosen such that computing discrete logarithms mod p is infeasible. Given the discrete logarithm algorithms known today, this means that p should be at least a 768-bit number. Also, primes of special forms for which certain DL algorithms such as the Pohlig-Hellman method (see Section 9.5) are particularly efficient must be avoided. As explained in Section 7.2.6, the best strategy is to use random primes.

It is also dangerous if $p \equiv 3 \bmod 4$, the primitive root g divides $p - 1$, and computing discrete logarithms in the subgroup of $(\mathbb{Z}/p\mathbb{Z})^*$ of order g is possible. This is discussed in Exercise 11.6.5. Therefore, g should not divide $p - 1$.

11.4.5 Choice of k

We show that for every new signature a new exponent k must be chosen. This is guaranteed if k is a random number.

Suppose that the signatures s_1 and s_2 of the documents x_1 and x_2 are generated with the same k. Then the number $r = g^k \bmod p$ is the same for both signatures. Therefore,

$$s_1 - s_2 \equiv k^{-1}(h(x_1) - h(x_2)) \bmod (p - 1).$$

From this congruence, k can be determined if $h(x_1) - h(x_2)$ is invertible modulo $p - 1$. From $k, s_1, r, h(x_1)$, Alice's secret key a can be determined since

$$s_1 = k^{-1}(h(x_1) - ar) \bmod (p - 1)$$

and therefore

$$a \equiv r^{-1}(h(x_1) - ks_1) \bmod (p - 1).$$

11.4.6   Existential forgery

If no hash function is used in the ElGamal signature system, then existential forgery is possible. Without a hash function, the verification congruence is

$$A^r r^s \equiv g^x \bmod p.$$

We show how r, s, x can be chosen such that this congruence is satisfied. To mount the existential forgery, Oscar chooses two integers u, v with $\gcd(v, p - 1) = 1$. Then he sets

$$r = g^u A^v \bmod p, \quad s = -rv^{-1} \bmod (p - 1), \quad x = su \bmod (p - 1).$$

With those values for r and s, the verification congruence

$$A^r r^s \equiv A^r g^{su} A^{sv} \equiv A^r g^{su} A^{-r} \equiv g^x \bmod p$$

holds.

This procedure also works if a collision resistant hash function is used. But since the hash function is a one-way function, it is impossible for Oscar to find a document x such that the signature generated is the signature of x.

As for the RSA signature scheme, the existential forgery described can also be prevented by using redundancy in the documents to be signed.

The condition $1 \le r \le p - 1$ is also crucial. If it is not required, then it is possible to generate new signatures from old signatures, as we now explain. Let (r, s) be the ElGamal signature of the document x. Let x' be another document. To sign x', Oscar computes

$$u = h(x')h(x)^{-1} \bmod (p - 1).$$

Here we assume that $h(x)$ is invertible mod $p - 1$. Oscar also computes

$$s' = su \bmod (p-1)$$

and, using the Chinese remainder theorem, he determines r' with

$$r' \equiv ru \bmod (p-1), \quad r' \equiv r \bmod p. \tag{11.7}$$

The signature of x' is (r', s'). The verification of this signature works because

$$A^{r'}(r')^{s'} \equiv A^{ru}r^{su} \equiv g^{u(ar+ks)} \equiv g^{h(x')} \bmod p.$$

We also show that $r' \geq p$ and therefore the condition $1 \leq r' \leq p-1$ is violated. On the one hand, we have

$$1 \leq r \leq p-1, \quad r \equiv r' \bmod p, \tag{11.8}$$

and on the other hand

$$r' \equiv ru \not\equiv r \bmod p - 1. \tag{11.9}$$

This follows from $u \equiv h(x')h(x)^{-1} \not\equiv 1 \bmod p - 1$ and from the fact that h is collision resistant. Now (11.9) implies $r \neq r'$ and (11.8) implies $r' \geq p$.

11.4.7 Efficiency

The generation of an ElGamal signature requires one application of the extended euclidean algorithm for the computation of $k^{-1} \bmod p - 1$ and one modular exponentiation mod p for the computation of $r = g^k \bmod p$. These are possible precomputations. They do not depend on the document to be signed. However, the result of the precomputation must be securely stored. The actual signature only requires two modular multiplications. It is extremely fast.

The verification of an ElGamal signature requires three modular exponentiations. This is considerably more expensive than an RSA signature verification. The verification can be sped up by using the congruence

$$g^{-h(x)}A^r r^s \equiv 1 \bmod p.$$

The exponentiation on the left-hand side can be carried out simultaneously as explained in Section 2.13. It follows from Theorem 2.13.1 that the verification requires at most $5 + t$ multiplications and $t - 1$ squarings mod p, where t is the binary length of p. This is only slightly more expensive than one modular exponentiation.

11.4.8 Generalization

Like the ElGamal cryptosystem, the ElGamal signature scheme can also be implemented in any cyclic group whose order is known. The implementation, including the security considerations, can be deduced from the implementation in $(\mathbb{Z}/p\mathbb{Z})^*$.

11.5 Digital Signature Algorithm (DSA)

The Digital Signature Algorithm (DSA) has been suggested and standardized by the National Institute of Standards and Technology (NIST) of the U.S. It is an efficient variant of the ElGamal signature scheme. The number of modular exponentiations in the verification is reduced from three to two and, more importantly, the number of digits in the exponents is 160 while in the ElGamal signature scheme the exponents have as many bits as the prime p (i.e., at least 768 bits).

11.5.1 Key generation

Alice chooses a prime number q with

$$2^{159} < q < 2^{160}.$$

Hence, q has binary length 160. Alice chooses a large prime p with the following properties:

- $2^{511+64t} < p < 2^{512+64t}$ for some $t \in \{0, 1, \dots, 8\}$,
- the prime number q, which was chosen first, divides $p - 1$.

The binary length of p is between 512 and 1024 and is a multiple of 64. Therefore, the binary expansion of p is a sequence of 8 to 16 bitstrings of length 64. The condition $q \mid (p-1)$ implies that the group $(\mathbb{Z}/p\mathbb{Z})^*$ contains elements of order q (see Theorem 2.20.1).

Next, Alice chooses a primitive root $x \bmod p$ and computes

$$g = x^{(p-1)/q} \bmod p.$$

Then $g + p\mathbb{Z}$ has order q in $(\mathbb{Z}/p\mathbb{Z})^*$. Finally, Alice chooses a random number a in the set $\{1, 2, \dots, q-1\}$ and computes

$$A = g^a \bmod p.$$

Alice's public key is (p, q, g, A). Her private key is a. Note that the residue class $A + p\mathbb{Z}$ is an element of the subgroup generated by $g + p\mathbb{Z}$. The order of this subgroup is approximately 2^{160}. Computing the secret key a from A requires the solution of a discrete logarithm problem in this subgroup. We will discuss the difficulty of this discrete logarithm problem below.

11.5.2   Signature generation

Alice wants to sign the document x. She uses the publicly known collision resistant hash function

$$h : \{0, 1\}^* \rightarrow \{1, 2, \dots, q-1\}.$$

She chooses a random number $k \in \{1, 2, \dots, q-1\}$, computes

$$r = (g^k \bmod p) \bmod q, \tag{11.10}$$

and sets

$$s = k^{-1}(h(x) + ar) \bmod q. \tag{11.11}$$

Here, k^{-1} is the inverse of k modulo q. The signature is (r, s).

11.5.3   Verification

Bob wants to verify the signature (r, s) of the document x. He gets Alice's authentic public key (p, q, g, A) and the public hash function.

Then he verifies that

$$1 \leq r \leq q - 1 \text{ and } 1 \leq s \leq q - 1. \qquad (11.12)$$

If this condition is violated, then Bob rejects the signature. Otherwise, Bob verifies that

$$r = ((g^{(s^{-1}h(x)) \bmod q} A^{(rs^{-1}) \bmod q}) \bmod p) \bmod q. \qquad (11.13)$$

If the signature is constructed according to (11.10) and (11.11), then (11.13) holds. In fact, the construction implies

$$g^{(s^{-1}h(x)) \bmod q} A^{(rs^{-1}) \bmod q} \equiv g^{s^{-1}(h(x)+ra)} \equiv g^{k} \bmod p,$$

which implies (11.13).

11.5.4 Efficiency

The DSA is very similar to the ElGamal signature scheme. As in the ElGamal scheme, precomputation makes the signature generation much faster.

   DSA verification is more efficient than ElGamal verification. On the one hand, only two exponentiations mod p are required, whereas ElGamal verification requires three exponentiations mod p. But this is not that important because ElGamal verification can be hastened if simultaneous exponentiation is used (see Sections 11.4.7 and 2.13). More important is the fact that the exponents in DSA are 160-bit numbers, whereas ElGamal exponents are as large as p (i.e., at least 768-bit numbers). This saves more than 600 squarings and multiplications mod p.

11.5.5 Security

As in the ElGamal signature scheme, it is necessary to choose a new random exponent k for each new signature (see Section 11.4.5). Moreover, the use of a hash function and checking condition (11.12) is mandatory to prevent possible existential forgery (see Section 11.4.6).

If Oscar can compute discrete logarithms in the subgroup H of $(\mathbb{Z}/p\mathbb{Z})^*$ generated by $g + p\mathbb{Z}$, then he is able to compute Alice's secret key a from her public key. He can then sign documents in Alice's name. This remains the only known general attack against DSA. But how difficult is the computation of discrete logarithm in the subgroup H, which, for efficiency reasons, is chosen much smaller than the residue class group $(\mathbb{Z}/p\mathbb{Z})^*$?

In principle, there are two methods of computing discrete logarithms in H. The first is to apply an index calculus algorithm in $\mathbb{Z}/p\mathbb{Z}$ (see Section 9.6). But it is unknown how index calculus algorithms can take advantage of the fact that a discrete logarithm in a subgroup of $(\mathbb{Z}/p\mathbb{Z})^*$ is to be computed. The running time of all known index calculus algorithms depends on the size of the prime number p, but p is chosen such that index calculus attacks are infeasible.

The second possibility is to apply a generic method that works for all cyclic groups. The most efficient generic methods in groups of prime order are due to Shanks and Pollard (see Sections 9.3 and 9.4). In a group of order q, they require more than $\sqrt{q}$ group operations. Since $q > 2^{159}$, this is infeasible with current technology.

11.6   Exercises

Exercise 11.6.1
Compute the RSA signature (without hash function) of $m = 11111$ with the RSA modulus $n = 28829$ and the smallest possible public exponent e.

Exercise 11.6.2
Is the low exponent or the common modulus attack on RSA a problem for RSA signatures?

Exercise 11.6.3
Describe a signature scheme that is based on the Rabin cryptosystem. Discuss its security and its efficiency.

Exercise 11.6.4
Compute the Rabin signature (without hash function) of $m = 11111$ with the Rabin modulus $n = 28829$.

Exercise 11.6.5
Let p be a prime number, $p \equiv 3 \mod 4$. Let g be a primitive root mod p and let $A = g^a \mod p$ be Alice's public key. Let g be a divisor of $p-1$ (i.e., $p-1 = gq$ with $q \in \mathbb{Z}$) and let $z \in \mathbb{Z}$ with $g^{qz} \equiv A^q \mod p$. Prove that for each document x the pair $(h(m), s = (p-3)(h(x) - qz)/2)$ is a valid ElGamal signature of m. How can this attack be prevented?

Exercise 11.6.6
Let $p = 130$. Compute a valid private key a and public key (p, g, A) for the ElGamal signature system.

Exercise 11.6.7
Let $p = 2237$ and $g = 2$. Assume that Alice's secret key is $a = 1234$. Let $h(x) = 111$ be the hash value of the document x. Compute the ElGamal signature with $k = 2323$ and verify this signature.

Exercise 11.6.8
Assume that in the ElGamal signature scheme the condition $1 \leq r \leq p-1$ is not required. Apply the existential forgery from Section 11.4.6 to construct an ElGamal signature of a document x' with hash value $h(x') = 99$ from the signature from Exercise 11.6.7.

Exercise 11.6.9
Use the same notation as in Exercise 11.6.7. Alice applies DSA, where q is the largest prime divisor of $p - 1$. She uses $k = 25$. What is the corresponding DSA signature? Verify it.

Exercise 11.6.10
Explain the existential forgeries from Section 11.4.6 for DSA.

Exercise 11.6.11
What is the verification congruence if in the ElGamal signature scheme s is computed as $s = (ar + kh(x)) \mod (p - 1)$?

Exercise 11.6.12
Modify the ElGamal signature system such that the verification only requires two exponentiations mod p.

12

CHAPTER

Other Groups

As we have described in Sections 7.4.4 and 11.4.8, the ElGamal cryptosystem and signature scheme can be implemented in groups in which the discrete logarithm problem is hard to solve. In this chapter, we describe a few possible groups. For more details, we refer the reader to the literature, for example to [17].

12.1   Finite Fields

We show that the ElGamal algorithms can be implemented in the unit group of any finite field, not only of the prime field $\mathbb{Z}/p\mathbb{Z}$ for a prime p.

12.1.1   Construction

The construction of a general finite field is similar to the construction of the prime field $\mathbb{Z}/p\mathbb{Z}$ for a prime number p.

Fix a prime number p and a polynomial f with coefficients in $\mathbb{Z}/p\mathbb{Z}$. This polynomial must be *irreducible*; that is, it is impossible to write $f = gh$, where g and h are polynomials in $(\mathbb{Z}/p\mathbb{Z})[X]$ whose degree is greater than zero. The elements of the finite field that we construct are the residue classes mod f. Those residue classes are similar to residue classes in $\mathbb{Z}$. The residue class mod f of the polynomial $g \in (\mathbb{Z}/p\mathbb{Z})[X]$ consists of all polynomials h in $(\mathbb{Z}/p\mathbb{Z})[X]$ such that $g - h$ is divisible by f (i.e., $g - h$ is a multiple of f). This residue class is written as $g + f(\mathbb{Z}/p\mathbb{Z})[X]$ since

$$g + f(\mathbb{Z}/p\mathbb{Z})[X] = \{g + hf : h \in (\mathbb{Z}/p\mathbb{Z})[X]\}.$$

By Theorem 2.19.2, each residue class mod f contains a uniquely determined representative that is either zero or whose degree is less than the degree of f. This representative can be determined by one division with remainder. If we want to decide whether the residue classes mod f of two polynomials are equal, then we compute those representatives for both classes and compare them.

We discuss operations on residue classes mod f. If $g, h \in (\mathbb{Z}/p\mathbb{Z})[X]$, then the sum of the residue classes of g and h mod f is defined as the residue class of $g + h$ mod f. Likewise, the product of the residue classes of g and h mod f is the residue class of the product gh mod f. Together with this addition and multiplication, the set of all residue classes mod f is a field with zero element $f(\mathbb{Z}/p\mathbb{Z})[X]$ and unit element $1 + f(\mathbb{Z}/p\mathbb{Z})[X]$. To invert a nonzero residue class $g + f(\mathbb{Z}/p\mathbb{Z})[X]$ we apply an analog of the extended euclidean algorithm. It finds a polynomial $r \in (\mathbb{Z}/p\mathbb{Z})[X]$ such that $gr + fs = 1$ with some other polynomial s. Then the inverse residue class is $s + f(\mathbb{Z}/p\mathbb{Z})[X]$.

If n is the degree of f, then the field that is constructed in this way has p^n elements. The reasons are that the residue classes of all polynomials whose degree is less than n are pairwise different and that any residue class contains such a polynomial.

If two fields are constructed in this way with polynomials of the same degree, then they are isomorphic. The isomorphism can be computed in polynomial time. Such a field is called the *Galois field* of degree n over $\mathbb{Z}/p\mathbb{Z}$. It is denoted by $\mathrm{GF}(p^n)$. In particular, we write $\mathrm{GF}(p) = \mathbb{Z}/p\mathbb{Z}$. The prime number p is called the *characteristic* of the field. The field $\mathrm{GF}(p)$ is called a *prime field*. For any positive integer n, the field $\mathrm{GF}(p^n)$ exists because there is an irreducible polynomial in $(\mathbb{Z}/p\mathbb{Z})[X]$ of degree n.

TABLE 12.1 Addition in GF(4).

+	0	1	α	$\alpha + 1$
0	0	1	α	$\alpha + 1$
1	1	0	$\alpha + 1$	α
α	α	$\alpha + 1$	0	1
$\alpha + 1$	$\alpha + 1$	α	1	0

TABLE 12.2 Multiplication in GF(4).

*	1	α	$\alpha + 1$
1	1	α	$\alpha + 1$
α	α	$\alpha + 1$	1
$\alpha + 1$	$\alpha + 1$	1	α

Example 12.1.1

We construct $GF(2^2) = GF(4)$. We need an irreducible polynomial f of degree 2 in $GF(2)[X]$. The polynomial $f(X) = X^2 + X + 1$ is irreducible since it has no zero (see Example 2.19.8).

The elements of $GF(4)$ are the residue classes of the polynomials 0, 1, X, and $X + 1$ mod f. Tables 12.1 and 12.2 are the addition and multiplication tables for $GF(4)$. Let $\alpha = X + f(\mathbb{Z}/2\mathbb{Z})[X]$. Note that α is a zero of $f(X)$ in $GF(4)$ (i.e., we have $\alpha^2 + \alpha + 1 = 0$).

12.1.2 DL problem

Let p be a prime number and let n be a positive integer. In Theorem 2.20.1, we have shown that the unit group of the finite field $GF(p^n)$ is cyclic. Its order is $p^n - 1$. If this order has only small prime factors, then the Pohlig-Hellman DL algorithm will efficiently compute discrete logarithms in this group (see Section 9.5). Otherwise, an index calculus algorithm can be applied (see Section 9.6). For fixed n, the number field sieve can be applied. For fixed p and growing n, the function field sieve is used. An overview can be found in [31]. Both algorithms have running time $L_q[1/3, c + o(1)]$ (see Section 8.4), where

c is a constant and $q = p^n$. If p and q grow simultaneously, then the best-known algorithm has only running time $L_q[1/2, c + o(1)]$.

12.2　Elliptic Curves

Elliptic curves can be defined over any field. In cryptography, elliptic curves over finite fields are of particular interest. To make things simple, we only describe elliptic curves over prime fields. For more details concerning elliptic curve cryptosystems we refer to [16], [23], and [7].

12.2.1　Definition

Let p be a prime number, $p > 3$ and let $a, b \in \mathrm{GF}(p)$. Consider the equation

$$y^2 z = x^3 + axz^2 + bz^3. \tag{12.1}$$

Its *discriminant* is

$$\Delta = -16(4a^3 + 27b^2). \tag{12.2}$$

We assume that Δ is nonzero. If $(x, y, z) \in \mathrm{GF}(p)^3$ is a solution of (12.1), then for any $c \in \mathrm{GF}(p)$ also $c(x, y, z)$ is a solution. Two solutions (x, y, z) and (x', y', z') are called *equivalent* if there is a nonzero $c \in \mathrm{GF}(p)$ with $(x, y, z) = c(x', y', z')$. This defines an equivalence relation on the set of all solutions of (12.1). The equivalence class of (x, y, z) is denoted by $(x : y : z)$. The *elliptic curve* $E(p; a, b)$ is the set of all equivalence classes of solutions of (12.1). Each element of this set is called a *point* on the curve.

We simplify the description of the elliptic curve. If (x', y', z') is a solution of (12.1) and if $z' \neq 0$, then $(x' : y' : z')$ contains exactly one element $(x, y, 1)$. Here (x, y) is a solution of the equation

$$y^2 = x^3 + ax + b. \tag{12.3}$$

Conversely, if $(x, y) \in \mathrm{GF}(p)^2$ is a solution of (12.3), then $(x, y, 1)$ is a solution of (12.1). Moreover, there is exactly one equivalence class of solutions of (12.1) which are all of the form $(x, y, 0)$. In fact, if $z = 0$, then we also have $x = 0$, so this equivalence class is $(0 : 1 : 0)$. Hence, we can write the elliptic curve as

$$E(p; a, b) = \{(x : y : 1) : y^2 = x^3 + ax + b\} \cup \{(0 : 1 : 0)\}.$$

We also write (x, y) instead of $(x : y : 1)$ and $\mathcal{O}$ instead of $(0 : 1 : 0)$, so

$$E(p; a, b) = \{(x, y) : y^2 = x^3 + ax + b\} \cup \{\mathcal{O}\}.$$

Example 12.2.1
We work in GF(11). The elements are represented by their smallest nonnegative representatives. Over this field, we consider the equation

$$y^2 = x^3 + x + 6. \tag{12.4}$$

We have $a = 1$ and $b = 6$. The discriminant is $\Delta = -16*(4+27*6^2) = 4$. Hence, (12.4) defines an elliptic curve over GF(11). It is

$$E(11; 1, 6) = \{\mathcal{O}, (2, 4), (2, 7), (3, 5), (3, 6), (5, 2), (5, 9), (7, 2),$$
$$(7, 9), (8, 3), (8, 8), (10, 2), (10, 9)\}.$$

12.2.2 Group structure

Let p be a prime number, $p > 3$, $a, b \in$ GF(p) and let $E(p; a, b)$ be an elliptic curve. We define the addition of points on that curve.

For a point P on the curve, we set

$$P + \mathcal{O} = \mathcal{O} + P = P.$$

Hence, the point $\mathcal{O}$ is a neutral element with respect to this addition.

Let P be a point different from $\mathcal{O}$, $P = (x, y)$. Then $-P = (x, -y)$ and we set $P + (-P) = \mathcal{O}$.

Let P_1 and P_2 be points on the curve that are different from $\mathcal{O}$ and satisfy $P_2 \neq \pm P_1$. Let $P_i = (x_i, y_i)$, $i = 1, 2$. Then the sum

$$P_1 + P_2 = (x_3, y_3)$$

is defined as follows. If

$$
\lambda =
\begin{cases}
\frac{y_2 - y_1}{x_2 - x_1}, & \text{for } P \neq Q, \\[2ex]
\frac{3x_1^2 + a}{2y_1}, & \text{for } P = Q,
\end{cases}
$$

then

$$
x_3 = \lambda^2 - x_1 - x_2, \qquad y_3 = \lambda(x_1 - x_3) - y_1.
$$

It can be shown that with this addition $E(p; a, b)$ is an abelian group.

Example 12.2.2
We use the curve from Example 12.2.1 and compute the sum $(2, 4) + (2, 7)$. Since $(2, 7) = -(2, 4)$, we have $(2, 4) + (2, 7) = \mathcal{O}$. Next, we compute $(2, 4) + (3, 5)$. We obtain $\lambda = 1$ and $x_3 = -4 = 7$, $y_3 = 2$. Hence, $(2, 4) + (3, 5) = (7, 2)$. Finally, we have $(2, 4) + (2, 4) = (5, 9)$, as the reader can easily verify.

12.2.3 Cryptographically secure curves

Again, let p be a prime number $p > 3$, $a, b \in GF(p)$ and $E(p; a, b)$ an elliptic curve. In the group $E(p; a, b)$, the Diffie-Hellman key-exchange system (see Section 7.4) and the ElGamal encryption and signature schemes (see Sections 7.4.4 and 11.4.8) can be implemented.

Those implementations are only secure if the discrete logarithm problem in $E(p; a, b)$ is difficult. Currently, the fastest DL algorithm on elliptic curves is the Pohlig-Hellman algorithm (see Section 9.5). This algorithm has exponential complexity. For special curves, the so-called *supersingular* and *anomalous* curves, faster algorithms are known.

To obtain an elliptic curve cryptosystem or signature scheme that is as secure as a 1024-bit RSA system, curves are used with approximately 2^{163} points. To prevent a Pohlig-Hellman attack, a prime factor $q \geq 2^{160}$ of the group order is required. We briefly describe how such a curve can be found.

The number of points on the curve $E(p; a, b)$ is estimated in the following theorem.

Theorem 12.2.3 (Hasse)
We have $|E(p; a, b)| = p + 1 - t$ with $|t| \leq 2\sqrt{p}$.

The theorem of Hasse guarantees that the elliptic curve $E(p; a, b)$ has approximately p points. To obtain a curve with 2^{163} points, we choose $p \sim 2^{163}$. If p is fixed, then the coefficients a and b are chosen at random. Then the order of $E(p; a, b)$ is determined. This is possible in polynomial time and takes a couple of minutes per curve. If the curve is supersingular, anomalous, or its order has no prime factor $q \geq 2^{160}$, then a new curve is generated. Otherwise, the curve is accepted.

There are more efficient ways of generating cryptographically secure curves.

12.2.4   Advantages of EC cryptosystems

There are several reasons to use elliptic curve cryptosystems.

Elliptic curve public-key systems are currently the most important alternative to RSA systems. Such alternatives are necessary since one day RSA may become insecure.

Elliptic curve systems have efficiency advantages over RSA and finite field systems. While in the latter systems modular arithmetic with 1024-bit numbers is used, the arithmetic on cryptographically secure elliptic curves works with 163-bit numbers. This is an efficiency advantage, although group operations on elliptic curves are more complicated than group operations in prime fields. Also, keys in elliptic curve systems are much smaller than keys in RSA and finite field systems.

12.3   Quadratic Forms

Class groups of binary quadratic forms or, more generally, class groups of algebraic number fields can also be used to implement cryptographic algorithms (see [9] and [10]). In some respects, class groups are different from the unit groups of finite fields and point groups of elliptic curves. The order of the unit group of GF(p^n) is $p^n - 1$. The order of an elliptic curve can be computed in polynomial time. But no efficient algorithm is known for computing the order of a class group. The known algorithms for solving this problem are closely related to DL algorithms in class groups and no more efficient. Also, class groups may be very small. However, if a class group is small it is very difficult to decide whether two elements in the class group are equal. In fact, there are cryptographic protocols whose security is based on the intractability of deciding equality in class groups. For more information on class group cryptography see [25].

12.4   Exercises

Exercise 12.4.1
Construct the finite field GF(9) with its addition and multiplication tables.

Exercise 12.4.2
1. Construct GF(125) and determine a generating element for the multiplicative group GF(125)*.
2. Determine a valid secret and public key for the ElGamal signature system in GF(125)*.

Exercise 12.4.3
Determine the number of points on the elliptic curve $y^2 = x^3 + x + 1$ over GF(7). Is the group of points on that curve cyclic? If it is cyclic, determine a generator of this curve.

Exercise 12.4.4
Let p be a prime number, $p \equiv 3 \bmod 4$, and let E be an elliptic curve over GF(p). Find a polynomial time algorithm that, given $x \in$ GF(p), computes a point (x, y) on E if it exists. Hint: use Exercise 2.22.21. Use this algorithm to find a point $(2, y)$ on $E(111119; 1, 1)$.

13

CHAPTER

Identification

In the previous chapters, two important basic mechanisms have been explained: encryption and digital signatures. In this chapter we describe a third basic technique: identification.

First, we present two examples for situations in which identification is necessary.

Example 13.0.5
Using Internet banking, Alice wants to find out how much money is left in her account. She must identify herself to the bank in order to prove that she is entitled to obtain that information.

Example 13.0.6
Bob works in a university where he uses a Unix workstation. When he comes to work, he identifies himself to his workstation in order to get access. The computer verifies Bob's identity and checks whether Bob is a legal user. If he is, access is granted to Bob. Typically, Bob proves his identity by presenting a secret password. This method of identification is not totally secure and will be discussed in Section 13.1.

Identification is required in many applications. Typically, the goal of an identification procedure is access control. Methods that permit identification are called *identification protocols*.

In an identification protocol, the *prover*, Bob, proves to the *verifier*, Alice, that it is really Bob who is communicating with Alice. Identification is a real-time problem.

In this chapter, we describe different identification protocols.

13.1　Passwords

Access to Unix or Windows NT is typically controlled by password systems. Each user picks his individual and secret password w. The computer stores the image $f(w)$ of the password w under a one-way function f. If the user wants access to his computer, he enters his name and password w. The computer determines $f(w)$ and compares the result with the stored value. If they are identical, then access is granted. Otherwise, the user is rejected.

Passwords are also used to control access to World Wide Web pages or to files that contain private encryption or signature keys.

The password file does not need to be kept secret since it contains only the images $f(w)$ of the passwords w and f is a one-way function. Nevertheless, password identification systems are not very secure.

A user must memorize his or her password. Therefore, many users choose the first name of their spouse or children as their password. An attacker can mount a dictionary attack. For all words w in a dictionary, he computes $f(w)$ and compares the result with the entries in the password file. If he finds an entry of the password file, he has determined the corresponding password. It is, therefore, recommended to use symbols such as $ or # in the the passwords. Then dictionary attacks are impossible, but it is also harder to memorize the passwords. It is also possible to store the password on a smart card. Instead of typing in his password, the prover inserts his smart card into the smart card reader. The verifier reads the password from the smart card. There is no need for the user to memorize or even know the password. On the contrary, if the user does not know his password he cannot give it away.

An attacker can also tap the connection between the prover and the verifier and can learn the password. This is particularly successful if there is a great distance between the prover and the verifier; for example, if a password system is used to protect World Wide Web access. Note that the use of smart cards does not prevent this attack.

Finally, the attacker can also replace an entry $f(w)$ in the password file with the image $f(v)$ of his own password v. Then, using the password v, he can get access. Therefore, the password file must be write protected.

13.2   One-Time Passwords

Using passwords is dangerous because an attacker can learn the passwords by tapping the connection between the prover and the verifier. With one-time passwords, this attack does not work. One-time passwords are used for one identification. For the next identification, a new one-time password is used.

A simple way of implementing one-time passwords is the following. The verifier has a list $f(w_1), f(w_2), \ldots, f(w_n)$ of images of passwords $w_1, \ldots, w_n$. The prover knows this list of passwords and uses its elements for the identifications. Since the prover must store all passwords in advance, an attacker could learn some or all of them.

It is also possible that the prover and the verifier share a secret one-way function f of an initial string w. Then the one-time passwords are $w_i = f^i(w), i \geq 0$. The prover can put the current password w_i and the one-way function f on a smart card. He does not need a large password file.

13.3   Challenge-Response Identification

Password identification protocols have the disadvantage that an attacker can learn passwords long before the actual identification. This is even true for one-time password systems.

Challenge response identification systems do not have this problem. Alice wants to identify herself to Bob in a challenge response system. Bob asks a question, the *challenge*. Alice computes the *response* using her secret key and sends it to Bob. Bob verifies the response using the same secret key or the corresponding public key.

13.3.1   Symmetric systems

We describe a simple challenge response identification system which uses a symmetric cryptosystem. We assume that the encryption key and the corresponding decryption key are the same. Alice and Bob share a secret key k. Alice wants to identify herself to Bob. Bob sends a random number r to Alice. Alice encrypts this random number by computing $c = E_k(r)$ and sends the ciphertext c to Bob. Bob decrypts the ciphertext; that is, he computes $r' = D_k(c)$ and compares the result with his chosen random number r. If $r = r'$, then he accepts the proof of identity; otherwise he rejects it.

This protocol proves that Alice knows the secret key at the time of the identification. It is not possible for Bob or an attacker to compute or obtain the correct response in advance. But since the verifier, Bob, also knows Alice's secret key, this key cannot be used for identification with another verifier since Bob can then pretend that he is Alice.

13.3.2   Public-key systems

Challenge response systems can also be based on public-key signature schemes. If Alice wants to identify herself, she obtains a random number from Bob and signs this random number with her private key. Bob verifies the signature, thereby verifying the identity of Alice.

In this protocol, Bob cannot pretend that he is Alice. He only knows Alice's public key. But it is necessary that Bob obtains the authentic public key of Alice. If the attacker, Oscar, can replace Alice's public key with his own, then he can convince Bob that he is Alice.

13.3.3   Zero-knowledge proofs

In a challenge response protocol, the prover proves that he knows a secret. If a symmetric cryptosystem is used, then the verifier also knows the secret. If a public-key signature system is used, then the verifier does not know the secret.

We now describe a *zero-knowledge* identification protocol. Again, the prover proves the knowledge of a secret, which the verifier does not know. During the protocol, the verifier learns nothing but the fact that the prover knows the secret. He gets no additional information about the secret. The protocol has the *zero-knowledge property*.

The protocol that we describe is the *Fiat-Shamir identification protocol*. As in the RSA scheme, the prover, Alice, chooses two large random primes p and q. Then she chooses a random number s from $\{1, \ldots, n-1\}$ and computes $v = s^2 \bmod n$. Bob's public key is (v, n). His secret key is s, a square root of $v \bmod n$.

In a zero-knowledge protocol, Alice proves to the verifier, Bob, that she knows a square root s of $v \bmod n$. This protocol works as follows.

1. Commitment: Alice chooses a random number $r \in \{1, 2, \ldots, n-1\}$ and computes $x = r^2 \bmod n$. She sends the result x to the verifier, Bob.

2. Challenge: Bob chooses a random number $e \in \{0, 1\}$ and sends it to Alice.

3. Response: Alice sends $y = rs^e \bmod n$ to Bob.

4. Verification: Bob accepts if and only if $y^2 = xv^e \bmod n$.

Example 13.3.1

Let $n = 391 = 17 * 23$. Alice's secret key is $s = 123$. Her public key is $(271, 391)$. In the identification protocol, Alice proves that she knows a square root of $v \bmod n$.

1. Commitment: Alice chooses the random number $r = 271$ and computes $x = r^2 \bmod n = 324$. She sends the result x to the verifier, Bob.

2. Challenge: Bob chooses the random number $e = 1$ and sends it to Alice.

3. Response: Alice sends $y = rs \bmod n = 98$ to Bob.

4. Verification: Bob accepts since $220 = y^2 \equiv vx \bmod n$.

We analyze the protocol.

If Alice knows the secret, the square root s of v mod n, then she can answer both possible questions correctly. We say that the protocol is *complete*.

If the attacker, Oscar, can compute a square root of v mod n, then he can also factor n. This was shown in Section 7.3.5. Because factoring integers is considered to be difficult, Alice's secret is secure.

But what happens if Oscar tries to impersonate Alice even though he does not know the secret? Then he cannot answer both possible questions correctly, as we will now show. Suppose that Oscar knows r and rs mod n. Then he can compute $s = rsr^{-1}$ mod n, so he knows Alice's secret. Because he does not know s, Oscar can only answer one question correctly. In fact, in order to be able to answer the challenge correctly for a fixed e, he chooses the commitment x as $x = y^2 v^{-e}$ mod n for some y. Then $y^2 = xv^e$ mod n. But, as we have seen, the knowledge of both answers implies the knowledge of a square root of v. Hence Oscar is not able to give the correct response for the other e. Therefore, the verifier notices with probability $1/2$ that Oscar is not Alice. After k iterations of the protocol, the verifier notices the fraud with probability $1 - 1/2^k$. This probability can be made arbitrarily close to 1. We say that the protocol is *correct*.

Finally we show that the Fiat-Shamir protocol has the *zero-knowledge property*. This means that the verifier, Bob, learns nothing from the protocol except that he is convinced that the prover knows Alice's secret. More technically, it means that Bob can simulate the protocol without Alice participating and obtains the same distribution on the messages as if he ran the real protocol with Alice. Since Bob gets all his information from the messages, he does not learn anything new. He can produce the message distributions himself.

Let us analyze the message distributions and then explain how the simulation works.

The commitment x is the square of a random number in $\{1, 2, \ldots, n-1\}$. The challenge e is a random number in $\{0, 1\}$. The response $y = rs^e$ mod n is a random number in $\{1, 2, \ldots, n-1\}$ because s is prime to n. Bob can simulate the protocol as follows. He chooses random numbers $y \in \{1, \ldots, n-1\}$ and $e \in \{0, 1\}$ and sets $x = y^2 v^{-e}$ mod n. Then $y^2 \equiv xv^e$ mod n as in the original protocol. The simulated commitment x is the square of a random number in

$\{1, 2, \ldots, n-1\}$. The challenge e is a random number in $\{0, 1\}$. The response y is a random number in $\{1, 2, \ldots, n-1\}$. Hence, the simulated protocol generates the same distributions on the messages as the original protocol.

Example 13.3.2
We start with the situation from Example 13.3.1. Bob simulates the identification protocol with Alice. He does not know a square root of 271 mod 391, so he starts by choosing the response $y = 271$. Then he chooses the challenge $e = 0$ and computes $x = y^2 \bmod n = 324$. Then the verification works.

For more details concerning zero knowledge, we refer the reader to [14].

13.4 Exercises

Exercise 13.4.1
Let p be a prime number, g a primitive root mod p, $a \in \{0, 1, \ldots, p-2\}$, and $A = g^a \bmod p$. Describe a zero-knowledge proof for the knowledge of the discrete logarithm a of A mod p to the base g.

Exercise 13.4.2
In the Fiat-Shamir scheme, let $n = 143$, $v = 82$, $x = 53$, and $e = 1$. Determine a valid response that proves the knowledge of a square root of v mod n.

Exercise 13.4.3 (Feige-Fiat-Shamir protocol)
The Feige-Fiat-Shamir protocol is a modification of the Fiat-Shamir protocol. In this protocol, a cheating verifier is discovered with much higher probability. A simplified version works as follows. Alice uses an RSA modulus n. She chooses random numbers $s_1, \ldots, s_k$ in $\{1, \ldots, n-1\}^k$ and computes $v_i = s_i^2 \bmod n$, $1 \le i \le k$. Her public key is $(n, v_1, \ldots, v_k)$. Her secret key is $(s_1, \ldots, s_k)$. To convince Bob of her identity, she chooses a random number $r \in \{1, \ldots, n-1\}$, computes the commitment $x = r^2 \bmod n$, and sends it to Bob. Bob

chooses a random challenge $(e_1, \ldots, e_k) \in \{0, 1\}^k$ and sends it to Alice. Alice sends the response $y = r \prod_{i=1}^{k} s_i^{e_i}$ to Bob. Bob verifies that $y^2 \equiv x \prod_{i=1}^{k} v_i^{e_i} \bmod p$. Determine the probability of success for a cheating verifier in one round.

Exercise 13.4.4

Modify the scheme from Exercise 13.4.3 such that its security is based on computing discrete logarithms.

Exercise 13.4.5 (Signatures from identification)

Find a signature scheme based on the protocol from Exercise 13.4.3. The idea is to replace the challenge by the hash value $h(x \circ m)$, where m is the message to be signed and x is the commitment.

14

CHAPTER

Public-Key Infrastructures

Since public keys in asymmetric cryptosystems need not be kept secret, key management in those systems is simpler than in symmetric schemes. Private keys, however, must be kept secret. Also, public keys must be protected from falsification and abuse. Therefore, appropriate *public-key infrastructures* (PKI) must be set up. They are responsible for key distribution and management. In this chapter, we describe how such public-key infrastructures work.

14.1   Personal Security Environments

14.1.1   Importance

If Bob wants to generate signatures or decrypt documents using a public-key system, then he needs a private key. Bob must keep this key secret because everybody who knows the key can sign messages in Bob's name or decrypt secret documents that were sent to Bob. Therefore, Bob needs a *personal security environment (PSE)* in which his private keys are securely stored. Since the private keys should not leave the PSE, the PSE also does the signing or decrypting.

Frequently, the PSE also generates the private keys. If the private keys are generated elsewhere, then at least the generating institution knows Bob's secret keys, which may corrupt the security of the system. On the other hand, secure key generation may require resources not present in the PSE. For example, for RSA keys random primes of a fixed bit length are required. In particular, the key generating environment must generate large, cryptographically secure, random numbers. If the random number generator of the PSE is weak, then the public-key system is insecure. It may therefore make sense to have the RSA keys generated by a trusted institution.

14.1.2   Implementation

The more sensitive the documents that are signed or encrypted, the more secure the PSE must be. A simple PSE is a file in Bob's home directory that can be accessed only after entering a secret password. This password may, for example, be used to decrypt the information. The security of a software PSE relies on the security of the underlying operating system. One may argue that operating systems must be very secure anyway and that they are therefore able to protect the PSE. Operating systems, for example, prevent unauthorized users from becoming administrators. On the other hand, it is well known that with sufficient effort the security of most operating systems can be successfully attacked. Therefore, a software PSE is not adequate for applications that require high security.

It is more secure to put the PSE on a smart card. Bob can carry his smart card in his wallet. If the card is in the smart card reader, it only permits very limited access. Manipulating its hardware or software is very difficult (although successful attacks have been reported). Unfortunately, computations on smart cards are still very slow. Therefore, it is impossible to decrypt large documents on a smart card, so public keys encrypt session keys which, in turn, are used to encrypt the documents. The encrypted session key is appended to the encrypted document. The smart card only decrypts the session key. The decryption of the document is then done on a fast PC or workstation.

14.1.3 Representation problem

Even if Alice uses a smart card for signing, there is still a severe security problem. If Alice wants to sign a document, she starts a program on her PC, which sends the document or its hash value to the smart card, where it is signed. With some effort, the attacker, Oscar, can manipulate the signing program on Alice's PC such that it sends a document to the smart card that is different from the one that Alice intended to sign. Because the smart card has no display, Alice is unable to detect this fraud. It is therefore possible that Alice could sign documents that she never wanted to sign. This problem is called the *representation problem* for signatures. The more important documents are for which digital signatures are accepted, the more dramatic the representation problem becomes. The problem is solved if Alice sees what she signs. For this purpose, Alice's PSE needs a display. One possibility is to use a cellular phone as a PSE. But its display is very small. Hence, the documents that can be signed securely on it are rather short. It depends on the solution of the representation problem whether digital signatures can be used to replace handwritten signatures.

14.2 Certification Authorities

If Alice uses a public-key system, it is not sufficient for her to keep her own private keys secret. If she uses the public key of Bob, she must be sure that it is really Bob's key. If the attacker, Oscar, is able to substitute his own public key for Bob's public key, then Oscar can decrypt secret messages to Bob and he can sign documents in Bob's name.

One solution of this problem is to establish trusted authorities. Each user is associated with such a *certification authority* (CA). The user trusts his CA. With its signature, the CA certifies the correctness and validity of the public keys of its users. The users know their CA's public key. Therefore, they can verify the signatures of their CA. We now explain in more detail what a CA does.

14.2.1 Registration

If Bob becomes a new user of the public-key system, then he is registered by his CA. He tells the CA his name and other relevant personal data. The CA verifies Bob's information. Bob can, for example, go to the CA in person and present some identification. The CA issues a user name for Bob that is different from the user name of all other users in the system. Bob will use this name, for example, if he signs documents. If Bob wants to keep his name secret, then he may use a pseudonym. Then, only the CA knows Bob's real name.

14.2.2 Key generation

Bob's public and private keys are generated either in his PSE or by his CA. It is recommended that Bob not know his private keys, because then he cannot inform others about those keys. The private keys are stored in Bob's PSE. The public keys are stored in a directory of the CA. Clearly, the keys must be protected while they are communicated between Bob and his CA.

For each purpose (for example, signing, encryption, and identification), a separate key pair is required. Otherwise, the system may become insecure. This is illustrated in the next example.

Example 14.2.1

If Alice uses the same key pair for signatures and challenge response authentication, then an attack can be mounted as follows. Oscar pretends that he wants to check Alice's identity. As a challenge, he sends the hash value $h(m)$ of a document m. Alice signs this hash value, assuming that it is a random challenge. But in fact Alice has signed a document, which was chosen by Oscar, without noticing.

14.2.3 Certification

The CA generates a *certificate*, which establishes a verifiable connection between Bob and his public keys. This certificate is a string, which is signed by the CA and contains at least the following information:

1. the user name or the pseudonym of Bob,

2. Bob's public keys,

3. the names of the algorithms in which the public keys are used,

4. the serial number of the certificate,

5. the beginning and end of the validity of the certificate,

6. the name of the CA,

7. restrictions that apply to the use of the certificate.

The certificate is stored, together with the user name, in a directory. Only the CA is allowed to write in this directory, but all users of the CA can read the information in the directory.

14.2.4 Archive

Depending on their use, keys in public-key systems must be stored even after they expire. Public signature keys must be stored as long as signatures generated with those keys must be verified. The CA stores certificates for public signature keys. Private decryption keys must be stored as long as documents were encrypted using those keys must be readable. Those keys are stored in the PSEs of the users. Authentication keys, private signature keys, and public encryption keys need not be put in archives. They must be stored only as long as they are used for authentication, generating signatures, or encrypting documents.

14.2.5 Initialization of the PSE

After Bob has been registered and his keys have been generated and certified, the CA transmits private keys to his CA, if they have been generated by the CA. The CA may also write its own public key and Bob's certificate to the PSE.

14.2.6   Directory service

The CA maintains a *directory* of all certificates together with the name of the owner of each certificate. If Alice wants to know Bob's public keys, she asks her CA whether Bob is one of its users. If Bob is registered with Alice's CA, then Alice obtains Bob's certificate from her CA's directory. Using the public key of her CA, Alice verifies that the certificate was in fact generated by her CA. She obtains the certified public keys of Bob. If Bob is not a user of Alice's CA, then Alice can obtain his public keys from another CA. This is explained below.

Alice may keep in her PSE certificates that she frequently uses. However, she must check regularly whether those certificates are still valid.

If a CA has many users, access to its directory may become very slow. It is then possible to keep several copies of the directory and to associate each user with exactly one copy.

Example 14.2.2

An international company wants to introduce a PKI for its 50,000 employees in five countries. The company only wants to maintain one CA. In order to make access to its directory more efficient, the CA distributes five copies of its directory to the five countries. Those copies are updated twice a day.

14.2.7   Key update

All keys in a public-key system have a certain period of validity. Before a key expires, it must be replaced by a new, valid key. This new key is exchanged between the CA and the users in such a way that it does not become insecure even if the old, invalid key becomes known.

The following key update method is insecure. Shortly before Bob's key pair becomes insecure, Bob's CA generates a new key pair. It encrypts the new private key using Bob's old public key and sends it to Bob. Bob decrypts that key using his old private key and replaces the old private key with the new one. If the attacker, Oscar, finds the old private key of Bob, then he can decrypt the message of the CA to

Bob that contains the new private key. Thus, he can find Bob's new private key if he knows the old one. The security of the new private key depends on the security of the old one. This makes no sense. Instead, variants of the Diffie-Hellman key-exchange protocol can be used that avoid the man-in-the-middle attack.

14.2.8 Revocation of certificates

Under certain conditions, a certificate must be invalidated although it is not yet expired.

Example 14.2.3
On a boat trip, Bob has lost his smart card. It contains Bob's private signature key, which he can no longer use for signatures since this private key is nowhere but on the smart card. Therefore, Bob's certificate is no longer valid since it contains the corresponding verification key. The CA must invalidate this certificate.

The CA collects the invalid certificates in the *certificate revocation list* (CRL). It is part of the directory of the CA. An entry in the CRL contains the serial number of the certificate, the date when the certificate was invalidated, and possibly further information, such as the reason for the invalidation. This entry is signed by the CA.

14.2.9 Access to expired keys

Expired keys are kept in the CA's archive and can be provided by the CA upon request.

Example 14.2.4
The CA changes the signature keys of its users each month. Bob orders a new car from Alice and signs this order. But three months later, Bob denies that he ordered the car. Alice wants to prove that the order was actually signed by Bob. She requests Bob's old public verification key from the CA. This key is kept in the archive since it is out of date.

14.3 Certificate Chains

If Bob and Alice do not belong to the same CA, then Alice cannot obtain the public key of Bob from the directory of her own CA but can obtain Bob's public key indirectly.

Example 14.3.1
Alice is registered with a CA in Germany. Bob is registered with a CA in the U.S. Hence, Alice knows the public key of her German CA but not the public key of Bob's CA. Now Alice obtains a certificate for the public key of Bob's CA from her own CA. She also obtains Bob's certificate either directly from Bob or from his CA. Using the public key of Bob's CA, which, in turn, is certified by her own CA, Alice can verify that she obtained a valid certificate for Bob.

As described in Example 14.3.1, Alice can use a *certificate chain* to obtain Bob's authentic public key, even if Bob and Alice belong to different CAs. Formally, such a chain can be described as follows. For a certification authority CA and a name U, denote by CA$\{U\}$ the certificate that certifies the public key of U. Here, U can either be the name of a user or the name of another certification authority. A certificate chain that for Alice certifies the public key of Bob is a sequence

$$CA_1\{CA_2\}, CA_2\{CA_3\}, \ldots, CA_{k-1}\{CA_k\}, CA_k\{Bob\}.$$

In this sequence, CA_1 is the CA where Alice is registered. Alice uses the public key of CA_1 to verify the public key of CA_2, she uses the public key of CA_2 to obtain the authentic public key of CA_3, and so on, until she finally uses the public key of CA_k to verify the certificate of Bob.

This method only works if trust is transitive (i.e., if U_1 trusts U_2 and U_2 trusts U_3, then U_1 trusts U_3).

References

[1] RFC 1750. Randomness requirements security. Internet Request for Comments 1750, December 1994.

[2] ISO/IEC 9796. Information technology - security techniques - digital signature scheme giving message recovery. International Organization for Standardization, Geneva, Switzerland, 1991.

[3] A. Aho, J. Hopcroft, and J. Ullman. *The Design and Analysis of Computer Algorithms*. Addison-Wesley, Reading, Massachusetts, 1974.

[4] E. Bach and J. Shallit. *Algorithmic number theory*. MIT Press, Cambridge, Massachusetts and London, England, 1996.

[5] F. Bauer. *Entzifferte Geheimnisse*. Springer-Verlag, Berlin, 1995.

[6] M. Bellare, S. Goldwasser, Lecture Notes on Cryptography, http://www-cse.usd.edu/users/mihir/pares/gb.ps.gz

[7] I.F. Blake, G. Seroussi, and N.P. Smart. *Elliptic curves in cryptography*. Cambridge University Press, Cambridge:England, 1999.

[8] J. Buchmann. Faktorisierung großer Zahlen. *Spektrum der Wissenschaften*, 9:80–88, 1996.

[9] J. Buchmann and S. Paulus. A one way function based on ideal arithmetic in number fields. In B. Kaliski, editor, *Advances in Cryptology – CRYPTO '97*, volume 1294 of *Lecture Notes in Computer Science*, pages 385–394, Berlin, 1997. Springer-Verlag.

[10] J. Buchmann and H. C. Williams. Quadratic fields and cryptography. In J.H. Loxton, editor, *Number Theory and Cryptography*, volume 154 of *London Mathematical Society Lecture Note Series*, pages 9–25. Cambridge University Press, Cambridge, England, 1990.

[11] H. Cohen. *A course in computational algebraic number theory*. Springer, Heidelberg, 1995.

[12] T.H. Cormen, C.E. Leiserson, and R.L. Rivest. *Introduction to Algorithms*. MIT Press, Cambridge, Massachudetts, 1990.

[13] N.G. de Bruijn. On the number of integers $\leq x$ and free of prime factors $> y$. *Indag. Math.*, 38:239–247, 1966.

[14] O. Goldreich. *Modern Cryptography, Probabilistic Proofs and Pseudorandomness*. Springer-Verlag, New York, 1999.

[15] D.E. Knuth. *The art of computer programming. Volume 2: Seminumerical algorithms*. Addison-Wesley, Reading, Massachusetts, 1981.

[16] N. Koblitz. *A Course in Number Theory and Cryptography*. Springer-Verlag, 1987.

[17] N. Koblitz. *Algebraic Aspects of Cryptography*. Springer-Verlag, 1998.

[18] A.K. Lenstra and H.W. Lenstra, Jr. Algorithms in number theory. In J. van Leeuwen, editor, *Handbook of Theoretical Computer Science, Volume A, Algorithms and Complexity*, chapter 12. Elsevier, Amsterdam, 1990.

[19] A.K. Lenstra and H.W. Lenstra Jr. Algorithms in number theory. In J. van Leeuwen, editor, *Handbook of theoretical computer science. Volume A. Algorithms and Complexity*, chapter 12, pages 673–715. Elsevier, 1990.

[20] A.K. Lenstra and H.W. Lenstra Jr., editors. *The Development of the Number Field Sieve*. Lecture Notes in Math. Springer-Verlag, Berlin, 1993.

[21] H.W. Lenstra, Jr. and C. Pomerance. A rigorous time bound for factoring integers. *Journal of the American Mathematical Society*, 5:483–516, 1992.

[22] LiDIA. **LiDIA** 1.3.1 - *a Library for Computational Number Theory*. Technische Universität Darmstadt, 1999. Available via anonymous FTP from `ftp.informatik.tu-darmstadt.de:/pub/TI/systems/LiDIA` or via WWW from `http://www.informatik.tu-darmstadt.de/TI/LiDIA`.

[23] A. Menezes. *Elliptic Curve Public Key Cryptosystems*. Kluwer Academic Publishers, Dordrecht, 1993.

[24] A. J. Menezes, P. C. van Oorschot, and S. A. Vanstone. *Handbook of Applied Cryptography*. CRC Press, Boca Raton, Florida, 1997.

[25] `http://www.informatik.tu-darmstadt.de/TI/forschung/nfc.html`

[26] E. Oeljeklaus and R. Remmert. *Lineare Algebra I*. Springer-Verlag, Berlin, 1974.

[27] H. Riesel. *Prime Numbers and Computer Methods for Factorization*. Birkhäuser, Boston, 1994.

[28] `http://csrc.nist.gov/encryption/aes/`

[29] J. Rosser and L. Schoenfeld. Approximate formulas for some functions of prime numbers. *Illinois Journal of Mathematics*, 6:64–94, 1962.

[30] R.A. Rueppel. *Analysis and Design of Stream Ciphers*. Springer-Verlag, Berlin, 1986.

[31] O. Schirokauer, D. Weber, and T. Denny. Discrete logarithms: the effectiveness of the index calculus method. In H. Cohen, editor, *ANTS II*, volume 1122 of *Lecture Notes in Computer Science*, Berlin, 1996. Springer-Verlag.

[32] D. Stinson. *Cryptography*. CRC Press, Boca Raton, Florida, 1995.

Solutions to the Exercises

Exercise 1.12.1

Let $z = \lfloor \alpha \rfloor = \max\{x \in \mathbb{Z} : x \leq \alpha\}$. Then $\alpha - z \geq 0$. Moreover, $\alpha - z < 1$, since $\alpha - z \geq 1$ implies $\alpha - (z+1) \geq 0$, which contradicts the maximality of α. Therefore, $0 \leq \alpha - z < 1$ or $\alpha - 1 < z \leq \alpha$. But there is only one integer in this interval, so, z is uniquely determined.

Exercise 1.12.3

The divisors of 195 are ± 1, ± 3, ± 5, ± 13, ± 15, ± 39, ± 65, ± 195.

Exercise 1.12.5

$1243 \bmod 45 = 28$, $-1243 \bmod 45 = 17$.

Exercise 1.12.7

Suppose that m divides the difference $b - a$. Let $a = q_a m + r_a$ with $0 \leq r_a < m$ and let $b = q_b m + r_b$ with $0 \leq r_b < m$. Then $r_a = a \bmod m$ and $r_b = b \bmod m$. Moreover,

$$b - a = (q_b - q_a)m + (r_b - r_a). \tag{14.1}$$

Since m divides $b-a$, it follows from (14.1) that m also divides $r_b - r_a$. Now, $0 \le r_b, r_a < m$ implies

$$-m < r_b - r_a < m.$$

Since m divides $r_b - r_a$, we obtain $r_b - r_a = 0$ and therefore $a \bmod m = b \bmod m$.

Conversely, let $a \bmod m = b \bmod m$. We use the same notation as above and obtain $b - a = (q_b - q_a)m$. Hence, m divides $b - a$.

Exercise 1.12.9
We have $225 = 128 + 64 + 32 + 1 = 2^7 + 2^6 + 2^5 + 2^0$. Hence, 11100001 is the binary expansion of 225. The hexadecimal expansion is obtained by dividing the binary expansion from the right into blocks of length four and by interpreting these blocks as hexadecimal digits. In our example, we obtain 1110 0001 (i.e., $14 * 16 + 1$). The hexadecimal digits are $0, 1, 2, 3, 4, 5, 6, 7, 8, 9, A, B, C, D, E, F$. Hence E1 is the hexadecimal expansion of 225.

Exercise 1.12.11
We must show that there are positive constants B and C such that $f(n) \le Cn^d$ for all $n > B$. We can, for example, choose $B = 1$ and $C = \sum_{i=0}^{d} |a_i|$.

Exercise 1.12.13
1. Each divisor of $a_1, \ldots, a_k$ is a divisor of a_1 and $\gcd(a_2, \ldots, a_k)$ and vice versa. This implies the assertion.

2. The assertion is proved by induction on k. For $k = 1$, the assertion is obviously correct, so let $k > 1$ and assume that the assertion is true for all $k' < k$. Then $\gcd(a_1, \ldots, a_k)\mathbb{Z} = a_1\mathbb{Z} + \gcd(a_2, \ldots, a_k)\mathbb{Z} = a_1\mathbb{Z} + a_2\mathbb{Z} + \ldots + a_k\mathbb{Z}$ by 1., Theorem 1.7.5, and the induction hypothesis.

3. and 4. are proved analogously.

5. The assertion is proved by induction using Corollary 1.7.8.

Exercise 1.12.15

We apply the extended euclidean algorithm and obtain the following table:

k	0	1	2	3	4	5	6
r_k	235	124	111	13	7	6	1
q_k		1	1	8	1	1	
x_k	1	0	1	1	9	10	19
y_k	0	1	1	2	17	19	36

Hence, $\gcd(235, 124) = 1$ and $19 * 235 - 36 * 124 = 1$.

Exercise 1.12.17

We use the notation from the extended euclidean algorithm. We have $S_0 = T_{n+1}$ and therefore $x_{n+1} = u_1$ and $y_{n+1} = u_0$. Moreover, S_n is the identity matrix. In particular, we have $u_n = 1 = r_n/\gcd(a, b)$ and $u_{n+1} = 0 = r_{n+1}/\gcd(a, b)$. Finally, we have seen in(1.8) that the sequence (u_k) satisfies the same recursion as the sequence (r_k). This implies the assertion.

Exercise 1.12.19

If (a, b) is multiplied with a positive integer, then each equation in the recursion of the euclidean algorithm is multiplied with the same number. In other words, the residue sequence is multiplied with this number and the quotients remain the same. If we divide a and b by a common divisor, the situation is analogous.

Exercise 1.12.21

By Corollary 1.7.7, there exist x, y, u, v with $xa+ym = 1$ and $ub+vm = 1$. Hence, $1 = (xa + ym)(ub + vm) = (xu)ab + m(xav + yub + yvm)$, which implies the assertion.

Exercise 1.12.23

If n is composite, then we can write $n = ab$ with $a, b > 1$. This implies $\min\{a, b\} \leq \sqrt{n}$. Since by Theorem 1.11.2 this minimum has a prime divisor, the assertion is proved.

Exercise 2.22.1
Simple induction.

Exercise 2.22.3
If e and e' are neutral elements, then $e = e'e = e'$.

Exercise 2.22.5
If e is a neutral element and $e = ba = ac$, then $b = be = b(ac) = (ba)c = c$.

Exercise 2.22.7
We have $4 * 6 \equiv 0 \equiv 4 * 3 \bmod 12$ but $6 \not\equiv 3 \bmod 12$.

Exercise 2.22.9
Let R be a commutative ring with unit element e and denote by R^* the set of all invertible elements in R. Then $e \in R^*$. Let a and b be invertible in R with inverses a^{-1} and b^{-1}. Then $aba^{-1}b^{-1} = aa^{-1}bb^{-1} = e$. Hence, $ab \in R^*$. Moreover, by definition the inverse of each element of R^* belongs to R^*.

Exercise 2.22.11
Let $g = \gcd(a, m)$ be a divisor of b. Set $a' = a/g$, $b' = b/g$, and $m' = m/g$. Then $\gcd(a', m') = 1$. Hence, by Theorem 2.6.2 the congruence $a'x' \equiv b' \bmod m'$ has a solution m' which is unique mod m'. If x' is such a solution, then $ax' \equiv b \bmod m$. This implies $a(x' + ym') = b + a'ym \equiv b \bmod m$ for all $y \in \mathbb{Z}$. Therefore, all $x = x' + ym'$, $y \in \mathbb{Z}$ are solutions of $ax \equiv b \bmod m$. We show that there is no other solution. Let x be a solution. Then $a'x \equiv b' \bmod m'$. Hence, $x \equiv x' \bmod m'$ by Theorem 2.6.2, and this concludes the proof.

Exercise 2.22.13
The invertible residue classes mod 25 are $a + 25\mathbb{Z}$ with $a \in \{1, 2, 3, 4, 6, 7, 8, 9, 11, 12, 13, 14, 16, 17, 18, 19, 21, 22, 23, 24\}$.

Exercise 2.22.15

Induction on the number of elements in X. If X contains one element, then Y also contains one element, namely the image of X. If X has n elements and if the assertion is proved for $n - 1$, then we choose an $x \in X$ and remove x from X and $f(x)$ from Y. Then we apply the induction hypothesis.

Exercise 2.22.18

a	2	4	7	8	11	13	14
ord $a + 15\mathbb{Z}$	4	2	4	4	2	4	2

Exercise 2.22.20

It follows from Theorem 2.9.5 that for each divisor d of $|G|$ there are exactly $\varphi(d)$ elements in G of order d. In particular, there is a cyclic subgroup of order d of G. By Theorem 2.9.5 it contains all elements of order d in G. Hence, there is exactly one such subgroup. It remains to be shown that all subgroups of G are cyclic. If H is a subgroup of G which is not cyclic then the number of elements in H is bounded by $\sum_{d | |H|, d < |H|} \varphi(d)$. But by Theorem 2.8.4 this number is less than $|H|$.

Exercise 2.22.22

By Theorem 2.9.2, the order of g is of the form $\prod_{p | |G|} p^{x(p)}$ with $0 \le x(p) \le e(p) - f(p)$ for all $p \mid |G|$. By definition of $f(p)$, we even have $x(p) = e(p) - f(p)$ for all $p \mid |G|$.

Exercise 2.22.24

By Corollary 2.9.3, the map is well defined. Clearly, the map is a homomorphism. Since g generates G, the map is surjective. Finally, the injectivity follows from Corollary 2.9.3.

Exercise 2.22.26

2, 3, 5, 7, 11 are primitive roots mod 3, 5, 7, 11, 13.

Exercise 3.15.1

The key is 8 and the plaintext is SECRET.

Exercise 3.15.3

The decryption function, restricted to the image of the encryption function, is the inverse function.

Exercise 3.15.5

Concatenation is obviously associative. The neutral element is the empty string ε. The semigroup is not a group since no element except for ε has an inverse.

Exercise 3.15.7

1. Not a cryptosystem because the encryption function is not injective. An example: Let $k = 2$. The letter A corresponds to 0, which is mapped to 0 (i.e., A). The letter N corresponds to 13, which is mapped to $2 * 13 \bmod 26 = 0$ (i.e., to A).

   2. A cryptosystem. The plaintext and ciphertext space are Σ^*. The key space is $\{1, 2, \ldots, 26\}$. If k is a key and $(\sigma_1, \sigma_2, \ldots, \sigma_n)$ a plaintext then $(k\sigma_1 \bmod 26, \ldots, k\sigma_n \bmod 26\}$ is the ciphertext. This describes the encryption function for key k. The decryption function i is the same, except k is replaced by its inverse mod 26.

Exercise 3.15.9

The number of bit permutations on $\{0, 1\}^n$ is $n!$. The number of circular left or right shifts on this set is n.

Exercise 3.15.11

The map that sends 0 to 1 and vice versa is a permutation but not a bit permutation.

Exercise 3.15.13
The group properties are easy to verify. We show that S_3 is not commutative. We have

$$\begin{pmatrix} 1 & 2 & 3 \\ 3 & 2 & 1 \end{pmatrix} \circ \begin{pmatrix} 1 & 2 & 3 \\ 1 & 3 & 2 \end{pmatrix} = \begin{pmatrix} 1 & 2 & 3 \\ 3 & 1 & 2 \end{pmatrix}$$

but

$$\begin{pmatrix} 1 & 2 & 3 \\ 1 & 3 & 2 \end{pmatrix} \circ \begin{pmatrix} 1 & 2 & 3 \\ 3 & 2 & 1 \end{pmatrix} = \begin{pmatrix} 1 & 2 & 3 \\ 2 & 3 & 1 \end{pmatrix}.$$

Exercise 3.15.15
ECB mode: 011100011100
 CBC mode: 011001010000
 CFB mode: 100010001000
 OFB mode: 101010101010

Exercise 3.15.18
If

$$A = \begin{pmatrix} a_{1,1} & a_{1,2} & a_{1,3} \\ a_{2,1} & a_{2,2} & a_{2,3} \\ a_{3,1} & a_{3,2} & a_{3,3} \end{pmatrix},$$

then $\det A = a_{1,1}a_{2,2}a_{3,3} - a_{1,1}a_{2,3}a_{3,2} - a_{1,2}a_{2,1}a_{3,3} + a_{1,2}a_{2,3}a_{3,1} + a_{1,3}a_{2,1}a_{3,2} - a_{1,3}a_{2,2}a_{3,1}$.

Exercise 3.15.20
The inverse is

$$\begin{pmatrix} 0 & 0 & 1 \\ 0 & 1 & 1 \\ 1 & 1 & 0 \end{pmatrix}$$

Exercise 4.8.1
1. The events S and $\emptyset$ are mutually exclusive. Therefore, $1 = \Pr(S) = \Pr(S \cup \emptyset) = \Pr(S) + \Pr(\emptyset) = 1 + \Pr(\emptyset)$. This implies $\Pr(\emptyset) = 0$.

2. Set $C = B \setminus A$. Then the events A and C are mutually exclusive, so $\Pr(B) = \Pr(A \cup C) = \Pr(A) + \Pr(C)$. Since $\Pr(C) \geq 0$, we have $\Pr(B) \geq \Pr(A)$.

Exercise 4.8.3

By K denote heads and by T tails. Then the sample space is {KK,TT,KT,TK}. The probability of every elementary event is 1/4. The event "at least one coin comes up heads" is {KK,KZ,ZK}. Its probability is 3/4.

Exercise 4.8.5

The event "both dice come up differently" is $A = \{12, 13, 14, 15, 16, 17, 18, 19, 21, 13, \ldots, 65\}$. Its probability is 5/6. The event "the sum of the results is even" is $\{11, 13, 15, 22, 24, 26, \ldots, 66\}$. Its probability is 1/2. The intersection of both events is $\{13, 15, 24, 26, \ldots, 64\}$. Its probability is 1/3. The probability of A given B is 2/3.

Exercise 4.8.7

We use the birthday paradox. We have $n = 10^4$. Hence, $k \geq 118.3 \geq (1 + \sqrt{1 + 8 * 10^4 * \log 2})/2$ people are sufficient.

Exercise 4.8.9

By the definition of perfect secrecy we must check whether $\Pr(\vec{p}|\vec{c}) = \Pr(\vec{p})$ for each ciphertext $\vec{c}$ and each plaintext $\vec{p}$. This is incorrect. We give a counterexample. Let $\vec{p} = (0, 0)$ and $\vec{c} = (0, 0)$. Then $\Pr(\vec{p}) = 1/4$ and $\Pr(\vec{p}|\vec{c}) = 1$.

Exercise 5.5.1

The key is

$K = $ 00010011001101000101011101111001100110111011110011011111111110001.

The plaintext is

$P = $ 000000010010001101000101011001111000100110101010111100110111101111.

Hence,

$$C_0 = 111100001100110010101010101111$$
$$D_0 = 010101010110011001110001111$$
$$v = 1$$
$$C_1 = 111000011001100101010101011111$$
$$D_1 = 101010101100110011100011110$$
$$v = 1$$
$$C_2 = 110000110011001010101010111111$$
$$D_2 = 010101011001100111100011101.$$

In the first round of the Feistel cipher we have

$$L_0 = 1100110000000001100110011111111$$
$$R_0 = 11110000101010101111000010101010$$
$$k_1 = 000110110000001011101111111111000111000001110010$$
$$E(R_0) = 011110100001010101010101011110100001010101010101$$
$$B = 011000010001011110111010100001100110010100100111.$$

S	1	2	3	4	5	6	7	8
Value	5	12	8	2	11	5	9	7
C	0101	1100	1000	0010	1011	0101	1001	0111

$$f_{k_1}(R_0) = 00000011010010111010100110111011$$
$$L_1 = 11110000101010101111000010101010$$
$$R_1 = 11001111010010110110010101000100.$$

In the second round of the Feistel cipher, we have

$$L_1 = 11110000101010101111000010101010$$
$$R_1 = 11001111010010110110010101000100$$
$$k_2 = 011110011010111011011001110110111100100111100101$$
$$E(R_1) = 011001011110101001010110101100001010101000001001$$
$$B = 000111000100010010001111011010110110001111101100.$$

S	1	2	3	4	5	6	7	8
$Value$	4	8	13	3	0	10	10	14
C	0100	1000	1101	0011	0000	1010	1010	1110

$$f_{k_2}(R_1) = 1011110001101010100001010010001$$
$$L_2 = 1100111101001011011001010101000100$$
$$R_2 = 01001100110000000111010110001011.$$

Exercise 5.5.3

We first prove the assertion for each round. It is easy to verify that $E(\overline{R}) = \overline{E(R)}$, where E is the expansion function of DES and $R \in \{0, 1\}^{32}$. If $i \in \{1, 2, \ldots, 16\}$ and $K_i(k)$ is the ith DES round key for the DES key k, then $K_i(\overline{k}) = \overline{K_i(k)}$. Hence, if k is replaced by $\overline{k}$, then all round keys K are replaced by $\overline{K}$. If in a round R is replaced by $\overline{R}$ and K by $\overline{K}$, then by(5.3) the arguments for the S-boxes are $\overline{E(R)} \oplus \overline{K}$. Now $\overline{a} \oplus \overline{b} = \overline{a} \oplus \overline{b}$ for all $a, b \in \{0, 1\}$. Therefore, the arguments for the S-boxes are $E(R) \oplus K$. Since the initial permutation commutes with the complement function, the assertion is proved.

Exercise 5.5.5

1. Let $K_i = (K_{i,0}, \ldots, K_{i,47})$ be the ith round key, and let $C_i = (C_{i,0}, \ldots, C_{i,27})$ and $D_i = (D_{i,0}, \ldots, D_{i,27})$, $1 \leq i \leq 16$. We have $K_i = \text{PC2}(C_i, D_i)$. The function PC2 chooses its argument bits according to Table 5.5. Denote the corresponding choice function for the indices by g. Then $g(1) = 14$, $g(2) = 17$, etc. The function g is injective but not surjective, since 9, 18, 22, 25 are not images of g. Denote the inverse function on the image of g by g^{-1}. Let $i \in \{0, \ldots, 26\}$. We have two cases. In the first case, $i+1 \notin \{9, 18, 22, 25\}$ (i.e., $i+1$ is not in the image of g). The first assertion of this exercise and $K_1 = K_{16}$ imply $C_{1,i} = C_{16,i+1} = K_{16,g^{-1}(i+1)} = K_{1,g^{-1}(i+1)} = C_{1,i+1}$. In the second case, we have $i+1 \in \{9, 18, 22, 25\}$. Then i is in the image of g and, as earlier, we have $C_{16,i} = C_{16,i+1} = K_{16,g^{-1}(i+1)} = K_{1,g^{-1}(i+1)} = C_{1,i+1}$ so we have shown that $C_{1,0} = C_{1,1} = \ldots = C_{1,8}$, $C_{1,9} = \ldots = C_{1,17}$, $C_{1,18} = \ldots = C_{1,21}$, $C_{1,22} = \ldots = C_{1,24}$ and $C_{1,25} = \ldots = C_{1,27}$. Analogously, but using $K_1 = K_2$, $C_{1,8} = C_{1,9}$, $C_{1,17} = C_{1,18}$, $C_{1,21} = C_{1,22}$,

and $C_{1,24} = C_{1,25}$ are shown. In the same way, the assertion for D_i is proved.

2. and 3, We can either set all bits of C_1 to 1 or to 0, and we have the same choices for D_1 so there are four possibilities.

Exercise 6.6.1

$2^{1110} \equiv 1024 \bmod 1111$.

Exercise 6.6.3

The smallest pseudoprime to the base 2 is 341. We have $341 = 11 * 31$ and $2^{340} \equiv 1 \bmod 341 = 1$.

Exercise 6.6.5

Let n be a Carmichael number. By definition, it is not a prime number and by Theorem 6.3.1 it is square-free, hence not a prime power. Therefore, n has at least two prime divisors. Let $n = pq$ with prime factors $p, q, p > q$. By Theorem 6.6.5, $p - 1$ is a divisor of $n - 1 = pq - 1 = (p - 1)q + q - 1$. Therefore, $p - 1$ is a divisor of $q - 1$. This is impossible since $0 < q - 1 < p - 1$. This proves the assertion.

Exercise 6.6.7

We write $340 = 4 * 85$. Now $2^{85} \equiv 32 \bmod 341$ and $2^{170} \equiv 1 \bmod 341$. Hence, 341 is composite.

Exercise 6.6.9

The smallest 512-bit prime is $2^{512} + 3$.

Exercise 7.6.1

If $de - 1$ is a multiple of $p - 1$ and $q - 1$, then it can be shown as in the proof of Theorem 7.2.4 that $m^{ed} \equiv m \bmod p$ and $m^{ed} \equiv m \bmod q$ for any $m \in \{0, 1, \ldots, n - 1\}$. From the Chinese remainder theorem, we obtain $m^{ed} \equiv m \bmod n$.

Exercise 7.6.3

Set $p = 223$, $q = 233$, $n = 51959$, $e = 5$. Then $d = 10301$, $m = 27063$, $c = 50042$.

Exercise 7.6.5

We sketch a simple divide-and-conquer algorithm. Let $m_0 = 1$, $m_1 = c$. We repeat the following computations until $m_1^e = c$ or $m_0 = m_1$. Set $x = \lfloor (m_1 - m_0)/2 \rfloor$. If $x^e \geq c$, then set $m_1 = x$; otherwise, set $m_0 = x$. If after the last iteration $m_1^e = c$, then the eth root of c is found; otherwise, there is no such root.

Exercise 7.6.7

16 squarings and multiplications are necessary.

Exercise 7.6.9

Compute the representation $1 = xe + yf$ and then $c_e^x c_f^y = m^{xe+yf} = m$.

Exercise 7.6.11

We have $p = 37$, $q = 43$, $e = 5$, $d = 605$, $y_p = 7$, $y_q = -6$, $m_p = 9$, $m_q = 8$, $m = 1341$.

Exercise 7.6.13

Since e is coprime to $(p-1)(q-1)$, we have $e^k \equiv 1 \bmod (p-1)(q-1)$, where k is the order of the residue class $e + \mathbb{Z}(p-1)(q-1)$. This implies $c^{e^{k-1}} \equiv m^{e^k} \equiv m \bmod n$. As long as k is large, this is no problem.

Exercise 7.6.15

Yes, since the numbers $(x_5 2^5 + x_4 2^4 + x_3 2^3 + x_2 2^2) \bmod 253$, $x_i \in \{0, 1\}$, $2 \leq i \leq 5$ are pairwise distinct.

Exercise 7.6.17

Low-exponent attack: If the message $m \in \{0, 1, \ldots, n-1\}$ is encrypted with the Rabin scheme using the coprime moduli n_1 and

n_2, then we obtain the ciphertexts $c_i = m^2 \bmod n_i$, $i = 1, 2$. The attacker determines a number $c \in \{0, \ldots, n_1 n_2 - 1\}$ with $c \equiv c_i \bmod n_i$, $i = 1, 2$. Then $c = m^2$ and m can be determined as the square root of c. The attack can be prevented by randomizing a few plaintext bits.

Multiplicativity: If Bob knows the ciphertexts $c_i = m_i^2 \bmod n$, $i = 1, 2$, then he can compute the ciphertext $c_1 c_2 \bmod n = (m_1 m_2)^2 \bmod n$. This attack can be prevented by using only plaintexts with redundancy.

Exercise 7.6.19
If $(B_1 = g^{b_1}, C_1 = A^{b_1} m_1)$, $(B_2 = g^{b_2}, C_2 = A^{b_2} m_2)$ are the ciphertexts, then $(B_1 B_2, C_1 C_2 = A^{b_1 + b_2} m_1 m_2)$ is the ciphertext that encrypts the plaintext $m_1 m_2$. This attack can be prevented by using only plaintexts with redundancy.

Exercise 7.6.21
The plaintext is $m = 37$.

Exercise 8.6.1
Since $x^2 \geq n$, it follows that $\lceil \sqrt{n} \rceil = 115$ is the smallest possible value for x. For this x, we must check whether $z = n - x^2$ is a square. If not, then we test $x + 1$. We have $(x + 1)^2 = x^2 + 2x + 1$. Therefore, we can compute $(x + 1)^2$ by adding x^2 and $2x + 1$. Finally, we find that $13199 = 132^2 - 65^2 = (132 - 65)(132 + 65) = 67 * 197$. Not every composite integer is the difference of two squares. Therefore, the algorithm does not always work. If it works, it requires $O(\sqrt{n})$ operations in $\mathbb{Z}$.

Exercise 8.6.3
We find the factorization $n = 11617 * 11903$ since $p - 1 = 2^5 * 3 * 11^2$ and $q - 1 = 2 * 11 * 541$. Therefore, we can set $B = 121$.

Exercise 8.6.5
By Theorem 6.1.6, the number of primes $\leq B$ is $O(B/ \log B)$. Each of the prime powers whose product is k is $\leq B$. Therefore, $k =$

$O(B^{B/\log B}) = O(2^B)$. By Theorem 2.12.2, the exponentiation of a with $k \bmod n$ requires $O(B)$ multiplications mod n.

Exercise 8.6.7

We have $m = 105$. With the sieving interval $-10, \ldots, 10$ and the factor base $\{-1, 2, 3, 5, 7, 11, 13\}$, we obtain $f(-4) = -2 * 5 * 7 * 13$, $f(1) = 5^3$, $f(2) = 2 * 13^2$, $f(4) = 2 * 5 * 7 * 11$, $f(6) = 2 * 5 * 11^2$ and $(106 * 107 * 111)^2 \equiv (2 * 5^2 * 11 * 13)^2 \bmod n$. Hence, $x = 106 * 107 * 111$, $y = 2 * 5^2 * 11 * 13$, and therefore $\gcd(x - y, n) = 41$.

Exercise 9.9.1

The DL is $x = 1234$.

Exercise 9.9.3

The DL is $x = 1212$.

Exercise 9.9.5

The smallest primitive root mod 3167 is 5, and we have $5^{1937} \equiv 15 \bmod 3167$.

Exercise 9.9.7

The smallest primitive root mod $p = 2039$ is $g = 7$. We have $7^{1344} \equiv 2 \bmod p$, $7^{1278} \equiv 3 \bmod p$, $7^{664} \equiv 5 \bmod p$, $7^{861} \equiv 11 \bmod p$, $7^{995} \equiv 13 \bmod p$.

Exercise 10.8.1

Let n be a 1024-bit Rabin modulus (see Section 7.3). The function $\mathbb{Z}_n \to \mathbb{Z}_n$, $x \mapsto x^2 \bmod n$ is a one-way function if n cannot be factored. This follows from the results of Section 7.3.5.

Exercise 10.8.3

The maximal value of $h(k)$ is 9999. This implies that the maximal length of the images is 14. A collision is $h(1) = h(10947)$.

Exercise 11.6.1
We have $n = 127 * 227$, $e = 5$, $d = 22781$, $s = 7003$.

Exercise 11.6.3
The signature is a square root mod n of the hash value of the document. The security and efficiency considerations are similar to those in Section 7.3.

Exercise 11.6.5
We have $A^r r^s = A^q (q^{(p-3)/2})^{h(m)-qz}$. Since $gq \equiv -1 \bmod p$, we obtain $q \equiv -g^{-1} \bmod p$. Moreover, $g^{(p-1)/2} \equiv -1 \bmod p$ because g is a primitive root mod p. Therefore, $q^{(p-3)/2} \equiv (-g)^{(p-1)/2} g \equiv g \bmod p$, so $A^r r^s \equiv A^q g^{h(m)} g^{-qz} \equiv A^q g^{h(m)} A^{-q} \equiv g^{h(m)} \bmod p$. The attack works because g divides $p - 1$ and the DL z of A^q to the base g^q can be computed. This must be prevented.

Exercise 11.6.7
We have $r = 799$, $k^{-1} = 1979$, $s = 1339$.

Exercise 11.6.9
We have $q = 43$. The generator of the subgroup of order q is $g = 1984$. Also, $A = 834$, $r = 4$, $k^{-1} = 31$, and $s = 23$.

Exercise 11.6.11
$g^s = A^r r^{h(x)}$.

Exercise 12.4.1
We need an irreducible polynomial of degree 3 over GF (3). The polynomial $x^2 + 1$ is irreducible over GF (3) because it has no zero. Therefore, residue class ring mod $f(X) = X^2 + 1$ is GF (9). Denote by α the residue class of X mod $f(X)$. Then $\alpha^2 + 1 = 0$. The elements of GF (9) are $0, 1, 2, \alpha, 2\alpha, 1 + \alpha, 1 + 2\alpha, 2 + \alpha, 2 + 2\alpha$. The addition table is obtained using arithmetic in $\mathbb{Z}/3\mathbb{Z}$. The multiplication table also uses $\alpha^2 = -1$.

Exercise 12.4.3
The points are $\mathcal{O}$, $(0, 1)$, $(0, 6)$, $(2, 2)$, $(2, 5)$. Therefore, the group is of order 5 and hence cyclic. Each point $\neq \mathcal{O}$ is a generator.

Exercise 13.4.1
Alice chooses a random exponent $b \in \{0, 1, \ldots, p-2\}$ and computes $B = g^b \bmod p$. She sends B to Bob. Bob chooses a random $e \in \{0, 1\}$ and sends it to Alice. Alice sends $y = (b+ea) \bmod (p-1)$ to Bob. Bob verifies $g^y \equiv A^e B \bmod p$. The protocol is complete since using her secret key Alice can successfully identify herself. If Oscar knows the correct y for $r = 0$ and $r = 1$, then he knows the DL a. If he does not know the secret key, his answer is correct with probability $1/2$. Hence, the protocol is correct. The protocol can be simulated by Bob. He chooses random numbers $y \in \{0, 1, \ldots, p-2\}$, $e \in \{0, 1\}$ and sets $B = g^y A^{-e} \bmod p$. Then the protocol works and the probability distributions on the messages are the same as in the original protocol.

Exercise 13.4.3
A cheater must produce x and y that satisfy the protocol. When he communicates x, he does not know the random $e = (e_1, \ldots, e_k)$. If he is able to come up with a correct y after knowing e, then he can compute square roots mod n. But this is not possible. Hence, he can only choose x such that y is correct for exactly one $e \in \{0, 1\}^k$. He can survive the identification only with probability 2^{-k}.

Exercise 13.4.5
The signer chooses r randomly and computes $x = r^2 \bmod n$, $(e_1, \ldots, e_k) = h(x \circ m)$ and $y = r \prod_{i=1}^k s_i^{e_i}$. The signature is (x, y).

Index

A

$\lfloor \alpha \rfloor$, 2
abelian, 33, 34
adaptive chosen-plaintext
    attack, 72
adjoint, 94
affine cipher, 89
affine linear block cipher, 96
affine linear function, 95
alphabet, 73
anomalous curve, 238
archive, 253
associative, 33
asymmetric cryptosystem, 71

B

baby-step giant-step algorithm,
    186
baby-steps, 187
bijective, 43

binary expansion, 5
binary length, 6
birthday attack, 208
bit permutation, 76
block cipher, 77
block length, 77
bounded, 2

C

Caesar cipher, 70
cancellation rules, 34
Carmichael number, 130
CBC mode, 81
certain event, 104
certificate, 252
certificate chain, 256
certificate revocation list, 255
certification, 252
certification authority (CA), 251
CFB mode, 84

challenge-response protocols, 243
characteristic, 234
chosen-ciphertext attack, 72
chosen-plaintext attack, 72
cipher feedback mode, 84
cipherblock chaining mode, 81
ciphertext, 69
ciphertext-only attack, 72
circular shifts, 77
coefficient, 57
collision, 207
collision resistant, 207
column, 91
common divisor, 9
common modulus attack, 168
commutative, 33–35
composite, 22
compression function, 206
concatenation, 75
congruence, 29
CRL, 255
cryptosystem, 69
cyclic group, 42
cycling attack, 168

D

decryption, 70
decryption exponent, 142
degree, 57
DES encryption, 115
determinant, 93
Diffie-Hellman key exchange, 158
Diffie-Hellman problem, 161
Digital Signature Algorithm (DSA), 228
digital signatures, 217
direct product, 54

directory service, 254
discrete logarithm, 159, 186
discrete logarithm problem, 159, 185
discriminant, 236
divisibility, 2, 36
division with remainder, 3, 59
divisor, 3, 36
DL problem, 185

E

ECB mode, 79
ECM, 181, 182
electronic codebook mode, 79
element order, 41
elementary event, 103
ElGamal encryption, 162
ElGamal signature, 223
elliptic curve, 236
elliptic curve method, 181, 182
empty sequence, 75
encryption, 69, 70
encryption exponent, 142
encryption scheme, 69
enumeration, 186
Euler φ-function, 39
event, 104
exclusive or, 81
exhaustive search, 72
existential forgery, 152, 220, 226

F

factor base, 176, 199
Feige-Fiat-Shamir protocol, 247
Feistel cipher, 115
Fermat numbers, 23
Fermat test, 129
Fiat-Shamir identification, 245

field, 36
finite field, 233

G

g-adic expansion, 5
Galois field, 234
gcd, 9
generator, 42
giant-steps, 187
greatest common divisor, 9
group, 34

H

hexadecimal expansion, 5
Hill cipher, 97

I

identification, 242
identification protocol, 242
identity matrix, 92
independent events, 105
index calculus, 198
index of a subgroup, 44
induction, 2
initial permutation, 117
initialization vector, 81
injective, 43
integer linear combinations, 10
integers, 1
inverse, 33
invertible, 33, 35
irreducible polynomial, 233

K

key, 69
key space, 214

key generation, 252
known-plaintext attack, 72

L

leading coefficient, 57
least common multiple (lcm),
        66
linear function, 95
linear recursion, 88
linear shift register, 89
low-exponent attack, 149

M

MAC, 214
man in the middle attack, 161
matrix, 91
message authentication code,
        214
message expansion, 164
Miller-Rabin test, 132
monoid, 33
monomial, 57
multiple, 3, 36
multiple encryption, 78
multiplicative group of residues,
        39

N

NFS, 182
null event, 104
number field sieve, 181, 182

O

Ω-notation, 6
O-notation, 6
OFB mode, 86

one-time password, 243
one-way function, 206
operation, 32
order of a group, 34
order of an element, 41
output feedback mode, 86

P

$\mathbb{P}$, 22
parameterized hash function, 214
password, 242
perfect secrecy, 108
permutation, 75
permutation cipher, 97
permutation cipher, 78
personal security environment, 249
PKI, 249
plaintext, 69
Pollard $p - 1$ method, 172
polynomial, 57
polynomial time, 9
power product, 48
power set, 104
primality test, 129
prime divisor, 22
prime factorization, 23
prime field, 234
prime number, 22
primitive root, 63
private key, 140
probability, 104
probability distribution, 104
prover, 242
PSE, 249
pseudoprime, 130
public key, 140
public key cryptosystems, 71

public key infrastructure, 249

Q

quadratic form, 239
quadratic Sieve, 173
quotient, 4, 60

R

Rabin encryption, 153
Rabin signature, 222
randomized encryption, 166
redundancy function, 221
registration, 252
relation, 200
remainder, 4, 60
representation problem, 251
representatives, 30
residue class, 30
residue class ring, 35
residue mod m, 30
ring, 35
row, 91
RSA, 141
RSA signature, 218
RSA-modulus, 142

S

sample space, 103
secret key, 140
semigroup, 33
session key, 140
sieve of Eratosthenes, 26
simultaneous congruence, 51
smooth, 176
smooth integers, 199
square roots mod p, 66
string, 75

subexponential, 178
subgroup, 42
substitution cipher, 77
supersingular curve, 238
surjective, 43
symmetric cryptosystem, 71

T

theorem of Lagrange, 44
transposition, 100
trial division, 128, 171
triple encryption, 78

U

uniform distribution, 104
unit, 35
unit element, 35
unit group, 35
unit vector, 97

V

verifier, 242
Vernam one-time pad, 110

W

weak collision resistant, 207
weak DES keys, 125
witness, 133
word, 75

X

XOR, 81

Z

zero knowledge, 245
zero knowledge proof, 245

Undergraduate Texts in Mathematics

(continued from page ii)

Hijab: Introduction to Calculus and Classical Analysis.

Hilton/Holton/Pedersen: Mathematical Reflections: In a Room with Many Mirrors.

Iooss/Joseph: Elementary Stability and Bifurcation Theory. Second edition.

Isaac: The Pleasures of Probability. *Readings in Mathematics.*

James: Topological and Uniform Spaces.

Jänich: Linear Algebra.

Jänich: Topology.

Jänich: Vector Analysis.

Kemeny/Snell: Finite Markov Chains.

Kinsey: Topology of Surfaces.

Klambauer: Aspects of Calculus.

Lang: A First Course in Calculus. Fifth edition.

Lang: Calculus of Several Variables. Third edition.

Lang: Introduction to Linear Algebra. Second edition.

Lang: Linear Algebra. Third edition.

Lang: Undergraduate Algebra. Second edition.

Lang: Undergraduate Analysis.

Lax/Burstein/Lax: Calculus with Applications and Computing. Volume 1.

LeCuyer: College Mathematics with APL.

Lidl/Pilz: Applied Abstract Algebra. Second edition.

Logan: Applied Partial Differential Equations.

Macki-Strauss: Introduction to Optimal Control Theory.

Malitz: Introduction to Mathematical Logic.

Marsden/Weinstein: Calculus I, II, III. Second edition.

Martin: The Foundations of Geometry and the Non-Euclidean Plane.

Martin: Geometric Constructions.

Martin: Transformation Geometry: An Introduction to Symmetry.

Millman/Parker: Geometry: A Metric Approach with Models. Second edition.

Moschovakis: Notes on Set Theory.

Owen: A First Course in the Mathematical Foundations of Thermodynamics.

Palka: An Introduction to Complex Function Theory.

Pedrick: A First Course in Analysis.

Peressini/Sullivan/Uhl: The Mathematics of Nonlinear Programming.

Prenowitz/Jantosciak: Join Geometries.

Priestley: Calculus: A Liberal Art. Second edition.

Protter/Morrey: A First Course in Real Analysis. Second edition.

Protter/Morrey: Intermediate Calculus. Second edition.

Roman: An Introduction to Coding and Information Theory.

Ross: Elementary Analysis: The Theory of Calculus.

Samuel: Projective Geometry. *Readings in Mathematics.*

Scharlau/Opolka: From Fermat to Minkowski.

Schiff: The Laplace Transform: Theory and Applications.

Sethuraman: Rings, Fields, and Vector Spaces: An Approach to Geometric Constructability.

Sigler: Algebra.

Silverman/Tate: Rational Points on Elliptic Curves.

Simmonds: A Brief on Tensor Analysis. Second edition.

Singer: Geometry: Plane and Fancy.

Singer/Thorpe: Lecture Notes on Elementary Topology and Geometry.

Smith: Linear Algebra. Third edition.

Smith: Primer of Modern Analysis. Second edition.

Undergraduate Texts in Mathematics

Stanton/White: Constructive
  Combinatorics.
Stillwell: Elements of Algebra:
  Geometry, Numbers, Equations.
Stillwell: Mathematics and Its History.
Stillwell: Numbers and Geometry.
  Readings in Mathematics.
Strayer: Linear Programming and Its
  Applications.
Thorpe: Elementary Topics in Differential
Geometry.

Toth: Glimpses of Algebra and Geometry.
  Readings in Mathematics.
Troutman: Variational Calculus and
  Optimal Control. Second edition.
Valenza: Linear Algebra: An Introduction
  to Abstract Mathematics.
Whyburn/Duda: Dynamic Topology.
Wilson: Much Ado About Calculus.